DANCING FROM PAST TO PRESENT

STUDIES IN DANCE HISTORY

A Publication of the Society of Dance History Scholars

Dancing from Past to Present

Nation, Culture, Identities

Edited by

THERESA JILL BUCKLAND

THE UNIVERSITY OF WISCONSIN PRESS

The University of Wisconsin Press
1930 Monroe Street
Madison, Wisconsin 53711

www.wisc.edu/wisconsinpress/

3 Henrietta Street
London WC2E 8LU, England

1   3   5   4   2

Printed in the United States of America

Library of Congress Cataloging-in-Publication Data
Dancing from past to present: nation, culture, identities /
edited by Theresa Jill Buckland.
p.   cm.—(Studies in dance history)
Includes bibliographical references and index.
ISBN 0-299-21850-3 (cloth: alk. paper)
ISBN 0-299-21854-6 (pbk.: alk. paper)
1. Dance—History.   2. Dance—Anthropological aspects.
I. Buckland, Theresa.   II. Series: Studies in dance history (unnumbered).
GV1601.D36   2006
793.3109—dc22   2006008620

CONTENTS

PREFACE

This book has two principal goals. First, it aims to stimulate debate on the combined use of ethnographic and historical strategies in investigating dance as embodied cultural practice. Second, it aims to expand the field of mainstream dance studies by focusing on examples beyond typically Eurocentric conceptualizations of concert dance. The eight essays presented here constitute a specially commissioned collection of case studies on dancing in Tonga, Java, Bosnia-Herzegovina, New Mexico, India, Korea, Macedonia, and England. Each author was asked to root discussion in her or his own long-term ethnographic inquiry and to reflect upon issues of past and present within the dance practice investigated. Authors were also invited to discuss their relationship to the research. The resultant collection provides examples not only of the making of histories and identities through bodily practices, but also of the part that disciplinary frameworks, methodology, and autobiography play in determining selection and interpretation. The balance of this collection lies with researchers of dance whose investigations did not begin with history; rather they turned toward the diachronic perspective in order to shed light on present cultural meanings.

Scholarly examination of "the past" might not immediately suggest the research focus of the human sciences as social scientists traditionally concentrate their attention on the present, initially at least. Such was the starting point for all the contributors to this volume. Traditionally too, social scientists are concerned more with understanding communal than individual practice. Again, this is a characteristic of the essays, apart from one example (Janet O'Shea), in which the practice of individuals is examined in relation to interpretations of shared pasts. Taken as a whole, the collection of essays sheds light upon continuities and disruptions in codified movement systems, interrogates attributions of significance and power to particular dance forms, and scrutinizes social and political agency behind a rhetoric that may foreground dance as cultural expression by reference to specific "past(s)." The inquiry has been undertaken through the explicit juxtaposition of ethnographic and historical frameworks. The concentration is on dance practices typically associated with particular cultural groups professing national, ethnic, or regional identities. Such identification may be challenged within the essays, and differing interpretations of the working processes of ethnographic and historical inquiry are evident. Nonetheless, the emphasis upon empirically based studies, resulting from long immersion in whatever constitutes the "ethnographic community," is a collective feature.

Not every writer in this volume, of course, would necessarily consider herself or himself first and foremost as a social scientist. Some contributors work in university dance departments or dance organizations and may have training that parallels or draws upon aspects of the social sciences; others do hold specific qualifications as social scientists and are institutionally situated in such disciplines. The resultant treatment of the selected dance practices across this volume addresses a number of research questions that reach across past and present documentation and interpretation of dance practices. In answering such questions, the research requires techniques and analytical models beyond those traditionally associated with a single framework of inquiry. What brings the authors together here is less a single shared theoretical vision and more an interest in issues and knowledge gained from dancing across both pasts and presents.

Obviously, the collection does not represent every academic discourse that utilizes ethnography as a major methodology. Evident absences are sociology and cultural studies, both fields that have made innovative contributions to advancing dance knowledge and understanding.[1] The principal academic frameworks used here are anthropology, dance ethnology, folk life studies, dance history, and performance studies. The essays demonstrate variation in the ways in which the researcher, as a result of his or her training, may relate to people and their practices. Even where the authors explicitly locate themselves within one disciplinary field, there exist differences of approach. Three essays are written from within anthropology (Adrienne Kaeppler, Felicia Hughes-Freeland, and Lynn Maners), but the specific treatment emerges from the separate schools of ethnoscience, social anthropology, and cultural anthropology, respectively. Dance ethnology may constitute the disciplinary base for the essays by Judy Van Zile and Elsie Ivancich Dunin, but each author's treatment of the overall theme by no means suggests a uniformity of engagement. The interpretations provide reminders that even if the writers have a declared "home" discipline, they also exercise individual theoretical and methodological preferences. Moreover, all authors respond to different influences in dealing with their material in relation to the book's theme. Interdisciplinary tendencies evident in this collection may result from the author's training in more than one academic discipline and/or her or his openness to engaging with literature beyond the declared home discipline.

Each case study is concerned with a dance practice that is popularly seen as "other" to Euro-American-derived concert dance. The specificities of each essay refute any overarching tendency toward monolithic conceptualizations of world dance cultures. Hughes-Freeland's study, for example, reveals the fluid diversity of dance practice that belies the current seeming stability and tightly defined notion of classical dance in Indonesia. O'Shea discusses differing beliefs between individuals who perform a genre that is often popularly and erroneously referred to in a generalized fashion as "Indian dance." Even within the arguably more familiar terrain of scholarship on dancing in Europe, the three essays by Maners, Dunin, and Theresa Buckland examine dancing that has developed within particular historical, socioeconomic, and political situations. The selection of dance forms and geographies in this volume, then, is intended to contribute to redressing the long-standing balance in dance studies, observed by many, that "classist and racist ideologies . . . assigned the past and present of the socioculturally powerful to 'history' and 'criticism,' and the past and present of everyone else to 'anthropology/ethnography.'"[2]

This situation is changing, albeit slowly. It might be argued that this particular assemblage of case studies in one volume perpetuates such a division. At this juncture in the early twenty-first century, however, the appearance of eight specialist essays within a mainstream book series that is dedicated to dance history is symptomatic of the increasing profile of the traditionally perceived "other" in dance academia. The volume highlights sustained inquiry around a particular theme; it is not designed as a collection of examples under the umbrella of "world dance," a term that has replaced, often without full critical interrogation, that of "ethnic dance." The essays presented here are representative of the regions that have been studied from both ethnographic and historical perspectives. The original conception included material on Africa and the African diasporas, but, regrettably, the few knowledgeable scholars working in this area were already pressed to contribute their research in a variety of avenues. Considerable effort was made to elicit a suitable essay, but both the timeframe and comparative paucity of research activity conspired against inclusion in this volume. Such a situation needs to be addressed in dance scholarship, not least to bear witness to the voices of minority scholars. It is hoped that the examples within this volume will prompt further publications on this theme of communal dancing pasts and presents; not least with respect to the various dance practices of Africa but also those of China, South America, and Australasia.

NOTES

1. See, in particular, the works of Helen Thomas, for example, *The Body, Dance, and Cultural Theory* (Basingstoke, Hampshire, and New York: Palgrave Macmillan, 2003); and those of Jane C. Desmond, an influential example being her "Embodying Difference: Issues in Dance and Cultural Studies," in *Meaning in Motion: New Cultural Studies of Dance*, ed. Jane C. Desmond (Durham and London: Duke University Press, 1997), 29–54.

2. Kent De Spain, "Review of Ann Dils and Ann Cooper Albright, eds., *Moving History / Dancing Cultures*," *Dance Research Journal* 34, no. 1 (2002): 106. See also John O. Perpner III's thoughtful critique, "Cultural Diversity and Dance History Research," in *Researching Dance: Evolving Modes of Inquiry*, ed. Sondra Horton Fraleigh and Penelope Hanstein (London: Dance Books, 1999), 334–51.

ACKNOWLEDGMENTS

The impetus for this collection began at the 20th Symposium of the International Council for Traditional Music Study Group on Ethnochoreology in 1998 when a major theme was traditional dance and its historical sources. In addition to new historical research, a number of often contrasting theoretical and methodological approaches to dance study was exposed at this international meeting. These differences were frequently the result of geographical circumstances and intellectual traditions in the practices of dance history and dance ethnography that cried out for more overt acknowledgment and sustained treatment. Since 1998, there has been ongoing expansion in scholarly investigation across dance practices worldwide. Such developments, I would argue, coupled with further questioning of how we conduct dance research, have made the potential of juxtaposing dance history and dance ethnography even more relevant to the future direction of dance studies.

I am therefore most grateful to the editorial board of the Society of Dance History Scholars, especially to Lynn Garafola, then its chair, for recognizing the value of such a project for inclusion in their highly regarded series on dance and for offering advice. Ann Cooper Albright as the new chair has continued to champion and advance the volume's production through helpful recommendations. Greatly appreciated too has been the generous advice and attention to detail received from the staff at the University of Wisconsin Press.

My thanks also go to my own institution, De Montfort University, Leicester, for ongoing support and financial help to facilitate completion of the project. Thanks too to all those colleagues, Thomas DeFrantz in particular, who came so quickly to my assistance in providing ideas and answers when chapter commissions unfortunately could not be realized. I would also like to thank Trvtko Zebec for his swift and effective help in selecting and providing photographs.

For a considerable period in this book's gestation, Georgiana Gore acted as coeditor until time pressures unfortunately prevented her continuing participation. This present collection would undoubtedly be much the poorer without her insightful editorial comments, sharp intellectual input, and stimulating discussions in the earlier phases. Several of the contributors to this volume and I have benefited greatly from her suggestions.

This book could never have been realized without the ongoing patience of the contributors, who have toiled tirelessly in response to sometimes lengthy and frequent editorial requests; my grateful thanks to all.

An invaluable figure in the background, but whose participation has been very much "hands-on," has been Chris Jones, whose critical editorial eye, expert advice, and unflagging commitment to the project have been faultless. Added to this, her unbelievable patience, good humor, and encouragement make her a treasured companion on any editorial journey.

Finally, I would like to express my appreciation to my husband for his unfailing support in listening and inspiring me to bring this volume to fruition.

DANCING FROM PAST TO PRESENT

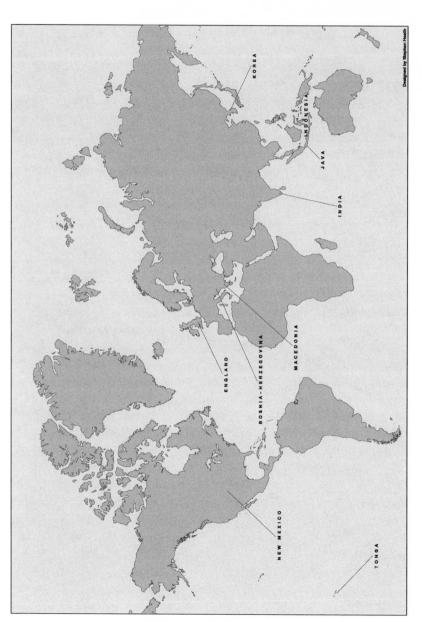

World map: Main locations cited in the text. Map by Stephen Heath.

I

Dance, History, and Ethnography

Frameworks, Sources, and Identities of Past and Present

THERESA JILL BUCKLAND

Ethnography and history, as methodologies through which dance may be researched, suggest contrasting spheres of space and time. For the dance ethnographer, her or his usual territory is that of the field, where source materials are created through the researcher's systematic description of the transient actions and words of people dancing in the present. For the dance historian, the familiar realm is the archive, where extant sources, often fragmentary and sparse, have been created by people other than the researcher, who now employs their surviving artifacts as testimony to the dancing of the past. Stereotypically, the dance ethnographer investigates the customary dance practices of an aggregate of people, such as an ethnic or cultural group. The dance historian more frequently focuses on individuals or perhaps a dance company, often seeking evidence of innovative rather than consensual activity.

In the twenty-first century, such a neat division into mutually exclusive territories no longer holds; nor indeed, as this book demonstrates, were such strict demarcations ever wholly operative in dance research. Some branches of ethnography, in the Eastern European and Scandinavian disciplines of ethnology, ethnography, and folk life studies, explicitly aimed to document dances from the past by seeking out older ways of life to record for posterity.[1] From the middle of the twentieth century, some historians of dance, influenced by Western European and North American practices of oral history, for example, similarly found sources among the living about dancing that was no longer performed.[2] In pursuing dance research, it has not always been easy, nor necessarily desirable, to ignore the potential benefits to be gained by combining synchronic and diachronic perspectives.

Both ethnography and history may be found interrelated in studies of dance that, for their theoretical and methodological frameworks, are located in anthropology, ethnology, cultural studies, social and cultural history, performance studies, sociology, ethnomusicology, and folklore studies. There are also the hybrid disciplines that clearly indicate their focus on dance, as in dance anthropology, dance ethnology, and ethnochoreology. As a comparatively new subject within academia, dance studies in general draws upon established disciplinary frameworks in which ethnographic and historical methods have already taken on distinctive hues that may not always be immediately evident to the dance researcher's eye. Very often the precise meaning of ethnography and history when applied within a particular discipline may be the result of certain intellectual traditions and geographical circumstances. There is, for example, no consensus about the meaning of the term "ethnography," even within its home disciplinary bases of the social sciences. It is beyond the scope of this introductory chapter to explore the detailed and diverse terrain of disciplinary legacies, differences, and correspondences in their application to dance. But some background to the older traditions of dance ethnography and dance history, together with some reflections on past and present sources and identities of dance, are presented here as a frame through which the essays that constitute this book may be viewed.

Disciplinary Frameworks and Questions of Context

The terms "ethnography" and "history" share the characteristics of referring simultaneously to their practice and to their end result. In most West European and North American practice, ethnography is a methodology that deals with the present and typically concludes in a book known as an ethnographic monograph or ethnography. History—or, more properly, the historical method—similarly signals a methodology but investigates the past to produce a history, also most often in book form. The practice of dance history and the production of dance histories were established features of mainstream dance scholarship for much of the twentieth century.

For most of that period, mainstream dance scholarship in North America concentrated on dance as an art form. This was certainly the case during the late 1960s when dancer and anthropologist Joann Kealiinohomoku wrote her seminal article on ballet as an ethnic form of dance.[3] Research that addressed consensual meanings and the sociocultural contextualization of dance was regarded as the sole concern of anthropologists. Anthropologists, unlike most dance scholars, predominantly studied supposedly oral, homogenous societies that were positioned as "other" to so-called civilized and literate white European and North American society.[4] Oral cultures were believed to possess no history since there were often no literary records to study their pasts. In any case anthropologists sought to understand the present of cultures as holistic systems, an aim for which the methodology of ethnography—documenting and explaining the present—was essential. Culture, in the broad anthropological sense of a discrete systematic totality of socially transmitted beliefs, values, institutions, and practices, became a hugely influential concept across academia in the later twentieth century, even if debate raged over its usefulness as an analytical construct both within and outside its home discipline.[5]

In the 1960s, though, for most dance scholars, the term "culture" had quite another meaning. Culture was instead understood as synonymous with "high" art. This meaning, as elucidated by Victorian literary critic Matthew Arnold, equated culture with "the best which has been thought and said."[6] Such a definition positioned popular or vernacular artistic expression in opposition, so that the category of culture as "high" accorded with the preferred arts of the aristocracy and bourgeoisie. Artifacts and practices eligible for the designation of "culture," furthermore, were evaluated by Eurocentric criteria for the label of "art." This socially hierarchical and evolutionist conception of culture continued to hold sway in the middle of the twentieth century, and most dance scholars were not unusual in professing it. In line with other arts and humanities subjects, those forms and practices deemed by society to possess high aesthetic value were granted primacy as sources for academic investigation.[7] Accordingly, dance forms other than ballet and modern dance were ranked lower in this order of aesthetic values and received less attention.

Those scholars interested in the arts of non-Western cultures, or in forms and practices other than those regarded as high culture, sought theoretical perspectives and methodologies that aimed to circumvent Eurocentric and evolutionist bias. Their work owed much to the outlook of the human sciences, particularly to the discipline of anthropology.[8] In these studies, following classical anthropology, the focus was upon contemporary manifestations of movement in societies that had been colonized and where the retrieval of history was not a priority. Classically trained anthropologists preferred to designate the field of study as that of culturally codified human movement systems. They thus highlighted the fact that the concept of dance was not necessarily universal and underscored anthropological concern with indigenous conceptualizations of dance and related phenomena.[9]

Anthropological thinking had a shaping influence on the discipline of dance ethnology in the dance department at the University of California, Los Angeles (UCLA). Unlike studies of dance conducted from within departments of anthropology, here there was greater use of literature from the European disciplines of ethnology, ethnography, and folk life studies.[10] In European ethnographic studies of dance, it was not necessary to question what conceptually constituted dance, since the object of inquiry was the dance of one's own culture. Another characteristic of European ethnographic study was the status of the past and its continuing relevance to the present.

In Eastern Europe, much of the research on dance was carried out within the long established and government-funded institutes of ethnology and ethnography, where the folk paradigm continues to dominate.[11] In North America and Western Europe, the concept of "the people" or "the folk" has been subject to considerable critique since the second half of the twentieth century, even where the disciplines of folklore studies and folk life studies have been maintained within the university sector.[12] In this academic context, the early-twentieth-century conceptualizations and practices of anthropology and folk studies have been the subject of political interrogation, especially with respect to their construction in and contribution to the maintenance of power inequalities. If the ongoing legacies of colonialism have been the source of much debate in classical anthropology, in folk studies the major dispute has concerned political affiliations with nationalism.[13] Through this examination, the concept of the folk has been revealed as an ideological construct whereby rural communities and their older practices were perceived by the intelligentsia as survivals from an ancient, pure culture.

This "folk culture" had become a resource for asserting specific ethnic and ultimately national identity and was principally constructed in opposition to European high culture. With respect to dance categorization, cosmopolitan genres such as ballet were positioned as comparatively recent, individually and consciously created sophisticated art forms, in contrast to primitive, simple "natural" folk dances that arose as a collective spontaneous expression of a people's spirit. The songs, dances, poetry, costume, dialect, and so on of the peasantry were collected as relics of antiquity since such expressive forms were believed to be dying out in the advance of modernity. The process and motivation behind this form of cultural rescue archaeology shared similar aims to that of nineteenth-century anthropological activities, and both shared an evolutionist perspective.[14] It was deemed essential to collect the signs of primitive and folk cultures for posterity, before they became contaminated by modern civilization and disappeared in the wake of urbanization and industrialization.

Given the significance of history in nation building and in articulating ancient ethnic identities, a diachronic perspective has been an integral part of folk studies for most of its existence. The political significance of history has ensured a continuous emphasis on selecting dance forms with long histories of performance tied to place or ethnicity. Largely as a result of the political situation when much pioneering work on dance was carried out in Eastern Europe during the Cold War years of 1945–89, the dominant attention was not so much on issues of sociocultural context but on the dance forms themselves.[15]

The past has been granted a differing status in classical forms of anthropology and folk studies, having been viewed as irrelevant to scholarly exegeses of cultural practices in the former and pivotal to those of the latter. As suggested above, however, this broad characterization does not reveal the nuances and exceptions in approach that came increasingly to the fore from the 1970s onward. In the extensive literature in anthropology that does engage with historical perspectives are a number of works on dance such as those by Adrienne Kaeppler, Cynthia Novack, Sally Ann Ness, and Zoila S. Mendoza.[16] In late-twentieth-century writings, proper attention to colonialist legacies has necessitated engagement with the past, not in a naive replacement of

the colonizer's histories with those of the colonized, but in a critical recognition of their mutually constitutive nature.[17] Within the broad frame
of folk studies, as pursued in North America, Britain, and Scandinavia
in particular, challenges to nationalist legacies in the scholarship have
resulted in critiques of dance scholarship and practice that have arisen
from examination of historical records, both written and oral.[18] Beyond
these more established paradigms of anthropology and folk studies,
ethnographic and historical perspectives on dance have been utilized
within the fields of cultural studies, performance studies, and sociology.
A clear indication of growing interest in ethnographic perspectives on
dance is the specialized designation of "dance ethnography." The application of this label emerged more purposefully from the New York
school of performance studies during the 1990s to indicate a specific
focus on dance as embodied cultural knowledge. Exploration of this
premise is realized through methodological and theoretical approaches,
drawn from feminism and postmodern anthropology to address the distinctive nature of an ethnographic practice that is "necessarily grounded
in the body and the body's experience."[19] Elsewhere, as in my own
usage of the term, the term "dance ethnography" has been employed as
an umbrella term to embrace a variety of intellectual traditions and
theoretical positions.[20]

There has been considerable cross-fertilization between disciplines
that have traditionally used ethnographic and historical perspectives in
the study of dance and increasingly so, following both the fall of the Berlin Wall in 1989 and the earlier shift toward dismantling disciplinary
boundaries in the arts and humanities in the late twentieth century.
Nonetheless, all terms and methodologies have legacies, and it must be
remembered that the selection of disciplinary context is fundamental to
both methodological procedures and analytical outcomes. The choice
of social context through which to investigate dance emerges from the
choice of disciplinary context. The social context, however defined,
whether as the anthropological understanding of "culture" or as ethnic
group in the concept of "the folk," provides both frame and resources
for interpretation. The problem with all contexts, of course, is that they
are "constructed for specific purposes and thus always negotiable, which
makes futile any attempts at defining contexts substantively."[21] This
means that it is imperative for researchers and readers to make public
the circumstances of their choice and to identify as far as possible ensu-
ing implications for their interpretation of dance.

Ethnography and History:
Methodologies and Sources for Dance

The differing contexts of "culture" and "folk," in whatever guise they are utilized as an interpretive framework, lead to differing practices in the methodology of ethnography and in the delineation of the field. Typically, ethnography in classical anthropology has entailed long periods of a year or more living within the selected society, which traditionally has been far from the researcher's normal country of residence. The focus continues to be on the present. In folk studies, in contrast, the researcher tends to work within her or his own country and undertakes more restricted field trips. This latter style is generally characteristic of ethnographic work undertaken in sociology, a discipline in which ethnography has been practiced since the early twentieth century. British sociologist Helen Thomas characterizes ethnography as an

> in-depth study of a culture, institution and context over a sustained period of time, which is usually longer for anthropologists than sociologists. Ethnographic research employs a range of methods and techniques such as participant-observation, interviews, filed [*sic* field] notes, audio and visual recordings and, in the case of dance, movement analysis. The aims of ethnography, the (far/near) relation between representation and reality and the observer and the observed, are subject to debate and largely depend on the theoretical, political and/or methodological stance of the individual researcher.[22]

One thing is clear: ethnography is not a set of methods to collect data. Nor is it value-free description. In anthropology and sociology, the aims of ethnography are to analyze and interpret the perspectives and evaluative concerns of insiders; it is not to impose judgments, explicit or implicit, that are derived from the researcher's own cultural position. In this approach, the fieldwork is normally conducted by an individual. In Eastern European ethnography, the aims have been to observe, document, and analyze the cultural forms as manifestations of past and present ethnic identities. More typically here, the research is conducted by a team composed of specialists in different cultural forms, such as music, song, and costume.[23]

Aside from distinctions relating to intellectual traditions across differing continents, over the twentieth century and into the twenty-first, ethnography has been utilized in a myriad of ways across a diverse range of disciplines. Within the narrower band of the social sciences as formulated in Western Europe and North America, it "escapes ready summary definitions. . . . [and] has become a site of debate and contestation within and across disciplinary boundaries."[24] Ethnography's exact interpretation and application have never been uniform in anthropology, sociology, and folk studies, but within these contexts ethnography has at least a common history of initial development within the positivist paradigms of the early twentieth century.[25] It was believed that if the fieldwork had been conducted properly in the first place with sufficient scholarly precision and objectivity, the results could be replicated on subsequent visits and by other equally proficient ethnographers. This "scientific method" underpins the ethnography practiced in much of Eastern Europe, where the very term of "ethnography" also signals a disciplinary framework that remains very much rooted within positivist sensibilities. The aim to document traditional rural culture for posterity relies upon belief in a past that can be systematically and objectively recorded.

In the wake of postmodernism, these once cherished certainties, believed to be indicative of true scientific method, have broken down in the practice of ethnography across much of Western Europe and North America. The post-positivist climate has led to recognition that however much rigor the ethnographer exercises, the field does not have a static existence in "reality"; results cannot be replicated. So, too, the once strict division between "insider informant" and "outsider researcher," positioned as such in the name of objective scholarship, has also undergone considerable criticism in the post-positivist climate. The notion of the field as a site of inquiry has itself been subject to much debate, being recognized as just as much a construction of historical, sociocultural, and personal circumstance as the data discovered within it. Despite the crises surrounding ethnography in Western Europe and North America, the methodology has emerged, having undergone the fires of intense criticism, still recognizable as a distinctive practice, if perhaps differently forged than earlier in the twentieth century.[26]

Such epistemological concerns have equally swept across the study of the past. The impact of post-positivist "new history" on dance historiography has enjoyed greater prominence in mainstream dance scholarship than that of reflexive ethnography, largely as a result of dance academia's traditions of scholarly interest.[27] Increasing engagement with ideas that the past can only be known through the present, that it is particularized and subject to manipulation, has opened up new territories for research and debate. In the new history, there can be no one "true" account of a historical event, as recognition of multiple perspectives reveals the complexities underlying what was once selected and interpreted as singular fact; for "when it comes to the historical record, there are no grounds to be found in the record itself for preferring one way of construing its meaning rather than another."[28]

Not only does the researcher shape the field of inquiry that is determined as the past or the present, but historical or ethnographic sources are inevitably part of that shifting process. Recognition of and engagement with issues and dilemmas raised by post-positivism, however, should not necessarily lead to anarchical clouds of unknowing in the pursuit of ethnographic and historical methodologies in studying dance. Nor should they ever be an excuse for not following precise scholarly procedures of critical evaluation and reflection upon source materials, whether they have been garnered in the past or present.

Evaluating Past and Present Sources for Dance

In moving from the present to the past in research into dance as cultural practice, the investigator has a number of source materials at her or his disposal, including personally recorded ethnographic field notes or those written by previous researchers; taped interviews; traditional historical sources such as journal entries, diaries, and letters; iconographic material such as paintings and photographs; audiovisual records of film and videotape; and personal memory in both its traditionally understood meaning as a product of "mind" and as an embodied manifestation.

Traditionally, written evidence has been deemed the province of historians; the oral, that of anthropologists and folklorists. The oral traditions of so-called folk and primitive cultures were judged through European literate eyes to be poor history and therefore rarely admissible as factual evidence. Since the mid-twentieth century, however, the discipline of history has largely rejected the former hierarchical relationship between oral and written testimonies.[29] Historians accept that the written is not necessarily any more reliable than the oral, both being situational records of perceived realities. Furthermore, within the disciplines of anthropology, folk studies, and history, there has been increased recognition that in the construction of histories, both written and oral, the interaction and interreliance of evidence stemming from both types of material is often richly complex.[30] To an extent, of course, ethnography is always history, in that the events recorded have already passed in time. But the ethnographer usually has the benefit of moving people to observe, imitate, and hopefully interact with when pursuing an investigation; not so the researcher of the past, the historian, who must locate and interpret sources that bear witness to the transient nature of dance.

In the majority of dance scholarship, both past and present, most of the documentation has been made by those external to the dancing itself, even if witnessed at source. Both anthropology and history as disciplines owe their existence to textualizing practices. The ethnographer commits her or his observations to a variety of texts, both written and visual, before drawing upon them to create the written monograph. The historian, as dance scholar and anthropologist Georgiana Gore observes, normally uses the records of other people. She points out that both anthropologist and historian require the legitimating "presence of the author."[31] This is a vital process of validation in both ethnographic and historical methodology, although the motivation and positioning of the author should always be subject to questioning. In distinguishing between first- and second-hand testimonies, "the source which in history is considered primary . . . would be generally considered secondary in anthropology."[32] An anthropologist or folklorist is the author of the written field notes, the taker of the photograph, the maker of the film, the notator of the dances, or the recorder of the interview. A historian's primary sources, on the other hand, have always been constructed by somebody else. Yet a further distinction occurs between the anthropologist and the folklorist in their written documentation. The folklorist's field notes have always been written for public consumption; she or he creates records as historical documents, in the sure knowledge of their future use in the archive. There has always been an intended audience. Not so the traditional anthropologist whose field notes and journals have typically been private documents.[33]

Traditional textual sources of the past frequently prove fragmentary, scattered, and sparse. In contrast, sources of the present may appear to offer a clear route to the lost past. Individual oral testimony has a long and rich history of being fruitfully mined in folk studies to recover past practices in dance. But testimonies articulated in language, whether in oral or written form, are not the only sources in the present. When conceived as a repository of cultural meanings both past and present, the moving body may be a source to be observed and documented from the outside.[34] Traces of the past may be discovered in the ways in which people execute particular movements and use their bodies; but caution needs to be exercised. Researchers of today do not possess the same bodies as those constituted in different material and symbolic circumstances of particular pasts.[35] When attempting to uncover cultural values of the past in present dance forms, other source materials need to be consulted in elucidating this archaeology of the body. The physical biography of the individual dancer may not always be the same as the idealized cultural notions of the dancer's body—age, injury, and health may transform earlier practices, and as a living, moving source, the body may not always replicate with exactitude the moves of the past. Treating "the body" as a text to be read carries inherent dangers of objectification and Cartesian dualities of inner/outer meaning. But new strategies have arisen in a seemingly phenomenologically driven approach to understanding the moving body from an ethnographic perspective.

In ethnographic descriptions of dancing in the present, it has become a favored technique since the 1990s to use the researcher's body as a means of access to information.[36] Cultural embodiment is explored through the researcher's participation in and reflection upon the dancing. Movement competence in the cultural forms on the part of the researcher has always been an essential strategy of dance scholarship since at least the 1950s, but as Sally Ann Ness makes clear, the later mode of participation as a research tactic is of a different order.[37] One obvious difference to the objectified ethnographic descriptions of the earlier inquiries has been the foregrounding of participation. The researcher's own movement experiences become part of the means of comparative analysis. Such an approach is not without its epistemological dangers, as anthropologist and semasiologist Brenda Farnell has argued.[38] Nonetheless, the "I" persona as a source, dancing and reflecting on sensation and meaning, has produced a significant extension and alternative to earlier objective modes of analysis. In this endeavor, the methodology of embodied practice in late-twentieth-century ethnography, despite obvious analogies, is not, according to Ness, phenomenological in its inquiry, since the aim is to gain, rather than to "bracket out" cultural understanding. In these examinations of the dancing self as culturally embodied, the individual's potential location in relation to the parameters and associated values of time and space operates within a largely consensual framework of meaning. The performance and representation of self in such studies, though, is not reduced to that of static and "perfect replicants of some cultural template."[39] Instead, the process affords opportunity to explore embodied cultural knowledge as temporally and spatially dynamic, situational in its meaning, and creative in the interstices of personal and communal histories that reach across experiences of researcher and researched. Such departures of inquiry are often inextricably, though not exclusively, linked with issues of identity.

Constructing Identities through Dance: Mythic Pasts and Cultural Memory

Postmodern scholarship has challenged notions of identity as being singular and essential in character, treating the performance of identity as historical and sociocultural. Since the 1980s, a considerable literature has viewed dance performance through the lenses of gender, race, ethnicity, nation, and age, all of which have diachronic trajectories to explore; "any activity or practice, the agents who engage in them and the patients who are their subjects, are themselves partly a consequence of, but are not fully determined by, past practices and activities."[40] Whether we construe the contexts of past(s) as culture, national heritage, tradition, local history, or oral history, affiliation to the particular construct and its use in the present often serves the needs and aspirations of personal and communal identities. The use of dance as a symbolic political strategy in shaping a future society was particularly evident in the often integrated aims of research and reconstruction in the institutes and state dance ensembles of Cold War Eastern Europe. This formula for collecting, selecting, and constructing once participatory dances for staged display has been pursued elsewhere in the world to various ends.[41]

The use of a dance form to evoke former or authentic contexts of performance may often be encountered in the public domain. Performances of traditional dances in international festivals and in tourist displays owe much to a twin embracing of the powers of nostalgia and exoticism. Audience and performers are locked in a mutually constitutive framework of interpretation and appreciation in which they, the modern, gaze at dance, the tradition.[42] In this respect dance is emblematic of another culture, or another past that the audience cannot access through normal travel. As such, the act of dancing has become a piece of repertoire, an object of aesthetic appreciation, and a symbol of a way of life. In such stagings, in a manner analogous to that of a traditional museum exhibition, the audiences' lack of access to the dances' former histories precludes them from recognizing their own positioning or from understanding the lived experience of its earlier dancers.[43] The historicity of the past is denied to the audience since all that is represented to them is a piece of theater with no ethnographic context. Often this is presented nonetheless as an authentic representation of another culture or a since vanished piece of history.

Critical literature on concepts of "cultural heritage" and "invented traditions" by historians David Lowenthal and Eric Hobsbawm has influenced considerable interrogation of how the past is represented in the present.[44] The move to debunk what has popularly been regarded as authentic history and traditions of origin has been particularly visible in studies of dance with professed ancient histories. Much discussed examples are the Indian genre of bharata natyam and the English morris, both of which appear in this book. Such analyses have certainly been useful correctives to an uncritical acceptance or failure to engage with mythic histories. Interrogations of "invented traditions" demonstrate that formerly unchallenged conceptualizations and performances of the past may have functional purposes for particular groups or agents in terms of power relations. The performance of memory, whatever the political discourse within which it is constructed, may also be considered through other analytical perspectives.

Anthropologist Paul Connerton's distinction between incorporation and inscription as modes of documentation offer important signposts to the study of cultural memory as embodied performance in which the practices of ethnography and history may be aligned.[45] His characterization follows classic divisions between bodily, ultimately transient modes of transmission (incorporation) and those of traditional textual practices that use language or visual delineation to fix the moment (inscription). Elsewhere I have suggested that "in traditional forms of danced display . . . longevity of human memory is publicly enacted, demonstrating the ethereality of human existence and the continuity of human experience, as successive generations re-present the dancing."[46] Not that exact replication is a necessary condition in every ethnographic community, and even then, as noted above, human bodies are never stable over time. Yet they may be perceived to be stable in some instances and viewed as an authentic conduit to a past and continuing performance identity. As one English dancer explained to me:

It's something that, you know, has been handed down and handed down and it's all been handed down by word of mouth and practical help in learning the steps. It's not something you can just go and pick a book up, read about, go and do it. Impossible.[47]

In such instances, the human body is both recipient and manifestation of a local history that claims authenticity through its mode of transmission. The quotation above is ultimately embedded in earlier dichotomies of tradition and modernity that were operative in the folk paradigm to designate primitive or folk cultures from the civilized. But nonetheless the significance of so-called tradition to modern life is not to be simply dismissed by dance scholars as redundant regurgitation of old evolutionist theory circulating within ethnographic communities. In constructing narratives of continuity in dance, dancers themselves often draw upon such theory, self-consciously or not, to situate themselves within a temporal framework that may differentiate their identities in opposition to those dancers with perhaps younger histories of performance.[48]

But the embodiment of the past in performance form may serve more concrete territorial needs. During the 1990s, tensions between contrastive cultural understanding of the role and significance of embodied documentation was highlighted in court cases concerning Australian aboriginal lands. The presentation of traditional performance as evidence to claim territorial rights was rejected as inadmissible evidence.[49] Yet such means of performance, as Connerton has discussed, help to bind people to their own history. Cultural memory as performance operates to construct and consolidate identities even if that cultural memory may be at odds with personal memory. Multiple voices of memory, however, tend to be quieter in such events where the performance is a recurrent public enactment. The performance of memory in collective terms consolidates an agreed interpretation of what happened or what is valued.[50]

The inclusion and positioning of voices within ethnographic and historical texts has undergone considerable discussion since the advent of postmodernism. The new benefits and drawbacks to understanding have been variously assessed—at worst, as evidence of a cultural relativism that evades material and moral responsibilities; at best, as a positive means of giving voice to the repressed, marginalized, or ignored.[51] Authentic representation of experience has been a driving factor in this scholarship, bringing to prominence the native ethnographer and historian. Interrelated questions of authentic identity and knowledge in speaking, writing, and dancing continue to circulate in ethnographic and historical studies of dance. In some respects, the "I" persona and the practice of placing the author's dancing body at the center of reflexive inquiry is a further symptom of the drive toward authenticity of representation. Ironically, of course, the concept of authenticity in contingent areas of ethnographic and historical practice is, at the same time, subject to intense critical scrutiny. While applauding and embracing the long-awaited integration of individual embodied histories and the experiential, it remains necessary to guard against naive belief in the body and in the native researcher as sources of "natural" unmediated knowledge.

Attempts to question and to understand the often complex and circuitous relationships between past and present are then inseparably constituted in present discourse and biography. Yet such recognition inspires dance scholars to acquire greater knowledge and insight of their own values in relation to those of others, whether past or present. Extreme positions in predicating the past as an extension of the present need to be critically examined, for if we argue, as J. D. Peel does, that "conceptions of the past are facts of the present," and that "the content of such conceptions of the past . . . may well be largely or entirely the product of particular present interests," then we are led "to the logical absurdity of unhinging the present from the past completely."[52]

Dancing pasts across several presents—for example, as an African Caribbean performing the quadrille in London or a Caucasian swinging in California—necessitate acts of selection, omission, exclusion, transformation, and creation in the embodied production of cultural memory.[53] And the study of dance as representative practice requires the skills and perspectives of history and ethnography, not only to explore legacies of colonialism and nationalism, but also to interrogate the continuing impact of globalization and the politics of identity articulation. Through reflexive and dialogic strategies, synthesizing synchronic and diachronic perspectives, we can exercise our cultural and political choices purposefully toward a more informed and imaginative future for dance and its scholarship.

NOTES

1. See, for example, László Felföldi, "Folk Dance Research in Hungary: Relations among Theory, Fieldwork, and the Archive," in *Dance in the Field:*

Theory, Methods, and Issues in Dance Ethnography, ed. Theresa J. Buckland (Basingstoke, Hampshire: Macmillan; New York: St Martin's Press, 1999), 55–70; and in the same volume, Egil Bakka, "'Or Shortly They Would Be Lost Forever': Documenting for Revival and Research," 71–81, on collecting in Norway.

2. See, for example, the Oral History Project and Archive of the New York Public Library Dance Collection from 1974 onward.

3. Joann Kealiinohomoku, "An Anthropologist looks at Ballet as a Form of Ethnic Dance," *Impulse* (1969–70): 24–33. It has deservedly been reprinted many times, most recently in *Moving History / Dancing Cultures: A Dance History Reader,* ed. Ann Dils and Ann Cooper Albright (Middletown, Conn.: Wesleyan University Press, 2001), 33–43. For an evaluation of this article, see Theresa Buckland, "All Dances Are Ethnic—But Some Are More Ethnic Than Others: Some Observations on Recent Scholarship in Dance and Anthropology," *Dance Research* 17, no. 1 (1999): 7–9.

4. There are innumerable books on the history of anthropology, but see, for example, Alan Barnard, *History and Theory in Anthropology* (Cambridge: Cambridge University Press, 2000).

5. Raymond Williams referred to the term "culture" as "one of the two or three most complicated words in the English language," in his *Keywords: A Vocabulary of Culture and Society* (London: Fontana Paperbacks, 1976), 87. For a critical overview of the use of the concept in anthropology, see Carla Pasquinelli, "The Concept of Culture between Modernity and Postmodernity," in *Grasping the Changing World: Anthropological Concepts in the Postmodern Era,* ed. Vaclav Hubinger (London: Routledge, 1996), 53–73.

6. Matthew Arnold, *Culture and Anarchy* (Cambridge: Cambridge University Press, 1960), 6. (First published in 1869.)

7. For a comparable history of music study, see Jonathan Stock, "New Musicologies, Old Musicologies: Ethnomusicology and the Study of Western Music," *Current Musicology* 62 (1998): 40–68.

8. For a history of these developments in North America, see Adrienne Kaeppler, "American Approaches to the Study of Dance," *Yearbook for Traditional Music* 23 (1991): 11–21.

9. This working definition is most often associated with Adrienne Kaeppler. See her "Structured Movement Systems in Tonga," in *Society and the Dance: The Social Anthropology of Process and Performance,* ed. Paul Spencer (Cambridge: Cambridge University Press, 1985), 92–93. See also Judith Lynne Hanna, *To Dance Is Human: A Theory of Nonverbal Communication* (Austin: University of Texas Press, 1979), 19.

10. For a history of the dance ethnology program at UCLA and its relation to cognate developments, see Elsie Ivancich Dunin in this book; and Allegra Fuller Snyder, "Past, Present, and Future," *UCLA Journal of Dance Ethnology* 16 (1992): 1–28.

11. See Anca Giurchescu and Lisbet Torp, "Theory and Methods in Dance Research: A European Approach to the Holistic Study of Dance," *Yearbook for Traditional Music* 23 (1991): 1–10. For light on the differences between respective schools in North America and Europe, see Colin Quigley, "Methodologies in the Study of Dance: Ethnology," in *International Encyclopedia of Dance*, ed. Selma Jeanne Cohen (New York: Oxford University Press, 1998), 4:372–76.

12. For a critical history, see Regina Bendix, *In Search of Authenticity: The Formation of Folklore Studies* (Madison: University of Wisconsin Press, 1997).

13. See Roger Abrahams, "Phantoms of Romantic Nationalism in Folkloristics," *Journal of American Folklore* 106 (1993): 3–37.

14. See Drid Williams, *Anthropology and the Dance: Ten Lectures*, 2nd ed. (Urbana: University of Illinois Press, 2004), for a detailed critique of evolutionist perspectives on dance. On the concept of folk in relation to dance, see Theresa J. Buckland, "'Th'Owd Pagan Dance': Ritual, Enchantment, and an Enduring Intellectual Paradigm," *Journal for the Anthropological Study of Human Movement* 11, no. 4, and 12, no. 1 (Fall 2001/Spring 2002; double issue): 418–20. See also Andrée Grau, "Myths of Origin," in *The Routledge Dance Studies Reader*, ed. Alexandra Carter (London: Routledge, 1998), 197–202.

15. See Anca Giurchescu, "European Perspectives in Structural Analysis of Dance," in *Dance—A Multicultural Perspective*, ed. Janet Adshead (Guildford, Surrey: National Resource Centre for Dance, University of Surrey, 1984), 33–48; and chapters by Anca Giurchescu and Grażyna Dąbrowska, and László Felföldi in Adrienne Kaeppler, ed., *Dance and Structural Analysis* (Budapest: Hungarian Academy of Sciences, forthcoming).

16. Adrienne L. Kaeppler, "Preservation and Evolution of Form and Function in Two Types of Tongan Dance," in *Polynesian Culture History: Essays in Honor of Kenneth P. Emory*, ed. Genevieve A. Highland et al. (Honolulu: Bernice P. Bishop Museum Special Publication 56, 1967), 503–36; Cynthia J. Novack, *Sharing the Dance: Contact Improvisation and American Culture* (Madison: University of Wisconsin Press, 1990), 22–113; Sally Ann Ness, *Body, Movement, and Culture: Kinesthetic and Visual Symbolism in a Philippine Community* (Philadelphia: University of Pennsylvania Press, 1992), 154–76; and Zoila S. Mendoza, *Shaping Society through Dance: Mestizo Ritual Performance in the Peruvian Andes* (Chicago: University of Chicago Press, 2000), 84–108.

17. See, for example, John and Jean Comaroff, *Ethnography and the Historical Imagination* (Boulder, Colo.: Westview Press, 1992), 235–63; and Georgiana Gore, "Present Texts, Past Voices: The Formation of Contemporary Representations of West African Dances," *Yearbook for Traditional Music*, 23 (2001): 29–36.

18. See, for example, Arzu Öztürkmen (who trained in North American approaches to folklore), "Modern Dance *Alla Turca*: Transforming Ottoman Dance in Early Republican Turkey," *Dance Research Journal* 35, no. 1 (2003): 46–51, and her "Politics of National Dance in Turkey: A Historical Reappraisal,"

Yearbook for Traditional Music, 23 (2001): 139–43; Catherine Foley, "Irish Traditional Step-Dance in Historical Perspective: Tradition, Identity, and Popular Culture," in *Dans Müzik Kültür, ICTM 20th Ethnochoreology Symposium Proceedings 1998*, ed. Frank Hall and Irene Loutzaki (Istanbul, Turkey: Boğaziçi University Folklore Club, 2000), 43–55.

19. Deidre Sklar, "On Dance Ethnography," *Dance Research Journal* 23, no. 1 (1991): 6. For a further characterization of dance ethnography, see Deidre Sklar, "Reprise: On Dance Ethnography," *Dance Research Journal* 32, no. 1 (2000): 70–77. Examples from the general field of performance studies include Margaret Thompson Drewal, *Yoruba Ritual: Performers, Play, Agency* (Bloomington: Indiana University Press, 1992); Barbara Browning, *Samba: Resistance in Motion* (Bloomington: Indiana University Press, 1995); and Deidre Sklar, *Dancing with the Virgin: Body and Faith in the Fiesta of Tortugas, New Mexico* (Berkeley: University of California Press, 2001).

20. See Theresa J. Buckland, "Introduction: Reflecting on Dance Ethnography," in *Dance in the Field*, ed. Buckland, 1.

21. Mark Hobart, "Texte est un con," in *Contexts and Levels: Essays on Hierarchy*, ed. R. H. Barnes, D. de Coppet and R. J. Parkin, Occasional Paper no. 4 (Oxford: JASO [Journal of the Anthropological Society of Oxford], 1985), 48.

22. Helen Thomas, *The Body, Dance, and Cultural Theory* (Basingstoke, Hampshire: Palgrave Macmillan, 2003), 67.

23. For insight into a field trip conducted from a typical institute of ethnology, see Andriy Nahachewsky, "Searching for Branches, Searching for Roots: Fieldwork in My Grandfather's Village," in *Dance in the Field*, ed. Buckland, 175–185.

24. Paul Atkinson et al., eds., "Editorial Introduction," in *Handbook of Ethnography* (London: Sage, 2001), 1.

25. For a succinct discussion, see Paul Willis, "Notes on Method," in *Culture, Media, Language*, ed. Stuart Hall et al. (London: Hutchinson, 1980), 88–95.

26. For reflections on ethnography written by one of its fiercest critics, see George E. Marcus, *Ethnography through Thick and Thin* (Princeton, N.J.: Princeton University Press, 1998).

27. See Susan Leigh Foster, ed., *Choreographing History* (Bloomington: Indiana University Press, 1995); Amy Koritz, "Re/Moving Boundaries: From Dance History to Cultural Studies," in *Moving Words, Re-writing Dance*, ed. Gay Morris (London: Routledge, 1996), 88–103; Norman Bryson, "Cultural Studies and Dance History," in *Meaning in Motion: New Cultural Studies of Dance*, ed. Jane C. Desmond (Durham: Duke University Press, 1997), 55–77; Shelley Berg, "The Sense of the Past: Historiography and Dance," in *Researching Dance: Evolving Modes of Inquiry*, ed. Sondra Horton Fraleigh and Penelope Hanstein (London: Dance Books, 1999), 225–48; Alexandra Carter, ed., *Rethinking Dance History: A*

Reader (London: Routledge, 2004). A sustained critical response to the new history can be found in Lynn Matluck Brooks, "Dance History and Method: A Return to Meaning," *Dance Research* 20, no. 1 (2002): 33–53.

28. Hayden White quoted in Richard J. Evans, *In Defence of History* (London: Granta Books, 2000), 100–101.

29. For insight into the methodology's own history and practice, see David K. Dunaway and Willa K. Baum, eds., *Oral History: An Interdisciplinary Anthology* (Nashville, Tenn.: American Association for State and Local History, 1984).

30. See D. W. Cohen, *The Combing of History* (Chicago: University of Chicago Press), 1994; and Buckland, "'Th'Owd Pagan Dance.'"

31. Georgiana Gore, "Traditional Dance in West Africa," in *Dance History: An Introduction*, ed. Janet Adshead-Lansdale and June Layson (London: Routledge, 1994), 64.

32. Ibid.

33. For discussion on field documentation, see Robert M. Emerson, Rachel I. Fretz, and Linda L. Shaw, *Writing Ethnographic Fieldnotes* (Chicago: University of Chicago Press, 1995); Roger Sanjek, ed., *Fieldnotes: The Makings of Anthropology* (Ithaca, N.Y.: University of Cornell Press, 1990). As an example of classic modes of documentation in folklore studies, see Kenneth S. Goldstein, *A Guide for Field Workers in Folklore* (Hatboro, Penn.: Folklore Associates, 1964).

34. See, for example, Joann W. Kealiinohomoku, "A Comparative Study of Dance as a Constellation of Motor Behaviors among African and United States Negroes," in *Dance Research Annual, VII: Reflections and Perspectives on Two Anthropological Studies of Dance*, ed. Adrienne Kaeppler (New York: CORD, 1976), 1–179; Theresa Buckland, "Dance, Technology, and Metaphors of Modernity," in *International Academic Conference on Dance: The Challenge and the Message in Dance*, ed. Malborg Kim (Seoul, Korea: KIDE '95 Committee and Yong-hu Park, 1995), 96–105; Andrée Grau, "Dancers' Bodies as the Repository of Conceptualisations of the Body with Special Reference to the Tiwi of Northern Australia," in *Semiotics around the World: Synthesis in Diversity*, ed. Irmengard Rauch and Gerald F. Carr (Berlin: Mouton de Gruyter, 1997), 929–32; and Jane C. Desmond, "Embodying Difference: Issues in Dance and Cultural Studies," in *Meaning in Motion: New Cultural Studies of Dance*, ed. Jane C. Desmond (Durham: Duke University Press, 1997), 29–54.

35. See Yvon Guilcher, "Du témoignage au document: Nécessité de la critique," *La Danse et ses sources, actes du colloque, Toulouse 31 Octobre 1992*, ISATIS Cahiers d'Ethnomusicologue Régionale, no. 2 (Toulouse: Conservatoire Occitan, Centre des Musiques Traditionnelles en Midi-Pyrénées, 1992), 45–48; and in the same volume, Theresa Buckland, "Le barbare et le pittoresque: Figures de danse d'un monde en movement," 15–16. For discussion with reference to concert dance, see Thomas, *Body, Dance, and Cultural Theory*, 110–12.

36. See, for example, Browning, *Samba;* Sklar, *Dancing with the Virgin.*

37. Gertrude Kurath's descriptions of Native American dances are an example of mid-twentieth-century approaches to participation as a research method. See Gertrude P. Kurath, *Half a Century of Dance Research: Essays by Gertrude Prokosch Kurath* (Flagstaff, Ariz.: Cross Cultural Dance Resources, 1986). Classic examples of participation occur in structural analyses of dance where personal movement competence is a necessary means of gaining understanding of indigenous conceptualizations and means of structuring movement. See Adrienne Kaeppler, "Method and Theory in Analyzing Dance Structure with an Analysis of Tongan Dance," *Ethnomusicology* 16, no. 2 (1972): 173–217; and George Martin and Ernő Pesovár, "A Structural Analysis of the Hungarian Folk Dance: A Methodological Sketch," *Acta Ethnographica Scientiarum Hungariae* 10 (1961): 1–40. See also Kate Ramsey's study of early methodological opposition in anthropology to participation, "Melville Herskovits, Katherine Dunham, and the Politics of African Diasporic Dance Anthropology," in *Dancing Bodies, Living Histories: New Writings about Dance and Culture,* ed. Lisa Doolittle and Anne Flynn (Banff, Alberta, Canada: Banff Centre Press), 196–216. Sally Ann Allen Ness identifies a new rationale for participation in her essay "Being a Body in a Cultural Way: Understanding the Cultural in the Embodiment of Dance," in *Cultural Bodies: Ethnography and Theory,* ed. Helen Thomas and Jamilah Ahmed (Oxford: Blackwell, 2004), 123–44.

38. Brenda M. Farnell, "Ethno-graphics and the Moving Body," *Man* 29, part 4 (1994): 936–37. Sklar in this book presents a theoretical case for the method.

39. Ness, "Being a Body in a Cultural Way," 139.

40. Mark Hobart, "As They Like It: Overinterpretation and Hyporeality in Bali," in *The Problem of Context,* ed. Roy Dilley (New York: Berghahn Books, 1999), 112–13.

41. See Anthony Shay, *Choreographic Politics: State Folk Dance Companies, Representation and Power* (Middletown, Conn.: Wesleyan University Press, 2002). There is a growing literature on this phenomenon, and the nature of transformation from field to stage is diverse. For a sample of the range of different approaches from field to stage and attitudes toward the phenomenon, see the discussion of Katherine Dunham in John O. Perpener III, "Cultural Diversity and Dance History Research," in *Researching Dance: Evolving Modes of Inquiry,* ed. Sondra Horton Fraleigh and Penelope Hanstein (London: Dance Books, 1999), 343–44; Catherine Foley, "Perceptions of Irish Step Dance: National, Global, and Local," *Dance Research Journal* 33, no. 1 (2001): 34–45; Sylvia Glasser, "Transcultural Transformations," *Visual Anthropology* 8, nos. 2–4 (1996): 287–309; Richard C. Green, "(Up)Staging the Primitive: Pearl Primus and 'the Negro Problem' in American Dance," in *Dancing Many Drums: Excavations in African American Dance,* ed. Thomas F. DeFrantz (Madison: University of Wisconsin

Press, 2002), 105–39; Sally A. Ness, "Originality in the Postcolony: Choreographing the Neoethnic Body of Philippine Ballet," *Current Anthropology* 12, no. 1 (1997): 64–108; Jacqueline Shea Murphy, "Lessons in Dance (as) History: Aboriginal Land Claims and Aboriginal Dance, circa 1999," in *Dancing Bodies, Living Histories*, ed. Doolittle and Flynn, 130–67; and Ann Cooper Albright, "Embodying History: Epic Narrative and Cultural Identity in African-American Dance," in her *Choreographing Difference: The Body and Identity in Contemporary Dance* (Middletown, Conn.: Wesleyan University Press, 1997), 150–78.

42. This discussion owes much to James Clifford's stimulating essay "On Collecting Art and Culture," in *The Predicament of Culture: Twentieth-Century Ethnography, Literature, and Art* (Cambridge, Mass.: Harvard University Press, 1988), 215–51.

43. See Theresa Buckland, "Multiple Interests and Powers: Authenticity and the Competitive Folk Dance Festival," in *Authenticity: Whose Tradition?* ed. László Felföldi and Theresa Buckland (Budapest: European Folklore Institute, 2002), 70–78; and Buckland, "Competing Interests: Culture, Histories, and Scholarly Appreciation in Adjudicating International Folk Dance," in preparation.

44. David Lowenthal, *The Past Is a Foreign Country* (Cambridge: Cambridge University Press, 1985) and *The Heritage Crusade and the Spoils of History* (Cambridge: Cambridge University Press, 1998); Eric Hobsbawm and Terence Ranger, eds., *The Invention of Tradition* (Cambridge: Cambridge University Press, 1983).

45. Paul Connerton, *How Societies Remember* (Cambridge: Cambridge University Press, 1989), 72.

46. Theresa Buckland, "Dance, Authenticity, and Cultural Memory: The Politics of Embodiment," *Yearbook for Traditional Music* 33 (2001): 1.

47. Derek Pilling, Britannia Coco-Nut Dancers, Bacup, Rossendale Valley, Lancashire, recorded interview, 21 April 1981.

48. Eric Martin Usner provides a fascinating case study of disjunction between past and present in "Dancing in the Past, Living in the Present: Nostalgia and Race in Southern California Neo-Swing Dance Culture," *Dance Research Journal* 33, no. 2 (2001): 87–101.

49. Dara Culhane, *The Pleasure of the Crown: Anthropology, Law, and First Nations* (Burnaby, British Columbia: Talonbooks, 1998), 123.

50. For work that includes dance as collective memory, see, for example, Dorothy Noyes and Roger D. Abrahams, "From Calendar Custom to National Memory: European Commonplaces," in *Cultural Memory and the Construction of Identity*, ed. Dan Ben-Amos and Liliane Weissberg (Detroit, Mich.: Wayne State University Press, 1999), 77–98; Susanne Kuchler and Walter Melion, eds., *Images of Memory: On Remembering and Representation* (Washington, D.C.: Smithsonian Institution Press, 1991); David M. Gordon, "The Cultural

Politics of a Traditional Ceremony: Mutomboko and the Performance of History on the Luapula (Zambia)," *Comparative Studies in Society and History* 46, no. 1 (2004): 63–83.

51. For critical responses to postmodernist approaches, see, for example, Ernest Gellner, *Postmodernism, Reason, and Religion* (London: Routledge, 1992) and Richard J. Evans, *In Defence of History* (London: Granta Books, 2000). More welcoming responses can be found in Norman K. Denzin, *Interpretive Ethnography: Ethnographic Practices for the 21st Century* (Thousand Oaks, Calif.: Sage, 1997) and A *New Philosophy of History*, ed. Frank Ankersmit and Hans Kellner (London: Reaktion Books, 1995). For other texts on this subject, see "Further Selected Reading" in this volume.

52. J. D. Y. Peel, "Making History: The Past in the Ijesha Present," *Man* 19, no. 1 (1984): 112.

53. Helen Thomas, "Mimesis and Alterity in the African Caribbean Quadrille: Ethnography Meets History," *Cultural and Social History: The Journal of the Social History Society*, 1, no. 3 (2004): 280–301; Usner, "Dancing in the Past."

2

Dances and Dancing in Tonga
Anthropological and Historical Discourses

ADRIENNE L. KAEPPLER

The study of dances as historical *and* cultural discourses can be an illuminating anthropological project. The combination, however, diverges from typical anthropological research and analyses where these two approaches are usually separated. Classic ethnographic research was based on extended fieldwork that attempted to present a picture and synchronic analysis of a contemporary society and usually resulted in a detailed account of the "ethnographic present." In contrast, late-nineteenth-century "armchair anthropologists" studied written accounts and theorized about diffusion or migration in the long ago. More recently, historians have researched historical records for societies usually reserved for the anthropological gaze. The twain did meet during the second half of the twentieth century when some anthropologists, such as Fernand Braudel and Marshall Sahlins, began to focus their attention on history and embarked on studies of "structures in the long run."[1]

Even though many anthropologists have felt that structure and history are opposing concepts, they have used history in their studies—especially the long view of history as taken from archaeology and oral history with its contributions to the study of myth and genealogy.

Because of the problematic heritage of evolutionism and diffusionism, however, anthropologists have generally shied away from history and especially from grandiose schemes. Those, such as Marshall Sahlins, who have attempted to bridge the gap between the structural/functional emphasis on synchrony and the historian's emphasis on diachrony, have carried out long-term fieldwork in contemporary societies and combed libraries and archives to place them in a historical perspective. Sahlins has demonstrated the possibilities and significance of combining structural analysis, history, event, and action in his structures in the long run and has concluded that "the historical process unfolds as a continuous and reciprocal movement between the practice of the structure and the structure of the practice."[2]

As a student in the 1960s, I became drawn to the vibrancy and importance of dance performances while carrying out anthropological fieldwork in Tonga. Why was dance so important? Who were the patrons, composers, performers, and audiences? How did these dances come to their present complexity? What could dance tell me about society? Over the years I have often focused my attention on dance (or on its broader application as "structured movement systems") and its relationships to social structure, authority, gender, and art, as well as more theoretical concepts such as the analogy of dance with language, style, and aesthetics. I have also, nonetheless, found it necessary to place these concepts into historical perspectives. Here I explore this combination of some historical and cultural aspects of dance.

That dance can be a form of historical and cultural discourse is not common in the study and analysis of dance; historically anthropologists have not often focused on dance, except for its use in ritual.[3] Dances are surface manifestations or exemplars of movement languages that convey information, just as speech sequences are surface manifestations of spoken languages. The analogy is a convenient one, but it is always necessary to point out that what movement and speech communicate may be similar *or* quite different. If discourse is "communication of thought" usually through conversation (as the dictionary tells us), how can bodies converse and convey history? And how can history help us to understand dance and other structured movement systems in the present?

The term "history" evokes the idea of a linear knowledge of what happened in the past that has been recorded in writing. But even in the best of times, written history records only select "moments" when someone happened to write down what she or he saw or was told. When we attempt to look at the history or historical processes of dance outside of the Euro-American traditions, we find that only occasionally did someone commit to writing information about dance performances. But history does not just depend on what was written down by outsiders or insiders. In this chapter, I pursue an anthropological approach to dance history and ethnography in the Kingdom of Tonga in the south Pacific that does not depend only on accounts that were written down, but rather on a variety of discourses derived from oral history, ethnohistory, ethnography, and movement itself. Dancing and its history are not just "out there" in some positivistic sense; it is the framing and interpretation of dancing that makes history for the present.

History, Politics, Oratory, Dance, and Aesthetics in Tonga

Ethnographic fieldwork often elicits a series of puzzles—puzzles that cannot be solved by the ethnographer without the use of historical sources and the dialectical engagement of the ethnographer with the ethnographer's mentors and hosts. My mentors and hosts in Tonga and their ancestors have been literate for more than a century, but they do not have a tradition of writing down their impressions of dance performances or the meanings of the dances to their contemporary lives. Nor do they have a tradition of written dance criticism. Indeed, the most important aspects of a dance are the sung text that the movements accompany and the skill with which this text is conveyed. Although many dance song texts are written down, their *interpretation* is in the oral tradition, and there are specialists who are skilled in such interpretation. These specialists became my mentors, and this chapter is the result of interaction with these dance specialists and interpreters of historic and contemporary events.

Because of the lack of written critical analyses of how specific works influence later works, dance historians often deny to non-Western productions the status of "works of art"; here I demonstrate that historic Tongan dances are known and do influence later works, and that they embed an aesthetic system that is widely recognized. Tongan dance is essentially an extension of the "oratorical voice." Oratory is the most important art form in Tonga; through oratory emotions are expressed and reciprocated. The job of the orator is to make people laugh and cry, by metaphorical (and sometimes direct) references to personified, yet abstract, objects of sympathy. To Tongans, oratory is a "high art," and dances that express the texts, with their oratorical power, are, in the words of Sherry Ortner, a "key elaborating symbol, extensively and systematically formulating relationships between a wide range of diverse cultural elements."[4] The oratorical art is central to social activity— constructing and imposing hierarchy and political potency. Through the oratorical voice fundamental cultural values are constructed and passed from generation to generation through the oral and written word. But *who* has the authority to project this oratorical voice and thereby to construct history for the present? Essentially, it was the aristocrats of the twentieth century, and especially Queen Sālote (1900–65), who objectified history into written form and codified the thinking of the nation to revere certain genealogical lines and their intermixture. It was the *selection* of historical and cultural information by those with the authority to do so that gave political potency to the status quo. Although the present powerful genealogical lines can be traced to the mythological charter of Tongan society and history and have the philosophical force of Mikhail Bakhtin's "epic," a study of oratory reveals how the past, present, and future can be shaped for political ends.[5] The concepts are embedded in the deep-seated Polynesian philosophy by which contested, or uncontested, genealogical links and historic events are brought to bear on contemporary authority and power.

Written poetic texts, the people who perform them in time and space, and the movements themselves are interpreted and explained in the oral tradition, thereby imposing knowledge about social order through an aesthetic medium that results in the shared values of the society.[6] Historic events, like Bakhtin's epics, have analogies in myth and can impose order on contemporary life. To Tongans, dance performances—like rituals—communicate messages that, for the most part, are already known. How social and political order are constructed from these messages is ever evolving depending on the contexts in which they are used for political action—an example of Sahlins's historical process unfolding "between the practice of the structure and the structure of the practice."[7]

Historic Dance Moments in Tonga

Since the first European descriptions of dance performances in Tonga made during the third voyage of Captain James Cook in 1777, observers have been fascinated by the coordinated performances of huge groups of men and/or women dancing in honor of the chiefs and visitors. The eightieth birthday of King Tāufaʻāhau Tupou IV, on 4 July 1998, was marked with dancing by large groups of villagers and whole islands. In the intervening two centuries after Cook's voyages, all important events (except funerals) have featured dance performances, and some of these events have been described in the literature. These descriptions can be considered sources for a history of Tongan dance. Instead of confining myself to the paradigm of linear written history, however, I want to enlarge our historical purview to suggest that dance history does not depend on accounts that were written down—usually by outsiders—but on a wider variety of historical sources that includes written history, oral history and cultural memory, ethnohistory, and ethnographic research. Even with this variety of sources, sometimes we know only about specific "moments." Moments, however, can be extended to represent a particular stage in something's development, or a stage in a course of events. As constructed here, a "moment" is essentially a historiographic abstraction, which can vary from a single written description of a specific performance to a period of years with intensive observations and numerous written sources.

I focus here on four moments in the history of Tongan dance and the importance of historical and ethnographic sources in our understanding of the transformations of the dance genre now known as *lakalaka*, the embodiment of history par excellence. It is the interpretation of these moments that makes "history" for the present—not only for the study of dance, but for the study of Tongan history. The first "moment" was a visit of the British explorer Captain James Cook to Tonga at the end of the eighteenth century and the descriptions and illustrations that resulted from the journal entries and drawings made in situ and their subsequent publication. This written and visual "history" (along with other eighteenth- and early-nineteenth-century written accounts and drawings by outsiders) is equally revealing about the outsiders and their points of view as it is about the dances. A second "moment" was the last third of the nineteenth century when the dances witnessed by Cook were transformed into the dance form now known as *lakalaka*. This moment combines oral history, accounts written by outsiders, and illustrations in the new medium of photography, as interpreted in the context of my own ethnographic research. It is an example of "ethnohistory." A third "moment" encompasses my continuing research on the *lakalaka* performing genre from 1964 until the present in which the method is the classic ethnographic participant-observation.[8] Finally, the fourth "moment" took place in July 1998 when elements of *lakalaka* were transformed once again, and during which I just happened to be an observer.

The first two moments are based on written historical accounts and on Tongan interpretations of written accounts and oral history. The third and fourth moments are based on my own ethnographic research as a participant-observer. This included talking to the composers, performers, patrons, and audience members, taking part in dance performances, and, with Tongan help, interpreting contemporary accounts from local newspapers and magazines, as well as photographs made by Tongans. Much of this ethnography has now become history. From this variety of accounts we see how language and points of view color what we see and do not see, and what knowledge is necessary to understand and interpret historic and contemporary accounts and illustrations.

Some Prehistory and History

Millennia ago, peoples from Asia and Southeast Asia began moving into Oceania, bringing with them musical, movement, literary, and theatrical ideas and concepts that evolved and became codified into "dances." These dances and the systems of knowledge in which they were embedded changed over time, owing to restyling from within and the influences of intercultural contact and later migrations.

During the late eighteenth century and the first part of the nineteenth century, Europeans began to travel to the Pacific and to write about and illustrate what they experienced. Eighteenth-century voyages of exploration were organized primarily by England, France, Holland, and Spain. The best early descriptions of dance were recorded by individuals who traveled with Captain Cook, especially in some areas of Polynesia. The published results of these encounters record descriptions of music, movement, and costume as seen from the outside. Though sketchy, early eyewitness accounts are invaluable sources when used in conjunction with later reports from missionaries, whalers, traders, tourists, beachcombers, anthropologists, and indigenous peoples.

An Eighteenth-Century Moment

An important historic moment is the first recorded description of a Tongan dance called *me'elaufola*. Performances of *me'elaufola* were described in Cook's journals during his visit in 1777 and were illustrated by the official artist on the voyage, John Webber. Webber made drawings of two large group dances, and professional engravers reworked these drawings into finished engravings. The two engravings depict "A Night Dance by Men in Hapaee" and "A Night Dance by Women in Hapaee." Descriptions of the dances became part of the official published version of the journal of the voyage. A description of the women's dance illustrates how we can learn about dance history from movement itself. Cook notes:

> The concert having continued about a quarter of an hour, twenty women entered the circle. Most of them had, upon their heads, garlands of crimson flowers of the China rose, or others; and many of them had ornamented their persons with leaves of trees, cut with a great deal of nicety about the edges. They made a circle round the chorus, turning their faces toward it, and began singing a soft air, to which responses were made by the chorus in the same tone; and these were repeated alternately. All this while, the women accompanied their song with several very graceful motions of their hands toward their faces, and in other directions[,] at the same time, making constantly a step forward, and then back again, with one foot, while the other was fixed. They then turned their faces to the assembly, sung some time, and retreated slowly in a body, to that part of the circle which was opposite the hut where the principal spectators sat. After this, one of them advanced from each side, meeting and passing each other in the front, and continuing their progress round till they came to the rest. On which two advanced from each side, two of whom also passed each other, and returned as the former; but the other two remained, and to these came one from each side, by intervals, till the whole number had again formed a circle about the chorus.
>
> Their manner of dancing was now changed to a quicker measure, in which they made a kind of half turn by leaping, and clapping their hands, and snapping their fingers, repeating some words in conjunction with the chorus. Toward the end, as the quickness of the music increased, their gestures and attitudes were varied with wonderful vigour and dexterity; and some of their motions, perhaps, would, with us, be reckoned rather indecent; though this part of the performance, most probably, was not meant to convey any wanton ideas, but merely to display the astonishing variety of their movements.[9]

The engraving based on Webber's drawing (see fig. 2.1) shows two groups of women, one on each side of the musicians. I have described

2.1. "A Night Dance by Women in Hapaee." Engraving after a drawing by John Webber in 1777. Photo courtesy of Smithsonian Institution.

elsewhere how this excellent description and illustration can be interpreted as an important arm-movement motif still used today and how the drawing suggests that Webber had actually distilled the essence of the most important arm motif for women used in the *meʻelaufola* dance genre.[10]

Webber's illustration of a men's dance shows a similar understanding of the arm movements. Again, there is a written description from Cook's journal:

> To this grand female ballet, succeeded one performed by fifteen men. Some of them were old; but their age seemed to have abated little of their agility or ardour for the dance. They were disposed in a sort of circle, divided at the front, with their faces not turned out toward the assembly, nor inward to the chorus; but one half of their circle faced forward as they had advanced, and the other half in a contrary direction. They, sometimes, sung slowly, in concert with the chorus; and while thus employed, they also made several very fine motions with their hands, but different from those made by the women, at the same time inclining the body to either side alternately, by raising one leg, which was stretched outward and resting on the other, the arm of the same side being also stretched fully upward. At other times, they recited sentences in a musical tone, which were answered by the chorus; and,

2.2. "A Night Dance by Men in Hapaee." Engraving after a drawing by John Webber in 1777. Photo courtesy of Smithsonian Institution.

at intervals, increased the motions of the feet, which however, were never varied. At the end, the rapidity of the music, and of the dancing, increased so much, that it was scarcely possible to distinguish the different movements; though one might suppose the actors were now almost tired, as their performance had lasted near half an hour.[11]

Webber's drawing of this or a similar performance (see fig. 2.2) again shows his understanding of the importance of the arm movements and has captured the essence of the most important arm movement motif for men—that is, with extended arms *(laufola)* the lower arm is rotated to alternate the palm facing from forward to back or from up to down.[12] I have elsewhere drawn attention to how the engraver of this drawing has misinterpreted Webber's original drawing of the arm movements.[13] These descriptions and illustrations have captured and conveyed the important movements and the differences between men's and women's movements in Tonga. The moment constitutes a historic base for all subsequent moments in Tongan dance. Webber's illustrations correspond to the journal description that "some of the gestures were so expressive, that it might be said they spoke the language that accompanied them, if we allow that there is any connection between motion and sound."[14]

A Nineteenth-Century Moment

Before the next "moment" occurred, Protestant missionaries arrived in Tonga and forbid dancing for their converts in the mistaken idea that dances were about religion and the gods, and were licentious and heathen. The Tongans, however, turned out to be much more clever than the missionaries. A historic moment in the late nineteenth century, recorded primarily in oral tradition, occurred when Tuku'aho (1858–97), the high chief of the village of Tatakamotonga, one of the Protestant villages, held a competition for the development of a new dance form. It is said that this competition was won by Fuapau of the northern island of Vava'u. The composers/choreographers *(punake)* of the time were familiar primarily with the *me'elaufola* described above and other traditional dances such as *me'utu'upaki* (a men's standing dance performed with small paddles) and *fa'ahiula* (a women's dance with complex arm movements), and they essentially transformed remnants of the old dance forms into a "new dance" that became known as *lakalaka*. Chief Tuku'aho worked in conjunction with a *punake* from his own village, Fineasi Malukava, to further develop the *lakalaka* and train the performers. "Malukava" became an inherited title, appointed by the king. A grandson of Malukava (Tevita Kavaefiafi) became the titleholder during the mid-twentieth century. This Malukava told me, "the *me'elaufola* was a form of *lakalaka* before the modern *lakalaka*, done by all women in which they stood and slowly performed *laufola* [outstretched arm movements]."[15] Although oral traditions do not record exactly what year this new dance was created, it is thought to have been in the late 1870s or early 1880s. By the mid-1880s, *lakalaka* became popular and spread throughout Tonga. In a description from 1885, the British vice-consul, Henry Francis Symonds, described a *lakalaka* performance in Neiafu on the northern Tongan island of Vava'u and its background:

> The Lakalaka is a dance that preserves some of the old forms of Tongan dancing united with what the Wesleyan missionaries have introduced as their idea of the proper way for natives to amuse themselves. The old dances, like all the old Tongan customs, were long ago prohibited by the Missionaries, apparently for no earthly reason than because they belonged to the days before the people were Wesleyans. . . . When Mr. Moulton assumed the direction of the Mission affairs (in 1881) being an educated man, he perceived the mistake that had been made,

2.3. *Lakalaka* performed at the wedding of King Tupou II in 1899. Photo from the voyage of the USS *Albatross*, under the command of the U.S. Fish Commission. Courtesy of the Naval Historical Center.

and consequently allowed them further latitude than they had hitherto been given, and the result is one of the prettiest and most graceful dances I have ever seen. . . . [T]he subjects embrace every conceivable thing; legends and war songs, descriptions of scenery, and tales of Foreign lands, and last but not least, love.[16]

Basil Thomson, visiting Tonga in 1900, noted that those *lakalaka* "that become popular may endure for many years. *Langa fale kakala* (Build a house of flowers), for example, . . . is as popular a favourite now as it was when I was in Mua in 1886."[17] Photographs of *lakalaka* performances are known from the nineteenth century. Figure 2.3 illustrates a *lakalaka* performed at the wedding of King Tupou II in 1899, and Figure 2.4 depicts the "King's Birthday Dances," probably from his great birthday celebration in 1893. On this occasion "there was a grand *lakalaka* (dancing) competition between the young men and women of Muʻa, Fuaʻamotu, Houma, and Hihifo. The Muʻa dancers . . . won the first prize."[18] Unfortunately, we do not know who did the judging, but

2.4. "The King's Birthday Dances," probably from the great birthday celebration of King Tupou II in 1893. Photographer unknown. Courtesy of Elizabeth Wood-Ellem.

the Mu'a dancers were those from the village of Tatakamotonga and were trained under the original dance master Malukava (Fineasi).

As noted above, the arm movements of *me'elaufola* appear to be the same kinds of movements now used in *lakalaka*. There are two major categories of arm movements *(haka)* recognized by Tongans. *Haka nonou* refers to movements in which the upper arms are held close to the body and are characteristic of certain movement motifs, used especially by women. The other category, *laufola*, describes movements in which the upper arms are extended forward and away from the body (see fig. 2.5). The term *me'elaufola* described the eighteenth-century dance form: *me'e* (dance) in which arm movements were *laufola*, extended. *Laufola* arm movements also became characteristic of the nineteenth-century form. The new name, *lakalaka*, is a word that means to walk quickly, "to step it out."[19] Whereas the term *me'elaufola* described the arm movements, *lakalaka* describes the leg movements.

I have argued elsewhere that *lakalaka* is a nineteenth-century evolved form of the pre-European *me'elaufola*, retaining the structural, vocal, and movement characteristics of the old form even though it has lost the instrumental accompaniment (of bamboo stamping tubes and struck idiophones, see figs. 2.1 and 2.2).[20] The vocal polyphony appears to be an evolved form of the traditional six-part polyphony, and although the

2.5. *Laufola,* outstretched arm positions, are performed by the women from the village of Kanokupolu. Princess Pilolevu performs as *vāhenga,* principal female dancer, and Baron Vaea performs as the male *vāhenga* at the presentation of the *lakalaka* to the ceremonial attendants for approval. Photo by Adrienne L. Kaeppler, 1975.

pitch intervals may have changed, the structure has not. In addition to retaining the arm and leg movements characteristic of *me'elaufola, lakalaka* incorporates changes in floor plan as dancers move from place to place on the dancing ground (also described in Cook's journals) and has developed the polyphonic and polykinetic prototypes found in early forms. From the similar, but separate, choreographies for men and women in *me'elaufola,* it was only a small step to simultaneously perform separate choreographies for men and women that became characteristic of *lakalaka,* in which the graceful movements of the women contrast with the more virile movements of the men (see figs. 2.5 and 2.6) illustrating the separate but interdependent roles of men and women in Tongan rank and social structure. *Lakalaka* did not simply incorporate the old forms but transformed them into something new. This transformation was carried out in accordance with the aesthetic principle on which Tongan poetry, music, and dance is based, *heliaki* (indirectness).

2.6. Princess Pilolevu and Baron Vaea perform as *vāhenga*, principal dancers, for the formal performance of the *lakalaka* of Kanokupolu in the 1975 *kātoanga*. Note the clothing differences between this performance and the "practice" performance in figure 2.5. Except for the two *vāhenga*, who wear special costumes, the performers wear barkcloth skirts and *maile*-leaf overskirts, the official costume of the *lakalaka* of Kanokupolu. Photo by Adrienne L. Kaeppler, 1975.

Heliaki means to say one thing but mean another, never stating something directly, but making reference by allusion and metaphor. For example, when referring to an individual, he or she is never named but is referred to as a bird, flower, wind, or place. Deeds are never detailed, but are referred to only indirectly. The transformation of *me'elaufola* into *lakalaka* was in itself a kind of *heliaki*.

An Ethnographic Moment

What I will consider an ethnographic moment is the time of my own participant-observation research on Tongan dance, beginning in 1964 and still continuing. By the middle of the twentieth century, *lakalaka* had become the most important performing genre, with *heliaki* becoming more and more complex, especially in *lakalaka* composed by such luminaries as King Tupou II, Queen Sālote Tupou III, Fakatava, Ve'ehala,

and a few others. Queen Sālote's *lakalaka* are the best known and over
the years have been revived, restaged, and repeated as examples of the
classical tradition of Tongan dance and as identity markers for members of the villages for which she composed them. By the 1950s the
transformation was complete; *lakalaka* were based on the style and structure promulgated by Queen Sālote, with their basis in *heliaki*.

The structure of a *lakalaka* is based on formal speechmaking, having
three sections: (1) an introductory *fakatapu*, which acknowledges the important family lines of the chiefs relevant to the occasion; (2) the main
lakalaka section, which conveys the theme, information about the occasion, genealogies of relevant people, history, or mythology of the village
performing, and other relevant information; and (3) the *tatau*, a closing
counterpart to the introductory *fakatapu*, in which the performers say
goodbye and again defer to the chiefs. One stanza may be a *tau*, a verse
that expresses the essence of the performance, during which the performers do their very best to compel the audience to pay strict attention.
This formal structure forms the outline of the composition. The overall
design, and thus the meaning of any specific composition, need not be
apparent until the end of the performance, however. The meaning is revealed as each verse, through verbal and visual allusions, builds on those
that went before, mediated through the aesthetic principle of *heliaki*.

The performers of *lakalaka* are both men and women, often two
hundred or more, arranged in two or more rows facing the audience.
The men stand on the right side (from the observer's point of view), the
women stand on the left. Men and women perform different movements that are consistent with the Tongan view of what is suitable and
appropriate for their sex. Women's movements are soft and graceful;
men's movements are strong and virile. Leg movements are minimal,
especially for women, who move only a few steps from side to side and
forward and back. Men may take larger steps, bend, turn, and sometimes strike or lay on the ground. Arm movements allude to the words
of the poetry—which are often allusions to a deeper meaning—creating
double abstractions much admired in Tongan performing arts.

The poetry of a *lakalaka* is a series of concepts and references rather
than a complete story and is usually composed for performance by a
specific group at a specific event. Poetic allusions are often to mythology
and genealogy—usually in a quite roundabout or indirect way—which
illustrates the Tongan ideal of *heliaki*. Although many of the allusions are
understood by everyone, others are understood only by other poets, and

the desire is often to take old allusions and transform them into something new. In order to understand the poetic transformations, one must "work from one's own knowledge," which has been gained through the study of genealogy, mythology, and history. It is necessary to listen to every word and watch every movement. Many of the references are common knowledge, but the association must be made instantaneously in order to go on to an understanding of the next allusion. The poetry is performed as a sung speech with choreographed movements, which in figurative language and allusive movements elevate the monarch and chiefs, paying them the highest possible respect and dignity. At the same time, the poetry also honors the performers and their villages. The texts become frames for interpreting history and the politics of prestige and power and encode knowledge about social order through an aesthetic medium that results in the shared values of the society. Metaphorical associations are made to specific places, residences (or former residences), trees, flowers and flower constructions, birds, winds, and *mātanga* (historic monuments or places associated with individuals of the past and present) as well as to the Christian god from whom they gained status as Christian aristocrats. The texts can be read in many ways, but especially as historical narratives relevant to contemporary politics.

The classic performance event for *lakalaka* is at a *kātoanga*, a public festivity or celebration. Large-scale government *kātoanga* are rare, but smaller *kātoanga* occur nearly every year and seem to have become more frequent. During the reign of Queen Sālote (1918–65) there were seven important *kātoanga*.[21] After Queen Sālote's death in 1965 the next *kātoanga* was the coronation of Tupou IV in July 1967.[22] The last important *kātoanga* of the twentieth century was the eightieth birthday celebration of Tupou IV in 1998.

Experiencing a *kātoanga* places the importance of performance and presentation into perspective and confirms the perpetuation of tradition in modern life. The presentations/performances described by Cook and others—such as J. H. Labillardière, D. Alejandro Malaspina, William Mariner, Basil C. Thomson, E. E. V. Collocott, Edward Winslow Gifford, Eric B. Shumway, Larry Shumway, Richard Moyle, 'I Futa Helu, and myself[23]—during the past two hundred years have continued to encompass some of the most important social and political events in modern Tonga. *Kātoanga* comprises several important performance activities including the mixing and drinking of *kava* (made from the infusion of a pepper plant called *kava*), the presentation of food and valuables, and the presentation of sung speeches with choreographed movements, primarily *lakalaka* that embed traditional rites and speeches and thereby confirm the importance of tradition in modern life. Ideally, a large segment of the men and women of each area of the kingdom perform, thereby involving every family in traditional allegiance. The central performers are the sons and daughters of the king, nobles, and chiefs who learn the rites and history of the lineage and villages they represent by enacting them and commenting on the event.

The complex verbal and visual performances of *lakalaka* display the social organization of the villages and the hierarchical structure of the kingdom embedded in metaphorical poetry delivered in an aesthetically charged atmosphere. The composition of these three-dimensional forms is done by specialists, and to learn and perform them requires a substantial investment of time and energy by the many performers and teachers. Researching a *kātoanga* lies in obtaining and comprehending the poetry of as many examples of *lakalaka* as possible, understanding how the movements project these sung speeches into visual form, analyzing the variations of the melodic contours and voice parts during as many practices and performances as possible, getting aesthetic evaluations during and after various performances, and placing the *kātoanga* into its total social context. Understanding such a complex event can only be attempted by immersion and in-depth research in a limited number of venues during the pre-*kātoanga* period, during the *kātoanga* itself, and during post-*kātoanga* evaluations. That is, long-term, in-depth ethnographic research is necessary for understanding "an ethnographic moment." My involvement in this ethnographic moment consisted of more than four years of fieldwork in Tonga as a participant-observer. In addition to interviewing hundreds of Tongans—ranging from Queen Sālote and members of the aristocracy to composers/choreographers to dancers and audience members—I took part in the *lakalaka* of the village of Ha'ateiho for the coronation of King Tupou in 1967. There were weeks and weeks of daily practices (with much personal interaction with other participants), a performance for the approval of the ceremonial attendants (when we were photographed by the *National Geographic* in our practice costumes[24]), the grand performance for the coronation, and numerous other performances in the following days (including one for the visiting Duke and Duchess of Kent, who represented the British monarch). Without such personal involvement, my description of this third moment would only have been as incomplete as the above descriptions of the first and second moments.

To experience a *kātoanga* is to be transported back in time to the rituals associated with propitiation of the descendant of the sky god Tangaloa, the sacred Tuʻi Tonga, or supreme ruler, whose function was to see to the continued fertility of the land and people. Continued fertility necessitated the offering of "first fruits" during an annual presentation of large quantities of *kava,* staple root crops, pigs, other foods, women's valuables *(koloa)* of mats and barkcloth, as well as music and dance performances. First fruits and women were sent to the supreme ruler, not only from all the Tongan islands, but also from a larger region over which Tonga held influence—Samoa, ʻUvea, Futuna, and other areas. Performances were also brought to honor and entertain the Tuʻi Tonga, the people, and the performers. A new composition might be presented to the Tuʻi Tonga in this extended "first fruits" category. Performances with new movements and musical settings were also brought from the far-flung territories of the Tongan Empire; some were added to the repertoire, and some were eventually Tonganized.

Kātoanga today continue these traditions in the court of the Tupou dynasty and include most of the same ingredients. The king's birthday celebrations and the annual agricultural show are contemporary expressions of the giving of first fruits and valuables to the king, who gives them a Christian blessing. They are then redistributed and used in his court. Dances are first performed with the food and valuables before they are publicly performed—usually during the public days of the *kātoanga* and the days leading up to it. Sons and daughters of the king and chiefs are often the central performers—they will be the next generation of chiefs and parents of future generations of chiefs.

In the court of the sacred Tuʻi Tonga, the presentations and performances included the *meʻelaufola* described above and *tauʻaʻalo* (work songs) in conjunction with food presentation. In 1800 the missionary George Vason described such a ceremony; approaching the Tuʻi Tonga "in regular rotations, in a slow, solemn pace, with a kind of monotonous song, and upon their bended knees, [they] presented the first production of their *abbees* [gardens]. . . . When the ceremony of the first fruits of their fields is completed, they usually have a dance."[25] The bestowing of titles was (and remains) an important event. Investiture of titles takes place during a ritual in which *kava* is mixed and served with great ceremony.

The manner of presentation of *kava*, food, valuables, and performances was, and still is, as important as the objects themselves—as Vason noted, "the manner of doing it rendered the present doubly valuable."[26] All of the niceties and etiquette continue today. In the court of the Tuʻi Kanokupolu, of which King Tāufaʻāhau Tupou IV is the twenty-second ruler, food and valuables are presented and counted in a most ceremonious manner, and the final offering is a music and/or dance performance—the most highly regarded are *lakalaka*.

A Moment of Change in 1998

This brings us to a historic moment when a *lakalaka* was transformed from *heliaki* in performance into a biographical "history." In the first week of July 1998 was a large-scale celebration in honor of the eightieth birthday of King Tāufaʻāhau Tupou IV. Although there have been several large-scale celebrations in recent years, this was the largest since the king's coronation in 1967, and much of it was planned and implemented by the king's only daughter, Princess Pilolevu (b. 1951). The princess is especially interested in the cultural life of Tonga and especially in dance. She performed as the principal dancer in the 1967 *kātoanga* for her father's coronation (see fig. 2.6) and in several *lakalaka* for her father's village Kanokupolu since that time. She has always had the benefit of someone to explain to her the complex *heliaki* of the poetry and movements. She is concerned, however, that because of the difficult *heliaki*, people of her generation and younger cannot understand the poetry. Thus, in 1998 she initiated the beginning of what may become another transformation in Tongan dance. This transformation included changes in the makeup of the performing group, changes in placement of the dancers, and especially changes in the literary content of the poetry.[27]

Lakalaka are traditionally performed by a single village that is the estate of a noble, or a few closely affiliated villages—either located near one another, or villages from different areas of Tonga that are the estates of the same noble. Princess Pilolevu's husband, Maʻulupekotofa, had recently been appointed governor of Vavaʻu, the northern area of Tonga. He was not yet a titleholder because his father, Baron Tuita, was still alive. The great island of Vavaʻu is made up of a large number of villages, including several that are the estates of important nobles, including the brothers of the princess. Princess Pilolevu thought it would be marvelous if all the Vavaʻu villages would perform together in a huge *lakalaka,* which would create a spectacular effect, and she asked them to perform in a grand new *lakalaka* composed for the event. This proposition was widely accepted by the village leaders and the villagers, and more than five hundred decided to participate.[28] Never before had villages of this variety performed together for a *lakalaka* for a government *kātoanga* and with such a large number of dancers.

The second transformation that took place during this moment was the choice and placement of the important dancers. The principal dancer, *vāhenga,* is classically the daughter of the village noble. For example, the noble of the village of Kanokupolu is the king, and in recent decades Princess Pilolevu, as daughter of the noble/king, was *vāhenga* (see figs. 2.5 and 2.6). In the 1998 *lakalaka* of Vava'u, instead of the daughter of a village noble, Lupepau'u Tuita, the daughter of the governor (and Princess Pilolevu), was *vāhenga.* But where would Princess Pilolevu stand? She is the daughter of the king and not simply the daughter of a Vava'u estate owner. She was the organizer of the *lakalaka* and is one of the most famous and respected dancers in the country. The people of Vava'u wanted to honor her. She chose to dance in the tenth place (from the center) on the ladies' side. Her husband, Governor Ma'ulupekotofa, chose to dance in the tenth place on the men's side. From this time forward, it is likely that the tenth place will be considered a place of honor.

The most radical change, however, was in the composition of the poetry. Although at least one new piece had already been created in traditional *heliaki* style by a composer for a Vava'u village, Princess Pilolevu wanted a different one and requested a little-known composer to attempt a new style. This was Mele Suipi Latu, the granddaughter of Fakatava, the famous composer from the area. Mele was requested to read a newly published biography of King Tupou and to create a *lakalaka* with little or no *heliaki*—that is, to speak directly, to tell the king's story so that everyone could understand it. She did, resulting in an extremely interesting new composition. Although the overall structure remained the same, *heliaki* (indirectness) was not incorporated into the text. The king's ancestors were named, and their deeds were described. The king's accomplishments were enumerated chronologically. His academic degrees and royal orders were listed, and his government positions were elaborated.[29]

In spite of rain during part of its performance, the *lakalaka* was a resounding success. Everyone loved it; they could understand the poetry;

2.7. Audience members bring gifts to the dancers of the *lakalaka* from Vava'u in the performance for the eightieth-birthday celebration of King Tupou IV. Cans of corned beef have been placed at the front of the performing space by the dancers. Photo by Pesi Fonua.

they enjoyed the visual impact of five hundred dancers, who even displayed signs printed with the king's degrees and royal orders; and they knelt and sat on the ground in order to convey poetic meaning visually. *Heliaki* had been transformed into poetically sung biography. New movement motifs were invented to convey the King's successes in the sports of pole vaulting and shotput.[30]

Even with these changes, *heliaki* was not completely abandoned. Before the performance, each dancer placed a six-pound can of corned beef at the front of the performing space (fig. 2.7) ostensibly as a gift to the court to help feed the visitors. The *heliaki* was not overlooked by the many knowledgeable audience members, who remembered comic allusions to a farmer from Leimatu'a village in Vava'u who attempted to plant corned beef hoping it would grow like vegetables. Also enlightening was a newspaper photo caption of the dancers.[31] The English caption was "Vava'u dancers enjoying a relaxing moment before performance" while the Tongan version, with traditional *heliaki*, noted that the dancers came from "Lolo 'a Halaevalu," the metaphorical name of the water in Vava'u harbor that is so calm it appears to be oil. Tongan speakers were expected to understand the metaphor, whereas English speakers had to be told that the dancers were from Vava'u.

Evaluating the Moment

What are we to make of these historic moments when changes were intentionally made by persons of authority—Chief Tuku'aho, Queen Sālote, and Princess Pilolevu? Each performance is only a *parole* or act (to use Ferdinand de Saussure's terms)—one instance or surface manifestation of the underlying system, that is, the deep structure, or *langue*—and in order to understand this, it is necessary to know the "structures of the *longue durée*."[32] In this examination of what can be discerned about a specific genre of Tongan dance over two centuries, we are able to see the historical process unfolding "as a continuous and reciprocal movement between the practice of the structure and the structure of the practice."[33] Each *parole* is a "performance" for which viewers need "competence" to understand—competence that has changed during the past two hundred years. Each instance (1770s, 1880s, mid-twentieth century, 1998) that manifested in the moment of a "dance system of knowledge" is only a small part of the system of sociocultural knowledge, which requires another level of competence. As levels of competence within a society in traditional forms change, the sociocultural context responds. The transformation of *me'elaufola* into *lakalaka* was a response to the outside influence of Protestant missionaries, and although the musical content of the dance changed, the dance movements and the values associated with poetry probably remained much the same (the level of competence among composers, performers, and viewers had not changed). The changes that elaborated *heliaki* into a complex aesthetic, promulgated by Queen Sālote and her contemporaries, was evolutionary. Indirectness had always been there, but from the 1930s to the 1960s it became more elaborated and systematized (the level of competence increased). The 1998 series of changes from within could have a more profound influence in the transformation of literary artistic style (the level of competence was thought to have diminished). On the other hand, the future may show that this was only a temporary change for a specific occasion that entered the historic stream of events simply because someone was there who chose to write about it.

History and Ethnography

It remains to suggest that a historical perspective in conjunction with ethnographic research has enlarged our understanding of what Tongan *lakalaka* can reveal about politics, power, poetry, music, movement, and aesthetics. As Sahlins has reminded us, when people of different cultures come in contact, events may convey quite different meanings to each group, and the reaction to the event is shaped by their different understandings of the occasion, which, in turn, may affect and transform basic structures of the society. Events are interpreted through the "structures of significance" that the people of a culture have derived from history.[34] By examining historic and ethnographic records of specific events and actions as well as oral traditions about them in Tonga, we can see that reactions to dance events were sometimes shaped by different intercultural understandings, such as the misunderstanding of the Protestant missionaries of the *me'elaufola*. Christianization affected and modified dance traditions along with religious and political structures that were transformed by outside contact—thus the origin of the *lakalaka*. For Queen Sālote, *lakalaka* gave her the opportunity to speak publicly on matters important to the nation, such as political independence and the retention of cultural traditions and aesthetics—matters that she promulgated as structures of significance for the mid-twentieth century.

Tongan *lakalaka* are socially realized cultural constructions of history, embedded in the aesthetic system. As we have seen by examining four historic moments, the more detail we have about each moment, the more we learn about cultural discourses of the time. The first two moments were interpreted with the aid of written history and oral tradition, whereas the two later moments used written history, oral tradition, and long-term ethnographic research.

The study of Tongan *lakalaka* and its history reveals a great deal about poetry, aesthetics, and Tongan society. Cloaked in *heliaki*, *lakalaka* distill Tongan historical, social, and political values in an artistic medium of heroic form. The poetics of history, prestige, and power are artistic refinements of the Tongan elite and especially those who have the ability and authority to present their interpretations of history publicly.

Since my anthropological studies of dance have always been informed by history, I can only agree with Sahlins: "Practice clearly has gone beyond the theoretical differences that are supposed to divide anthropology and history. Anthropologists rise from the abstract structure to the explication of the concrete event. Historians devalue the unique event in favor of underlying recurrent structures. And also paradoxically, anthropologists are as often diachronic in outlook as historians nowadays are synchronic."[35]

NOTES

Research in Tonga was carried out for more than four years between 1964 and 2003, funded by the Wenner-Gren Foundation for Anthropological Research, the National Institute of Mental Health, the Bishop Museum, and the Smithsonian Institution, to all of whom I wish to express my warmest appreciation. I am indebted to the government of Tonga under their majesties the late Queen Sālote Tupou III and King Tāufaʻāhau Tupou IV, and to the many Tongans who helped me to understand the data presented in this chapter, especially the late Queen Sālote, King Tupou IV, the late Prince Tuʻipelehake, Queen Mataʻaho, Princess Pilolevu, Princess Nanasipauʻu Tukuʻaho, His Royal Highness Prince ʻUlukālala-Lavaka-Ata, Princess Siuʻilikutapu, Sister Malia Tuʻifua, the late Vaisima Hopoate, Tuʻimala Kaho, Baron Vaea, the late Honorable Veʻehala, the late ʻAtiu Kalanivalu, and many others.

1. Fernand Braudel, "Histoire et sciences sociales: La longue durée," *Annales: Économies, Sociétés, Civilisations* 13 (1958): 725–53; Marshall Sahlins, *Historical Metaphors and Mythical Realities: Structure in the Early History of the Sandwich Islands Kingdom* (Ann Arbor: University of Michigan Press, 1981).

2. Sahlins, *Historical Metaphors and Mythical Realities*, 72.

3. See, for example, Maurice Bloch, "Symbols, Song, Dance and Features of Articulation: Is Religion an Extreme Form of Traditional Authority?" *Archives Européenes de Sociologie* 15 (1974): 55–81.

4. Sherry B. Ortner, "On Key Symbols," *American Anthropologist* 75 (1973): 1343.

5. Mikhail Bakhtin, *The Dialogic Imagination: Four Essays*, ed. M. Holquist (Austin: University of Texas Press, 1981).

6. See James Fernandez, "The Exposition and Imposition of Order: Artistic Expression in Fang Culture," in *The Traditional Artist in African Societies*, ed. Warren L. d'Azevedo (Bloomington: Indiana University Press, 1973), 197.

7. Sahlins, *Historical Metaphors and Mythical Realities*, 72.

8. Adrienne L. Kaeppler, "The Mystique of Fieldwork," in *Dance in the Field: Theory, Methods and Issues in Dance Ethnography*, ed. Theresa J. Buckland (Basingstoke, Hampshire: Macmillan; New York: St. Martin's Press, 1999), 13–25.

9. James Cook, *A Voyage to the Pacific Ocean*, 3 vols. (London: Strahan, 1784), 1:250–51.

10. Adrienne L. Kaeppler, "Preservation and Evolution of Form and Function in Two Types of Tongan Dance," in *Polynesian Culture History: Essays in Honor of Kenneth P. Emory*, ed. Genevieve A. Highland et al., Special Publication no. 56 (Honolulu: Bernice P. Bishop Museum, 1967), 503–36.

11. Cook, *Voyage to the Pacific Ocean*, 1:251–52.

12. Cook's description notes that fifteen men danced, whereas Webber's illustration depicts many more men dancing.

13. Adrienne L. Kaeppler, "Moments in the History of Tongan Dances from Captain Cook to the 80th Birthday of King Tāufaʻāhau Tupou IV," in *Dans Müzik Kültür, ICTM 20th Ethnochoreology Symposium Proceedings 1998*, ed. Frank Hall and Irene Loutzaki (Istanbul: Boğaziçi University Folklore Club, 2000), 73–91.

14. Cook, *Voyage to the Pacific Ocean*, 1:254–55.

15. Malukava, personal communication, May 1966. Kaeppler field notes.

16. Quoted in Niel Gunson, "Manuscript XIV Part 2," *Journal of Pacific History* 31, no. 2 (1996): 223.

17. Basil C. Thomson, "Appendix Tongan Music," in *Savage Island* (London: John Murray, 1902), 226.

18. Eseta Fulivai Fusitua, "King George II and the Government of Tonga" (M.A. thesis, Australian National University, 1976), 59.

19. Maxwell C. Churchward, *Tongan Dictionary* (London: Oxford University Press, 1959), 278.

20. Kaeppler, "Moments in the History of Tongan Dances from Captain Cook to the 80th Birthday of King Tāufaʻāhau Tupou IV"; Kaeppler, *Poetry in Motion: Studies of Tongan Dance* (Nukuʻalofa: Vavaʻu Press, 1993).

21. These *kātoanga* were listed in the Tongan language version of the government newspaper *Kalonikali* in December 1965 in the obituary of Queen Sālote, which detailed the important events of her reign: the centennial celebration of the coming of Christianity (1926), the centennial celebration of the installation of Tupou I (1945), the double wedding of the present king and his brother (1947), the golden jubilee of the treaty between Tonga and Great Britain (1951), the traveling of Queen Sālote to London for the coronation of Queen Elizabeth II (1953), the visit of Queen Elizabeth and the Duke of Edinburgh to Tonga (1953), and the centennial celebration of the "emancipation" (1962).

22. Other important *kātoanga* during the reign of Tupou IV were the 1975 centenary of the Tongan constitution, during which the crown prince was

invested with the noble title Tupouto'a, and the 1990 silver jubilee of the reign of Tupou IV and his brother Tu'ipelehake as prime minister, during which the king's youngest son was invested with his Ata title. Other *kātoanga* included the 1976 wedding of the king's only daughter, Princess Pilolevu; the 1986 centenary celebration of Roman Catholic education in Tonga; and the seventieth birthday celebration of King Tupou in 1988; as well as several smaller *kātoanga* for church conferences, opening of new churches, other birthday celebrations of the king, and his fiftieth wedding anniversary in 1997.

23. J. H. Labillardière, *An Account of a Voyage in Search of La Pérouse* (London: Uphill, 1802); D. Alejandro Malaspina, *La vuelta al mundo . . . desde 1789 a 1794* (Madrid, 1885); John Martin, M.D., *An Account of the Natives of the Tongan Islands in the South Pacific Ocean, compiled and arranged from the Extensive Communications of Mr. William Mariner,* 3rd ed. (Edinburgh, 1827); Thomson, "Appendix Tongan Music"; E. E. V. Collocott, *Tales and Poems of Tonga,* Bulletin no. 46 (Honolulu: Bernice P. Bishop Museum, 1928); Edward Winslow Gifford, *Tongan Society,* Bulletin no. 61 (Honolulu: Bernice P. Bishop Museum, 1929); Eric B. Shumway, "Ko e fakalangilangi: The Eulogistic Function of the Tongan Poet," *Pacific Studies* 1 (1977): 25–34; Larry Shumway, "The Tongan *lakalaka:* Music Composition and Style," *Ethnomusicology* 25, no. 3 (1981): 467–79; Richard Moyle, *Tongan Music* (Auckland: Auckland University Press, 1987); 'I Futa Helu, *Critical Essays: Cultural Perspectives from the South Seas* (Canberra: *Journal of Pacific History,* 1999); and Kaeppler, *Poetry in Motion.*

24. *National Geographic* 133, no. 3 (1968): 326–27.

25. J. Orange, *Narrative of the Late George Vason of Nottingham* (Derby: Henry Mozley and Sons, 1840), 163.

26. Ibid., 160.

27. Kaeppler field notes of interviews with Princess Pilolevu. The dancing at this 1998 *Kātoanga* is documented in the video *Haka he Langi Kuo Tau* (We Dance in the Ecstasy of Singing), produced for the government of the Kingdom of Tonga by the Institute for Polynesian Studies, Brigham Young University–Hawai'i, 2000.

28. Excluded were a few individuals such as the traditional composers for some of the villages and a few performers who might have had more prominent positions in their own village dances, but who now just became one of many dancers.

29. For the poetry in Tongan and English, see Adrienne L. Kaeppler, *From the Stone Age to the Space Age in 200 Years: Tongan Art and Society on the Eve of the Millennium* (Nuku'alofa: Vava'u Press for the Tongan National Museum, 1998), 54–57. Poems translated into English by Tau'atevalu (Siosiua Fonua).

30. Kaeppler field notes of interviews with Tau'atevalu, special protocol assistant to Princess Pilolevu, and with dancers and audience members.

31. *Kalonikali, Tongan Chronicle,* 16 July 1998: 6.

32. Braudel, "Histoire et sciences sociales: La longue durée"; Sahlins, *Historical Metaphors and Mythical Realities*, 8.

33. Sahlins, *Historical Metaphors and Mythical Realities*, 72.

34. Ibid., 8.

35. Marshall Sahlins, *Islands of History* (Chicago: University of Chicago Press, 1985), 72.

3

Constructing a Classical Tradition

Javanese Court Dance in Indonesia

FELICIA HUGHES-FREELAND

The Republic of Indonesia is politically and culturally dominated by the island of Java, which has reputedly enjoyed an unchanging history of court performance dating back hundreds of years. Subject to colonial rule, principally by the Dutch from the seventeenth to the early twentieth centuries, the Indonesian archipelago of several thousand islands has a complex history of invasion, rebellion, and division. In the middle of the eighteenth century, the Islamic kingdom of Mataram (1582–1749) in Central Java was divided into two principalities, each with their city and royal court: Yogyakarta and Surakarta, or Yogya and Solo, as the cities are popularly known today. When the independent nation-state of Indonesia was declared in 1945, the city and principality of Surakarta became absorbed into the province of Central Java, whereas Yogyakarta was preserved as a special province and city, with Sultan Hamĕngkubuwana IX (1939–88) as its governor. Both royal courts of Yogyakarta and Surakarta support a distinctively styled performance tradition and rival one another in their claims to antiquity and cultural superiority. This chapter considers the historical claims for and present practice

3.1. The Special Region of Yogyakarta.

of the performance tradition of Yogyakarta from the perspective of a British social anthropologist.

Indonesia includes a wide diversity of histories and ethnic groups. During the New Order period (1966–98), President Suharto began to emphasize the development of a national culture based on regional traditions. Despite this emphasis on regional diversity, it was the history and values of the Javanese, the largest ethnic group, that were used to promote Indonesian nationhood. During this period the movement styles of court performance assumed significance in Indonesian educational policy, and Javanese court dance was transformed into the Indonesian classical tradition. Continuity and longevity are emphasized in written histories of classical court dance in Java and in stories about the

origins of the dances. Local historians play down processes of change
and construct the dances as genres that are defined by essential and
unchanging qualities. My anthropological research into contemporary
performances, on the other hand, revealed that in practice, rather than
being fixed as discrete genres, dances varied over time according to the
context. Such fluidity made problematic any attempt to classify and secure the dances as belonging to wholly separate genres. Experience of
this difficulty led me to look more closely at contemporary local histories
of Javanese classical dance traditions and the historical sources upon
which they were based. Might, indeed, such histories indicate more
about present-day cultural policies and their future application than an
explicit focus on the past might suggest?

A major problem encountered by any researcher is how to treat and
to understand speculative mythic histories that have accrued to genres
of performance. Such stories about the historical origins of the court's
dance repertoire in fact formed part of the political rhetoric about Indonesian national identity and the place of Javanese culture within the
modern state. I explore here some of the interpretive processes that
produced the performance repertoire and its mythology in the sultan's
court in the city and province of Yogyakarta. I consider, in particular,
the elaborate and lengthy ceremonial dances known as the Bĕdhaya
dance tradition, normally performed today by nine women. It is a performance tradition that has been especially associated with the power of
the ruler in Java and, as such, has been particularly subject to mytho-
historical constructions.[1]

Reading Histories

Before my first period of research in Yogyakarta (1979–86), I prepared
for fieldwork by reading across the disciplines everything I could about
Javanese performance, especially the dances of the sultan's court, written in English, Dutch, French, and Indonesian. During fieldwork I continued to read published and unpublished studies, in Indonesian and
Javanese, as well as dance manuscripts in many libraries, including
those of the sultan's palace and the Institute of Indonesian Arts (then
named ASTI, the Indonesian Academy of Performing Arts). My initial
research aimed to discover the reality behind what had struck me as

romanticized accounts by Western travelers and scholars that were colored by stereotypes of the Orient as representing ancient and authentic traditions redolent of primeval sacrality. At that time the classic model of anthropological explanation, structural functionalism, had already been under radical criticism for its neglect of the historical dimensions of contemporary experience.[2] Looking back, I was still under the impression that by being a participant-observer in Java I would see the total significance of dance without having recourse to the systematic methodologies of the historian. In fact, I spent many long hours working in court libraries, but archival and manuscript work was marginal to the central methodologies I employed: these constituted learning embodied practices and working interpretively to establish an indigenous discourse of dance. As well as dancing and talking to local people, I read writings by contemporary Indonesian historians and social and political scientists on performance and culture, which would contribute to my understanding of that discourse. In attempting to deconstruct the mystique produced by the writing of outsiders through these methods, however, I ended up being faced in these local authors' writings with local ideologies about dance that were as much part of mythologizing structures as outsider accounts had been.

I came to understand that modern Indonesian culture is a response to a perceived modernization that calls on the ideology of the traditional to act as a panacea to the negative face of change. A further characteristic of Indonesian culture is the separation of connected performance practices into discrete elements, each identified in past documentation and artifacts. Attributions of origin and the implementation of what has come to be viewed as traditional with regard to standards or styles, I realized, needed to be treated with caution. The common practice of fixing a name to a genre that drew on prior conventions and that was then subsequently presented as traditional underlined the fact that tradition is a process, not a thing. Indeed, tradition should not necessarily be understood as referring to customs that are authentic, indigenous, and long established, although there may be particular instances, but rather as an ideology that attributes precedents to practices that may have recently been revived, recast, or reinvented, even if the label or contents refer back to a previous practice. As Eric Hobsbawm and Terence Ranger famously pointed out in their study of tradition and the emergence of the nation-state, so-called traditions may often be comparatively recent inventions; the rhetoric of wholeness and authenticity associated with traditional practices are not so much matters of fact but rather political strategies associated with legitimization.[3]

Making History

During Indonesia's New Order period, stories about the continuity of cultural traditions together with a projected long and stable political past became especially significant, with historians playing a key role in their construction. In attempting to understand local concepts of history and the significance of cultural traditions, the Western researcher has to come to terms with how the brute facts of Java's past—disruption, discontinuity, contingency, and adaptation to numerous cultural impacts, including Hinduism, Buddhism, Islam, Dutch colonization, postcolonial westernization, and now globalization—are treated in local written and oral historiography. These factors have been transformed into elegant cyclical patterns, with events imbued with a sense of inevitability based on allegorical connections with myths. An effect of these uses of history is to provide myths of origin for different dance forms to give legitimacy to the Central Javanese courts, a legitimacy that has now been absorbed by the Indonesian state.

Writing about the past in Java has long been understood to inform the political present, which is why writing history in Indonesia continues to be a powerful tool, and why particular historical interpretations have been favored. Writing history was also about writing the future. Even before and during the colonial period, Javanese historians became adept at re-presenting the past to represent the present, drawing on particular patterns and excluding others that did not support the orthodoxy.[4] Establishing the longevity of traditions contributes to the maintenance of the dominant culture as well as constructing a legitimate past. In his important study on how court literature became formalized and mythologized as a political strategy in the establishment of the kingdom of Yogyakarta in 1755, the Dutch historian Merle Ricklefs observes that it "seems possible that this schematization then had a reciprocal effect upon political behavior, which tended to fit the pattern. Events had been rewritten to become tradition, and the tradition then molded events to fit itself."[5] In a similar manner, the re-modeling of the diversity of performance practices as discrete and stable traditions was constructed through the attribution of mythic history and through the selective use of old records. The result was that well before the New Order period, the invented traditions had become naturalized and their constructedness forgotten.

This phenomenon is typical of the colonial and postcolonial situation, where history and culture may be collapsed into "cultural heritage." Such conceptual constructions deny local complexities and local modes of understanding the past. As Nicholas Dirks observes, history in colonial situations is "a metaphor for the subtle relationships between power and knowledge, between culture and control."[6] Colonialism creates both the conditions that make "culture" a conceptual necessity and the templates of practice that provide political cultural markers in any postcolonial reordering. Cultural manipulation is thus a response to the disruptions and the negation of local history brought about by colonization. When those in power talk about culture, their interest is not in the purportedly long-standing and enduring practices per se but rather in shifting these practices into new frameworks to address the needs of the present and the future.

In Indonesia, as in most postcolonial nations with a plural population, cultures are used for political purposes and are in turn constituted through those actions. The political dominance of Java means that the construction of Indonesian culture is both assisted and motivated by this (re)construction of history. If government policies during the New Order emphasized the development of a national culture based on regional traditions, the debates about Indonesian culture were crosscut by Javanese claims to be the true bearers of the ancient national heritage.

Much court performance in Java is, in fact, relatively modern. During the early nineteenth century, John Crawfurd, the British Resident (an official colonial post) in Yogyakarta, was struck by the lack of historical depth to court practices, noting that "[e]ven tradition does not pretend to an antiquity of above a few centuries."[7] Such a statement reveals much about his preconceptions and expectations; yet historians in Java were also to be preoccupied with projecting an ancient past for court performances. The relative shallowness of the history of the Central Javanese courts and the fractured complexity of Indonesia have been compensated for with stories that trace lineages from ancient history, asserting in particular the influence of Indian culture over a thousand years ago. The Hindu-Javanese period, so-called because powerful rulers in the island were influenced to varying degrees by religion, administration, and culture from India, originated with trade connections

between the subcontinent and the Sriwijaya kingdom (ca. 400–ca. 1300).
(The Buddhist kingdom of Sriwijaya was not established in Java, but in
the city of Palembang on the island of Sumatra, but it is nonetheless regarded as the mother empire of the Indonesian archipelago.) These
links continued through the first kingdom of Mataram (seventh to tenth
centuries) until the end of the Majapahit kingdom (ca. 1222–1451).[8]

The relation of performance and politics was already established
during the Hindu-Javanese period. Before the tenth century, drama was
employed to demonstrate to the population the might of the government and the role of the king,[9] and god-kings *(dewa-raja)* sponsored ceremonial dances and spectacles as offerings to deities and to honor and
impress other human beings. That there were concrete links between
the Indian subcontinent and Indonesian kingdoms is evidenced by in-
scribed charters as early as 840 that refer to mask plays with actors from
as far away as Sri Lanka and Southern India.[10] These charters also refer
to other performances such as shadow plays and fighting dances.

Of particular interest is how these sources, together with other cultural products from the fifth to the fifteenth centuries, have been used to
equate past performance practices with present ones. Specialists in Indonesian performance pay close attention to the poses of the carved
dancing figures at Borobudur, the Buddhist temple, and at Prambanan,
the Hindu temple, both built during the first Mataram kingdom. Parallels are drawn with the *Nāṭyaśāstra*, the classical Sanskrit canon for performance, as evidence of a direct link between the performance traditions of India and Java. This connection remains speculative but is highly
influential in the Indonesian histories of dance and also in Western
scholarship.[11]

Another important model for present national aspirations also
dates from the late Hindu-Javanese period. This is the *Nāgarakṛtāgama,* a
court chronicle of events between 1359 and 1365 in the kingdom of
Majapahit.[12] Detailed descriptions of performances have undoubtedly
been important for understanding what the court performance culture
of Majapahit might have been like, but they are also employed to give
meaning to the present-day court repertoire. Traits evident in these
early descriptions are often presented as having been crystallized over
time into a distinctive Yogyakartan tradition.

The kingdom of Majapahit was defeated by Java's first Islamic kingdom, Demak (ca. 1478–ca. 1550), which was itself defeated by the kingdom of Pajang (1568–82), which in turn was overcome by the second

kingdom of Mataram (1582–1749).[13] Although more information about performance is available for these centuries, the sources are fragmented, rarely contemporaneous, and heavily mythologized.

The second kingdom of Mataram has been significant in providing models of leadership for the twentieth-century Indonesian state, especially in the figure of Sultan Agung (1613–45), who, it is claimed by historians, "invented" the female ceremonial dance tradition of Bědhaya.[14] In the late seventeenth century, Rijklof Van Goens, the Dutch governor-general (1678–81), noted both the militaristic ethos of the court and its female dancers, features that were subsequently perceived as significant in tracing the lineage of the Bědhaya tradition as practiced in twentieth-century Yogyakarta.[15]

In the same period, the Englishman Edmund Scot referred to a royal circumcision ceremony at which he saw duels with pikes, figures in masks, "tumbling tricks" by men and women, and other "prettie shews" that had been taught to the "Javans" by Chinese, Gujeratis, Turks, and other traders.[16] This description of a culturally varied and carnavalesque event is interesting because such diversity in performances patronized by a ruler has been overlooked by recent historians. Instead, they define past repertoires according to contemporary ones and create origin stories for contemporary performance culture by tracing a single history for each dance tradition back to the Hindu-Javanese kingdom of Majapahit in order to represent the quintessence of Javanese culture in Yogyakarta.

Competition at the Cultural Heartland

Local distinctiveness in the performance traditions of Yogyakarta has been represented historically by the difference between the culture of the sultan's court in Yogyakarta and that of the *susuhunan* or *sunan* (the local term of respect for the ruler) in Surakarta. This distinction, evident even in the different titles for the rulers, dates back to the division of the kingdom in 1755, when Prince Mangkubumi rebelled against the accession of Pakubuwana III and established the separate court of Yogyakarta. Taking the name of Haměngkubuwana I, he became its first sultan and founded a dynasty that has continued to the present day. Two minor or junior courts associated with each of the principal royal courts were also established: the Mangkuněgaran in Surakarta in 1757 and the Pakualaman in Yogyakarta in 1813.

The split of Central Java into two royal courts produced duplication of a power base characterized as the center of the cosmos. As a result, legitimacy in historical interpretations about court practices needed to be determined. The competition between the traditions of Yogyakarta and Surakarta to represent Javanese culture might appear to the outside eye to be a competition between the performance of an identical set of cultural practices—however, the distinction is apparent to insiders. Yogyakarta's dance movement is described locally as controlled, disciplined, and authoritative, in contrast to Surakarta's softer, sensual, romantic style. In Yogyakarta, the contrast in style epitomizes differences that carry moral weight endorsed by history: the militaristic ethos is proudly associated with the revolt that led to Yogyakarta's foundation.

During the 1980s, there was a feeling of urgency about establishing a distinct Yogyakartan dance style to sustain traditions and the sense of *naluri,* or traditional basis for identity. This was because since the 1960s the state academies in Indonesia had taught not only Yogyakarta-style performance, but also Surakarta-style, Balinese, West Javanese, and, by the late 1980s, other Javanese regional traditions. "Javanese dance" had become associated with the Surakarta style because Soekarno, the first president of Indonesia, had preferred it. Similarly, his successor, although born close to the city of Yogyakarta, had allied himself with the court traditions of Surakarta, through his wife's connections with the junior court of Mangkunĕgaran. Such affiliations intensified the debate about origins and authenticity, and the children, nephews, and nieces of Sultan Hamĕngkubuwana VIII (1921–39) and their children put considerable energy into distinguishing a Yogyakartan style in order to produce discrete forms of culture. As a well-known aristocrat and dancer put it, "Because I was born a Yogyakartan, I feel obliged to sustain my *naluri.* I don't use that word in a fanatical way, but in Surakarta, many are continuing their *naluri,* and if I support theirs as well, it means that the ones here will be lost."[17]

The Creation of Yogyakarta's Heirlooms

The attribution of legitimacy to cultural practices in Javano-Indonesian culture can be compared metaphorically to the process of an object or activity being designated as an heirloom. Practices and objects classed as heirlooms include oral traditions of knowledge, skill in all kinds of performance, weaponry, musical instruments, furniture, items of clothing, ritual prescriptions and relics, and books. Performances may be heirlooms in themselves; they may use objects that are heirlooms; or they may be inspired by texts that are heirlooms. Heirlooms have provided the Central Javanese courts with their power and continue to provide comparatively recent practices with historical depth. To ensure their power, though, all heirlooms require "feeding." In the case of the heirloom of the Javanese dagger, or *kĕris*, this maintenance is achieved through an annual "ritual" meal of oil and arsenic. In a less concrete but nonetheless equally essential fashion, all heirlooms, even in the form of oral and embodied traditions, need conversations and debates to feed them. Oral traditions and, indeed, published writings keep such practices alive in the social memory and give them political substance. Thus, the principle of continuity is central to the heirlooms' status, but the possibility does exist that old heirlooms may be displaced by new heirlooms that are more intensely charged with identifications. This is a complex process that is assisted by argument, gossip, and interpretation.

The eighteenth-century split presents a problem for the relative antiquity and power of the two court traditions of performance, which are explained in two stories. The first tells how Hamĕngkubuwana I (1749–92) of Yogyakarta personally created the new fighting dances and dance drama that are performed today.[18] The second story relates how Pakubuwana III (1749–88) of Surakarta gave the old forms and objects to Yogyakarta so that he could create new and more powerful ones in his court. This supports the frequent claim in Yogyakarta that it has the older, more authentic performance traditions reaching back to Sultan Agung and beyond, to the Majapahit kingdom. Both these stories, however, lack documentary evidence and do not take into account the considerable movement of people and ideas between the two courts for the first thirty years after the division. Polarization has since been crosscut by intermarriages and cultural exchanges, and also by the founding of the junior courts, each of which developed dance styles reflecting that of the senior courts of the rival principality. Apart from polarizing differences between the two court centers, stories about performance overlook likely changes within performance practices and the fact that more recent court practices are the result of a process of formalization. Nonetheless, the search for origins to endorse distinctiveness between the two courts through the ideology of heirlooms remains a compelling trait in Javanese historiography and oral tradition. The precedence of the past

3.2. Close of Bĕdhaya at the Kraton Festival, Yogyakarta, August 1994. Photo by Felicia Hughes-Freeland.

to authenticate present practice through the selective interpretation of documentary evidence and through mythic history is particularly note-worthy in the elaborate and lengthy formal women's dance tradition known as Bĕdhaya.

Bĕdhaya and Women's Dance

Javanese has no generic word for "dance," and evidence for the histori-cal relationships between different forms of Javanese court performance is extraordinarily complex. The attribution of a mythic past that serves present ideological interest is a further complicating factor. There is an extensive and tangled web of references and sources to explain the origins and antecedents for the performances of the court. The term "Bĕdhaya" may refer to the female dancers, the dance genre, and spe-cific dances within the genre. Performed at both royal courts of Yogya-karta and Surakarta, Bĕdhaya is typically enacted by nine dancers, al-though there is a Bĕdhaya dance performed at Mangkunĕgaran, the junior court of the latter, which requires only seven dancers. Particu-larly revered are the Bĕdhaya Kĕtawang, performed annually in the palace of Surakarta on the anniversary of the ruler's accession, and the

Bĕdhaya Sĕmang, performed in the court of Yogyakarta. Srimpi is a related but less grandiose form of women's court performance, enacted by four women.

The formalization of "women's dance" in the senior courts has followed the mythologizing pattern of the creation of heirlooms. As noted above, the Bĕdhaya tradition is said to have been created by Sultan Agung in the seventeenth-century kingdom of Mataram; yet Sultan Agung is a semi-mythical figure when judged by Western criteria of historicity. He is believed to have married the Queen of the South Sea, a goddess, with whom he lived at the bottom of the sea and who, it is said, inspired the Bĕdhaya Sĕmang.[19] This dance was performed in Yogyakarta for the birthdays of the sultan and of the crown prince until the reign of Hamĕngkubuwana VII (1877–1921). Significantly, it was always performed at the heart of the court in the Bangsal Kĕncana, the chief ceremonial hall of the sultan's palace, where the court heirlooms were stored. It ceased to be performed in 1914 for a number of reasons, not least of which was the fear of the goddess.

Women's Dance and Numerical Formalization

Prior to 1918 (when the first school of training in Yogyakartan court performance was established), the Bĕdhaya with nine dancers was not allowed to be performed outside the Yogyakartan court unless the sultan gave special permission.[20] It could, however, be enacted in Yogyakarta with seven dancers. The precise number of dancers to perform Bĕdhaya is perceived by Javanese and Indonesian historians to be an important factor in tracing the lineage of this courtly performance. They have sought out references to nine female dancers, performing at court prior to the establishment of the Yogyakartan sultanate, in the drive to establish antiquity and continuity for the Bĕdhaya tradition as danced in the twentieth century. The fixing of the number of dancers at nine correlates with the sacred connotations of the number nine both for Hindu-Buddhism and for Islam, and the number has been a key factor in making connections between present practices and past texts. Some origin myths link Bĕdhaya to the seven heavenly nymphs of Hinduism as in the Mangkunĕgaran version. The discrepancy of seven rather than the later nine dancers is explained by the claim that it was Sultan Agung who later increased the number. The contents of historical documents, however, do not necessarily support the prevalent assumption about contemporary performances and their past.

Evidence for the creation of Bědhaya by Sultan Agung is drawn from court manuscripts and for its appearance from the writings of Rijklof Van Goens, the Dutch governor-general who visited Sultan Agung's court in the seventeenth century. According to Van Goens, he witnessed ceremonial women's dancing, in which five to nineteen young dancing girls, dressed in green and red, black and green, white and red, and white and green, performed to the accompaniment of flutes and violins. When Van Goens's record was published in 1956, his description produced a problematic generic essentialization. His original text refers simply to "daer eerst Koninghs jonge dansmaechden" (the king's young dance maidens), but the Dutch scholar H. J. de Graaf provided the explanation of "de bedaya's" and decided that Van Goens's reference to nineteen was a clerical error for nine.[21] Thus de Graaf interpreted what Van Goens saw in the mid-seventeenth century according to the conventions of the mid-twentieth-century female court performance of Bědhaya. This interpretation has since fed into Indonesian accounts of Bědhaya's historical origins as being from the time of Sultan Agung. It is highly unlikely that Van Goens saw anything as elaborate as the twentieth-century Bědhaya dance, which, I would argue, emerged as a result of later court formalization.

A particularly problematic interpretation concerns attempts to construct an enduring tradition of court performance culture from the earlier Majapahit kingdom of the thirteenth to fifteenth centuries. In his 1960s translation of the fourteenth-century court chronicle the *Nāgarakṛtāgama*, referred to above, the scholar Theodore Pigeaud explains the word *nawanātya*, used to describe the king's performance, as "the Nine Physiognomies." Pigeaud then links this to the nine dancers who perform the "sacral" Bědhaya Kětawang in front of the enthroned ruler at Surakarta.[22] The scholar R. A. Kern's later interpretation of this word as "nine dances" rather than "nine dancers" has added a further complication.[23]

Connections have also been postulated between the Bědhaya dancers and the *devadasi*, or sacred temple dancers of South India.[24] Such claims now need to be reconsidered in the light of Stuart Robson's more recent translation of the *Nāgarakṛtāgama* in which he transcribes *nawanātya* as "The Nine Principles of Drama," the title of a specific Sanskrit treatise.[25] Robson emphasizes that the term refers not to the number of dancers, but to qualities of drama, such as farce *(hasya)* and pathos *(karuna)*. In this reading, then, the number "nine" has lost its supposed ancient link with the performances during the Hindu-Javanese Majapahit kingdom, but this has not yet been registered by dance historians in their interpretations of Bĕdhaya. Although there is evidence of Sanskritic aesthetics in Hinduized Javanese courts, there is no account of Bĕdhaya-like dances being performed.

Other textual evidence shows that the number of Bĕdhaya dancers in court performances has varied over time and according to context. Sultan Amangkurat IV (1719–26) gave his son costumes for seven dancers, and in June 1726 a Dutch official saw fourteen groups of seven dancers, followed by nine dancers of the king, and then another group of seven royal dancers.[26] These accounts suggest that by 1726 nine and seven dancers had become signs of relative status in the Mataram court. Another source, however, claims that in 1755 the regent *(bupati)* of Ponorogo had seven groups of nine Bĕdhaya dancers.[27] To confuse the matter, in the early nineteenth century, Thomas Stamford Raffles (lieutenant-governor of Java, 1811–16) saw eight Bĕdhaya dancers.[28] It is then wiser not to assume that nine had become standard for court Bĕdhaya until some point during the nineteenth century, despite the claims of Indonesian and Javanese historians.[29]

Women's Dance and Controls on Female Sexuality

In addition to the search to correlate the present number of dancers in the Bĕdhaya tradition with examples from the past, there has been a similar effort to fix the gender of its performers as having been unchanged throughout history. At the *sunan's* palace in Surakarta, Bĕdhaya dancers were a hereditary professional group of court dancers, whereas Srimpi dancers were often related to the ruler. My research indicates that it became conventional in the Yogyakarta court from probably the nineteenth century until 1922 for female dancers of Bĕdhaya to be the daughters of court officials who lived in the female quarters and often became unofficial wives of the ruler. As such, they were subject to more stringent rules of purity and protection than the Srimpi dancers, who were often the children and grandchildren of the Sultan. Between 1840 and 1914, Srimpi dances could also be performed by men at the Yogyakartan court. Indeed, until the start of Hamĕngkubuwana VIII's reign in 1921, both Bĕdhaya and Srimpi were performed either by women or by men in female dress.[30]

Asserting historical continuity on the basis of gender is problematic, particularly when we consider terminological variation across time and space. The word "bĕdhaya" on the north coast of Java (Pasisir) means "taledhek," a woman who sings and dances. In the East Java towns of Prabalingga and Lumajan the word "bĕdajan" refers to a dance by a man dressed as a woman.[31] Amid this confusion of gendering it may be of significance that in Cirebon, in West Java, the kingdom from which Sultan Agung took his wife and various cultural forms, "badhaya" refers to female dancers[32]—a possible origin for the current Central Javanese court usage and even for Bĕdhaya itself? These regional variations indicate that gender ascription of performance has been less predictable in the past and even now should not be taken as fixed.

It is evident that in the early twentieth century, the process of formalization, including rules on the gender of participants in court performance, is related to changing patterns of control over female sexuality. Furthermore, it is aligned with the creation of a second opposition over and above that of the two courts of Surakarta and Yogyakarta. This second opposition concerns the idea of an "inside" Javanese court tradition that contrasts absolutely with an "outside" culture in order to serve as a model for a high classical Indonesian art dance tradition. Because of the emphasis on the court as a distinctive performance sphere separated from outside, it has been ideologically expedient to overlook another possible genealogy for women's court dance. This is the tradition of healing performance found throughout the Malay archipelago, such as *sanghyang* dances in Bali in which young girls possessed by deities perform to protect the community or cure epidemics, and *tayuban*, a kind of "village dancing party" and ritualized performance, still enacted today to the southeast of Yogyakarta, in which professional female singer-dancers *(taledhek, ledhek)* heal or protect babies and animals with face powder.[33] The *(ta)ledhek* also dance with men, a contrasting aspect to the women's court performances and one that has earned them a reputation of prostitution. The dancing is, however, a gift to the protective spirit in exchange for well-being. In the past, healing roles no doubt gave women status in the community—a status that would have been severely undermined, although not totally eradicated, much earlier by the coming of Islam in the fifteenth century.[34]

3.3. A rowdy *tayuban* in a village on the borders of Central and East Java, 1989. Photo by Felicia Hughes-Freeland.

The existence of historical records that reveal potentially close analogies between the present-day *tayuban* and former court performances is undoubtedly problematic for Indonesian historians. Certainly, the absence of male partners in Van Goens's account in the seventeenth-century court of Sultan Agung suggests that what he saw was not a *tayuban*. There is, however, an intriguing Javanese reference to a court performance that predates this influential description of women's ceremonial performance. Here, female dancing in the late sixteenth-century court of Senapati in the Pajang kingdom did take the form of a *tayuban* where professional dancers would dance with male guests and serve them drinks.[35] There is even earlier evidence. The *Nāgarakṛtāgama* of the fourteenth-century Majapahit court describes a female performer, Juru i Angin, who makes jokes with another performer, sings, and dances humorously, and then serves drinks to the king. Robson has recently radically suggested that the eight noble *"tĕkĕs"* in the Majapahit *rakĕt* play with whom the king jokes, sings, and dances are female, "his minor wives," and not male as previously claimed.[36] Humor, eroticism, and alcohol have been excluded from female court performance in Yogyakarta but were clearly present in the 1300s. Whether or not such exclusions began in Sultan Agung's Islamicizing reign, when Hindu traditions were also preserved, must remain speculation. But it provides grist to the mythmaker's mill. The historical sources suggest that the changing status of women is marked by the appearance in the courts of a form of ceremonial dance that, unlike women's ceremonial temple dance in Bali, has no religious function independent of the royal cult of glory.

It is noteworthy that even in the nineteenth century female singers in the court included *taledhek*.[37] Well-known singer-dancers used to be invited to train in Bĕdhaya inside the court or to dance in *tayuban*s in the residences of princes and the prime minister, skillfully guiding their male partner through the dance. A *(ta)ledhek* could become a performer, inside the court, and Hamĕngkubuwana II even married one. Nyai Riya Larasati, one of Yogyakarta's most esteemed female singers, performed until 1942 as a singer-dancer in a princely residence, where she had learned to sing. She did not dance inside the court but only in the houses of nobles: in the court she only sang, and after independence she worked professionally for Indonesian Republic Radio.[38] In the New Order period, *tayuban* came to be seen as rowdy and erotic, epitomizing the culture of "outside" and undesirable female behavior, in contrast to polite feminine behavior, represented quintessentially in court performance and the culture of "inside." The pattern of Nyai Riya Larasati's career is symptomatic of the general move after Indonesian independence to control female performance and, indeed, in some respects reflects attempts to abolish dance as a professional activity outside the control of the court and its sanctioned training schools. The perception of the tradition of *tayuban* has been constructed to stand in opposition to that of court performance, which might, unlike the informal *tayuban*, be strictly controlled by men as "culture."

Healing dancers, rather than the conjectured Hindu *devadasi*-like models, as suggested by Th. B. Van Lelyveld in 1931, might seem feasible as a historical source for contemporary female court performers.[39] By the twentieth century, however, such a genealogy had become unspeakable because of the formalization of the "inside" and the formalization of the "feminine" dance mode in the court as the only dance mode for women. Formalization of court culture has involved a process of exclusion. The contemporary Yogyakartan view of feminine court dance excludes erotic, magical, and humorous elements, and recognizes the control by the sultan over female sexuality. In the days when the dancers provided sexual services for the sultan, of course, the restraint on sexuality was a matter of the power of ownership, rather than an aesthetic based on the exclusion of sexuality. Unlike the commoditized performance of *ledhek,* who take money for their dancing, contemporary court dance as exemplary culture rests on a transcendental, nonmaterial ideology of honor as the basis for exchange, an ideology connected to the dissimulation or deflection of any physical expression of sexuality. Dance teachers, like the court choreographer B. R. Ayu Yudanĕgara, explain that sinuous and sensual as the Yogyakarta court's female movement traditionally has been, the quality of gentle refinement *(alus)* requires the strict exclusion of eroticism, flirtatiousness, and coyness. Female dancers are taught to control their gaze, lowering it to a point on the floor at a distance of not more than twice their height, to secure the aesthetic effect of sexual detachment. Subtle and oblique, this aesthetic rests on the absence of any overt signs of sexuality, in direct contrast with the "outside" performances of *ledhek,* which, I suggest, continue to be marked by the eroticism and sociality of the dance of the fourteenth-century performer Juru i Angin. The construction of a particular history has been achieved by a repression: these "outside" dancers were described by my informants as the polar opposite to what women's dance in the court, exemplified by Bĕdhaya (and Srimpi), should be like.

The gendering of court performance to express an essentialized and distinctive Yogyakartan court cultural aesthetic is also formulated in opposition to feminine performance in the *sunan's* palace in Surakarta. In Yogyakarta, the Surakartan feminine dance style—the exposed shoulders, the arm movements revealing the armpit (concealed in Yogyakarta normally by a more modest costume and always by a lower position for the elbows) and the unlowered eyes—was denigrated for being unseemly. The dance was altogether too lively *(linca).* Of course, both courts exercise strict control over female sexuality, though Surakarta court performance traditions in general have been less immured than those of Yogyakarta. Female dance in Surakarta is not contrasted with the performance of *ledhek* outside the court, but is perceived as being on a continuum. What has been "purified" from the Yogyakartan court remains in the Surakarta courts. The immured dance, performed by *ledheks* to open *tayuban*s in villages, forms part of the court repertoire, referred to by Yogyakarta diehards as the "Surakarta palace *tayuban.*" K. R. T. Hardjanĕgara, a senior official of the *sunan's* palace in Surakarta, suggested that these different court ideologies of female performance reflect the conditions under which the courts were founded. Surakarta is agrarian and maintains its links to rites of fertility, while Yogyakarta celebrates its origins in rebellion and military prowess.[40] The heirlooms of Surakarta are related to farming, and court performance is associated with fertility and thanksgiving, expressed through themes of marriage and sexual union in Bĕdhaya Kĕtawang and in plays performed from the Pañji and Damarwulan story cycles. In Yogyakarta, on the other hand, military themes from the Mahābhārata are the most popular, and love and marriage only come into the story as a result of abductions occurring in warfare.[41]

To summarize, the modern gendering and genres of dance are the result of change and innovation, not repetition of fixed past practices. Long-standing traditions of cross-dressing in ritual performance have been replaced by fixed identifications between performers and forms, giving women more scope to perform, albeit within a strictly controlled ethos. The female court dancers are at once the opposite of *ledhek* and their purged incarnation. Women's court dance provides a model for Indonesian women's dance and has been articulated in terms of an opposition to village and professional performance, an opposition that is seen by people in Yogyakarta as being weakly maintained in Surakarta, and that thus articulates the second opposition, between Yogyakarta and Surakarta. What was once a control of sexuality and rights over reproduction by the sultan has been transformed into an indirect control of female sexuality, which is given generalized aesthetic exemplary value in the contemporary Javano-Indonesian culture.

A Skeptical Attitude

Performance histories in Indonesia have worked to naturalize contemporary practice with reference to the past, just as traditional Javanese historiography mythologized events to produce impressions of preordained order and continuity. In the case of female performance, the demarcation between "inside" and "outside," which contemporary Yogyakartan commentators use to distinguish the practices of its court, has come about by a process of monopolization and formalization expressive of strict control. It is likely that Sultan Agung's dance maidens had more in common with *ledhek* than with contemporary Bĕdhaya dancers, but we will never know, unless some new manuscript evidence comes to light. This is why it is also the case that the significance of present practices gains weight and power from resonances with practices referred to in writings of the past. Bĕdhaya dances have been a particularly effective resource for enhancing the mystique of Javanese rulers and their courts, and the martial ethic in Yogyakarta has given rise to a modern aesthetic.

The uses of history and anthropology for dance research as illustrated in this account require a skeptical attitude because sources, which became fact by status or iteration, have to be interpreted from a different standpoint. During my fieldwork in the 1980s, Indonesian historians and intellectuals espoused strongly rationalistic scientific models of explanation in order to build a foundation of knowledge that would be appropriate for the development of the postcolonial state. The agenda among dance experts was to establish a positivist factual history—but as my research has revealed, this did not necessarily prevent the selective use and interpretation of documentary evidence by local and Western researchers. My example shows time and again how scholarly research by foreigners made points that have been taken up by Indonesian scholars—who themselves have read the works of foreign scholars and been trained by them.

The visibility of dance makes it particularly appropriate in the invention of tradition through a process in which appearances come to symbolize cultural reality.[42] So dance has been and remains particularly susceptible to attracting discourses that contribute to that reality and inform how those embodied practices are perceived and valued. When the New Order ended in 1998, cultural politicians in the courts and ministries started to take stock of political and economic contingencies and are still waiting to see where things might go. As people begin to discuss more openly the stories and myths promoted during the New Order years, they are also wondering which ones it will be expedient to promote in the future, and from where the inspiration for those inventions of tradition will come.

Meanwhile, the analysis of historiography in Western theory has recognized increasingly the mythic fictional dimensions that have characterized the making of history and that remain present in contemporary practices, under the guise of a factual "modern" approach.[43] As this chapter has demonstrated, my own attempt to get behind the representations of outsiders and insiders and to piece together another story to show dance as something other than that represented in the language of power—without beginning to slip back into the very mythologizing I was questioning—remains problematic, or maybe even impossible.

NOTES

1. Judith Becker, *Gamelan Stories: Tantrism, Islam and Aesthetics in Central Java* (Tempe: Arizona State University, 1993). For a description of Bĕdhaya as performed in the late twentieth century, see Miriam J. Morrison, "The Bĕdhaya-Serimpi Dances of Java," *Dance Chronicle* 2, no. 3 (1978): 188–212. Influential historical overviews of Yogyakartan court performance are R. M. Soedarsono, *Wayang Wong, the State Ritual Dance Drama in the Court of Yogyakarta* (Yogyakarta: Gadjah Mada University Press, 1984), and Jennifer Lindsay, "Klasik, Kitsch or Contemporary: A Study of the Javanese Performing Arts" (Ph.D. thesis, Sydney University, 1985).

2. Talal Asad, ed., *Anthropology and the Colonial Encounter* (London: Ithaca Press, 1973); Eric Wolf, *Europe and the People without History* (Berkeley: University of California Press, 1982).

3. Eric Hobsbawm and Terence Ranger, eds., *The Invention of Tradition* (Cambridge: Cambridge University Press, 1983).

4. Soedjatmoko, ed., *An Introduction to Indonesian Historiography* (Ithaca, N.Y.: Cornell University Press, 1965); Nancy Florida, "Reading the Unread in Traditional Javanese Literature," *Indonesia* 44 (1987): 1–15.

5. Merle C. Ricklefs, *Jogjakarta under Sultan Mangkubumi, 1749–1792: A History of the Division of Java* (London: Oxford University Press, 1974), 176.

6. Nicholas Dirks, ed., introduction to *Colonialism and Culture* (Ann Arbor: University of Michigan Press, 1992), 11.

7. John Crawfurd, *History of the Indian Archipelago*, 3 vols. (Edinburgh: Archibald, Constable, 1820), 2:295.

8. These dates are approximate. D. G. E. Hall, *A History of South-East Asia*, 4th ed. (London: Macmillan, 1991).

9. Jan Wisseman-Christie, "Raja and Rama: The Classical State in Early Java," in *Centers, Symbols, and Hierarchies: Essays on the Classical States of Southeast Asia*, ed. Lorraine Gesick (New Haven, Conn.: Yale University Southeast Asia Studies, 1986): 9–44.

10. Claire Holt, *Art in Indonesia: Continuities and Change* (Ithaca, N.Y.: Cornell University Press, 1967), 281–89.

11. See, for example, Edy Sedyawati Hadimulyo, "The Question of Indian Influence on Ancient Javanese Dance," *Review of Indonesian and Malaysian Affairs* 16, no. 2 (1982): 59–82; and Alessandra Iyer, *Prambanan: Sculpture and Dance in Ancient Java: A Study in Dance* (Bangkok: White Lotus Press, 1997).

12. Soemarsaid Moertono, *State and Statecraft in Java: A Study of the Later Mataram Period, 16th–19th Centuries* (Ithaca, N.Y.: Cornell University Press, 1968); Benedict O'Gorman Anderson, "The Idea of Power in Javanese Culture," in *Culture and Politics in Indonesia*, ed. Claire Holt (Ithaca, N.Y.: Cornell University Press, 1972).

13. Theodore G. Th. Pigeaud and H. J. de Graaf, *Islamic States in Java* (The Hague: Martinus Nijhoff, 1976). For dance at this time, see also B. P. A. Soerjadiningrat, *Babad lan Mekaring Djogèd Djawi* (Yogyakarta: Kolf-Buning, n.d. [1912]), 9–10, 16–17.

14. Sultan Agung consolidated the Islamic kingdom of Mataram with a ritual culture that was "both Islamic and Javanese." Anthony Reid, *Expansion and Crisis*, vol. 2 of *Southeast Asia in the Age of Commerce, 1450–1680* (New Haven, Conn.: Yale University Press, 1993), 178. The story of these events is recorded in a corpus of legends. W. L. Olthoff, ed., *Babad Tanah Jawi* (The Hague: Martinus Nijhoff, 1941). See also Merle C. Ricklefs, *War, Culture and Economy in Java, 1677–1726* (London: Allen and Unwin, 1993).

15. H. J. de Graaf, ed., *De Vijf Gezantschapsreizen van Rijklof van Goens naar het Hof van Mataram, 1648–1654* (The Hague: Martinus Nijhoff, 1956), 235, note 7, and 236, note 3.

16. Edmund Scot, "A Discourse of Java and the First English Factory There, with Divers Indian, English, and Dutch Occurents," in *Purchas His Pilgrimages in Five Books*, The First Part (Book 3), Samuel Purchas the Elder (London: William Stansby for Henry Featherstone, 1625), Chapter 4: 181, 182.

17. Author interview with R. M. Wisnu Wardhana, 30 September 1983.

18. Felicia H. Freeland, "Revivalism as a Defining Stand in Yogyakartan Court Dance," *Indonesia Circle* 37 (1985): 38. The standard historical interpretation of this period is Ricklefs, *Jogjakarta under Sultan Mangkubumi*.

19. The Sĕmang dance was probably devised in the reign of Hamĕngkubuwana II (1792–1812). See Jan Hostetler, "Bĕdhaya Sĕmang: The Sacred Dance of Yogyakarta," *Archipel* 24 (1982), 139. See also Clara Brakel-Papenhuyzen, *The Bĕdhaya Court Dances of Central Java* (Leiden: E. J. Brill, 1992), 274.

20. G. B. P. H. Suryobrongto, "Tinjauan Umum Mengenai Tari Klasik Gaya Yogyakarta," in *Mengenal Tari Klasik Gaya Yogyakarta*, ed. Fred Wibowo (Yogyakarta: Dewan Kesenian Propinsi DIY, 1981), 32.

21. De Graaf, ed., *De Vijf Gezantschapsreizen van Rijklof van Goens*, 235, note 7, and 236, note 3.

22. Theodore G. Th. Pigeaud, *Java in the Fourteenth Century: A Study in Cultural History. The Nāgarakṛtāgama by Rakawi Prapañca of Majapahit, 1365 A.D.*, 5 vols. (The Hague: Martinus Nijhoff, 1960–63), 4:326–28.

23. Cited in Holt, *Art in Indonesia*, 286.

24. For an example of this general approach see Th. B. Van Lelyveld, *De Javanaansche Danskunst* (Amsterdam: Van Holkema and Warendorf, 1931).

25. Stuart O. Robson, trans., *Deśawarṇana (Nāgarakṛtāgama) by Mpu Prapañca* (Leiden: KITLV Press, 1995), 147.

26. Ricklefs, *War, Culture and Economy in Java*, 213, 392.

27. B. P. A. Soerjadiningrat, *Babad lan Mekaring Djogèd Djawi* (Yogyakarta: Kolf-Buning, n.d. [1912]).

28. Thomas Stamford Raffles, *The History of Java* (Kuala Lumpur: Oxford University Press, 1978), 342 (first published in 1817).

29. Isaac Groneman, *In de Kedaton te Jogjakarta: Oepatjara, Ampilan en Tooneeldansen* (Leiden: E. J. Brill, 1888).

30. Felicia Hughes-Freeland, "Dance and Gender in a Javanese Palace Tradition," in *"Male" and "Female" in Developing South East Asia*, ed. Wazir-Jahan Karim (Oxford: Berg, 1995), 181–206.

31. Theodore G. Th. Pigeaud, *Javaanse Volksvertoningen: Bijdrage tot de Beschrijving van Land en volk* (Batavia: Volkslectuur, 1938), paragraphs 273–74 and 277.

32. Irawati Durban Arjo, "Women's Dance among the Sundanese of West Java, Indonesia," *Asia Theater Journal* 6, no. 2 (Fall 1989): 168–78.

33. Felicia Hughes-Freeland, "Golek Menak and Tayuban: Patronage and Professionalism in Two Spheres of Central Javanese Culture," in *Performance in Java and Bali*, ed. Ben Arps (London: School of Oriental and African Studies, 1993).

34. Reid, *Expansion and Crisis*, 161–63.

35. Soerjadiningrat, *Babad lan Mekaring Djogèd Djawi*, 16–17.

36. Robson, *Deśawarṇana (Nāgarakṛtāgama) by Mpu Prapañca*, 92; Pigeaud, *Java in the Fourteenth Century* 4:315.

37. Isaac Groneman, *In de Kedaton te Jogjakarta: Oepatjara, Ampilan en Tooneeldansen*, 37. A useful discussion of the court's twentieth-century censorship of *tayuban*-like dancing is found in Peggy Choy, "Texts through Time: The Golèk Dance of Java" in *Aesthetic Tradition and Cultural Transition in Java and Bali*, ed. Stephanie Morgan and Laurie J. Sears (Madison: Center for Southeast Asian Studies, University of Wisconsin, 1984), 55–57.

38. Author interview with Nyai Riya Larasati, Yogyakarta, November 1989.

39. Van Lelyveld, *De Javaansche Danskunst*.

40. Author interview with K. R. T. Hardjanĕgara, Surakarta, November 1989.

41. Author interview with B. R. Ayu Yudanĕgara, Yogyakarta, July 1992.

42. Felicia Hughes-Freeland, "Dance, Dissimulation, and Identity in Indonesia," in *An Anthropology of Indirect Communication*, ed. Joy Hendry and C. W. Watson, ASA Monographs no. 37 (London: Routledge, 2001).

43. See references in notes 4–6, and Michel de Certeau, *The Writing of History*, trans. Tom Conley (New York: Columbia University Press, 1988).

4

Utopia, Eutopia, and E.U.-topia

Performance and Memory in Former Yugoslavia

LYNN D. MANERS

Cultural performances may signal differing meanings according to changing political and symbolic economies. The use of dance, particularly folk dance, to project various images of nationalism and ethnonationalism in Eastern Europe has a long history dating back to the nineteenth century. In this chapter, I consider symbolic representation and the play of memory in the performance of folklore ensembles in the former Yugoslavia, from the Second World War to the early years of the twenty-first century. This period witnessed a transition from a politically unified Communist state under General Tito to the country's violent collapse and virtual dismemberment in the civil wars of the 1990s. Throughout, and in the uneasy peace of the following decade, staged and seemingly spontaneous performances of folk dance took place, thus posing questions with regard to representations of nationalism and ethno-nationalism. Based on the conceit of utopia—a perfect and harmonious world—this chapter narrates the shifting meanings and tensions of such performances within three broadly delineated periods, in order to underline the relationship between the ideological goals and experienced realities of changing political economies and the memories and meanings these performances of folk dance held for their participants and local audiences.

Bridging History, Symbol, and Memory: An Ethnographic Moment Crystallizes

An interesting phenomenon occurred during live television coverage by Cable News Network (CNN) of the bombing of the capital of Belgrade by the North Atlantic Treaty Organization (NATO) during the Yugoslav war of the 1990s.[1] Rather than engage in an indiscriminate bombing campaign that might have resulted in a politically unacceptable level of civilian casualties, NATO embarked instead on a deliberate air campaign aimed at destroying or disabling Belgrade's infrastructure. In fact, one of NATO's goals was to avoid casualties altogether. As a result, the Yugoslav government acted defensively to protect the city's infrastructure by surrounding it with people, thus hoping to dissuade NATO attacks. In Belgrade, this tactic focused on the city's bridges. Night after night civilians pinned paper targets onto their clothing and stood on the bridges of Belgrade.

One of those nights stands out in my memory. As the camera panned through the milling ranks of Belgraders, dressed for a cool night spent standing on a bridge, its gaze fell upon three young women dressed in the typical folk costume of Sumadija, a rural area in north central Serbia. Amid the drab browns and blacks of coats and jackets, these three young women, linked hand to elbow, stood out as they danced a traditional *kolo,* a dance form characterized by a circular or curvilinear pattern. Although the video clip was a short one, these young women were clearly good dancers, seemingly perfectly acquainted with the standardized choreography of the stage performance of this dance (body position and linkage, curved path, and so on), and the bystanders obviously approved of both their appearance and their performance. Since these young women were evidently not nineteenth-century rural women dancing together after church on Sunday, nor did they appear to have ridden in on the bus from Sumadija in order to defend the bridges of the capital, one might well ask just what were these young women doing there and what did they represent to those surrounding them? The answer to this question lies in an anthropological analysis of the role of folk dance performance in creating a type of social and cultural memory,

4.1. Southeastern Europe showing Republics of Former Yugoslavia. Map by Stephen Heath.

contributing, in both a symbolic and actual sense, to the formation of modern nation-states and to what we might call one form of an "imagined community."[2]

The relationship between dance and political economy has been explored by dance folklorist Anthony Shay in the Yugoslavian context and elsewhere. Using LADO (the Croatian professional folk dance company) as one example, he has examined some of these types of professional state-sponsored performance ensembles in their role as representations of the state.[3] His historical and folkloristic perspective focuses on examples from anti-liberal, authoritarian states or those that have had fragile democracies. I propose that an alternative future research direction, from a more anthropological perspective, is to investigate the types of political economies that result in the creation of a state-sponsored, professional folklore ensemble. Such a line of questioning needs to be pursued along with an analysis of the processes by which some dances are selected for representation, while others are rejected.[4] The ethnographic research that underpins my argument in this chapter uses a

North American, cultural anthropological paradigm, which tends to emphasize the constructivist role of culture and its idealist, as opposed to materialist, nature. Specifically, the research is situated within that body of work through which North American scholars have viewed the expressive cultures of Eastern Europe. My work has largely focused on analyzing the relationship between folk dance performances and the political economies within which they are embedded and has been primarily centered on Bosnia-Herzegovina, the one non-ethnic-majority republic of former Yugoslavia.[5]

Bosnia and Herzegovina, the symbolic and geographic center of the country, from which the Yugoslav state was formally constituted in 1942, was the only republic in which no one group was in the majority.[6] The other five republics had eponymous ethnic majorities: Serbs were the majority in Serbia, Slovenes in Slovenia, Croatians in Croatia, Montenegrins in Montenegro, and Macedonians in Macedonia. In the post–Second World War Yugoslav federation, an additional two autonomous provinces, Kosovo and Vojvodina, which were formally incorporated within Serbia, held a majority of ethnic Albanians (in Kosovo) and a mixed population of Serbs, ethnic Hungarians, and other national minorities (in Vojvodina). Thus, of the full republics in the post–Second World War Yugoslav federation, Bosnia's predominantly Muslim population was not of one ethnic group. Rather than being ethnic Turks left behind when the Ottoman Empire retreated, the Muslims were the descendants of Christians, Serbian Orthodox and Croatian Roman Catholics, whose ancestors had converted to Islam, if for no other reason than to avoid Ottoman taxes on non-Muslims. I have had many conversations over the years with native chauvinists attempting to "prove," often using ethnographic, cadastral (documents pertaining to taxation), or historical data, that Bosnian Muslims are "really" Serbs or Croats. It is because of the unique nature of the republic of Bosnia and Herzegovina within the Yugoslav polity that the attempt at the creation of a national memory was most important, most easily ascertainable, and had the greatest potential to succeed. I make the argument here that folk dance performance had, and still has, an important symbolic and actual role to play in the construction of national memory.

In Marcel Proust's classic novel *Remembrance of Things Past*, a madeleine pastry serves as an aid to memory in order to link the protagonist with his own past. Dance performances, specifically those of amateur and professional folklore ensembles in former Yugoslavia, played a similar part in helping to build three kinds of Yugoslav nation-state. The first relates to an imagined Yugoslav *utopian* past. Utopia signifies an idealized, romanticized society and is used here to represent the post-revolutionary stage of building state socialism, undertaken in accordance with the goals of Yugoslav policy and practice after the Second World War. The second kind of nation-state relates to a *eutopian* recent present. Here, *eutopia* refers to the actual conditions under the Yugoslav variant of state socialism, especially from about 1960 until the dissolution of the Yugoslav state in the early 1990s. The third and final characterization I identify as *E.U.-topian*—an imagined post-Yugoslav European Union (E.U.) future. This designates the end of the Yugoslav experiment, seen clearly in retrospect as beginning with the death of Tito in 1980, accelerating along with the geopolitical repercussions of the fall of the Berlin Wall in 1989, and culminating in the 1992–95 Bosnian War and violent dismemberment of the country. The post-1989 events, including the eventual collapse of the Soviet Union, subsequently led to the demise of all the national variants of state socialism in Eastern Europe. In the Yugoslav case, the country itself disintegrated into separate nation-states, each of which now independently seeks ultimate accession to the imagined "paradise" of the European Union. In each of these periods—that is, the utopian, eutopian, and E.U.-topian—the performance of folk dance and the founding and organization of ensembles had, and has, an important role as a symbol for Yugoslav and post-Yugoslav society. The "topia" are not intended to represent discrete periods in the following discussion but act as heuristic devices to stimulate thought on the relation between performance as an aesthetic production and as political economy.

In a sense, group expressive behaviors, formalized and enshrined in public performances, have served as a sort of social memory in twentieth-century Yugoslavia. This social memory through public performance simultaneously interpreted the past, explained how the present should be, and projected a future. Particularly under Communist ideological direction, the past, present, and future were ideologically reinterpreted through national cultural policy, much as occurred elsewhere in Eastern Europe and the Soviet Union. The pre-Communist past was invoked in two ways: first, through the distorting lens of a sort of pernicious negative nostalgia directed at urban elites, and second, as a romanticized image of a bucolic rural life. Meanwhile, the present was conceptualized as progress toward the perfection of the future. These social memories created through folklore performance are in the mode of historian Eric Hobsbawm's "invented tradition" in that they "seek to inculcate certain values and norms of behavior by repetition, which automatically implies continuity with the past. In fact, where possible, they normally attempt to establish continuity with a suitable historic past."[7] In the Yugoslav instance, dance and music performances, as manipulated by the state, tried also to establish a link with a socialist utopian future.

In the post–Second World War Yugoslavia of Tito, as in the 1920s and 1930s, cultural elites attempted to direct the creation of a supranational culture, a Yugoslav identity. From 1945 to roughly 1960, the Yugoslav government played a central role in the development and implementation of cultural policy. Slavic literary historian Andrew Wachtel points out that the separate national cultures were allowed to exist at what he felt was characterized as the "harmless level of folk culture."[8] While this folk stratum may have been perceived as harmless in other Eastern European countries, I believe this was less so in the multinational Yugoslav polity, where nationalism and ethno-nationalism were ultimately able to appropriate symbols of folk culture, including dance and music.

A Yugoslav Utopia

Although attempts to create a Yugoslav utopia, or at least a common Yugoslav culture, date at least to the 1840s when the Romantic nationalism of the era spread to the Balkans,[9] the Second World War marked a decisive break with previous attempts. From 1945 to the early 1960s, the creation of an ideologically driven socialist utopia was a goal of the state that was reflected in cultural policy. In this post–Second World War period, following the Marxist/Leninist model of national/state development, all significant cultural organizations and activities were subsumed under the rubric of the state. State agencies quickly utilized the model provided by the Soviet Union in which no activity was allowed to develop that might allow an alternate view of the state or an alternative base of power. This resulted in what social scientist and media critic Miklos Haraszti calls "directed culture" in which the state holds a monopoly on art and the official aesthetic.[10] As encapsulated by the classic Stalinist formula, culture could be "nationalist in form" as long as it was "socialist in content." Folk dances, with their ability to be appropriated and transformed for the stage, were significant cultural grist for this ideological mill. As a result, and with the emphasis on the importance of the urban proletariat, socialism often attempted to render ideologically harmless the more rural-oriented folklore through a process of fossilization, festivalization, and antiquarianization. These related terms, which I broadly adapt here from folklore-oriented studies, refer to reducing the variation in performance (fossilization), orienting those performances toward formally sanctioned and sometimes competitive events, separating audiences from performers (festivalization), and displacing referents in the performance backward in time/space (antiquarianization).[11] Under the guise of preserving folklore, the former state of Yugoslavia decontextualized several of these group expressive behaviors, sanitizing them ideologically and transforming dance and music into passive entertainment for urban audiences. A number of formal performance events, such as festivals and folk concerts, were established as venues for the performance of folklore, rather than for participation in folklore. At the International Folklore Festival in Zagreb, for example, "Plešite s nama" (Dance with Us) is presented as an opportunity for the audience and dancers of various groups to dance folk dances together on the outdoor stage. This participatory aspect, however, occurs only after the live television broadcast of the festival ceases. In the nonparticipatory events aimed at urban, national, or, indeed, international audiences, dance and music have become re-presentations of the ubiquitous and anonymous "folk." The models created for performance serve both as a social experience, that is, of integration in a common experience of performance for the performers, and as a form of public entertainment for audiences.

In developing a distinctive Yugoslav form of Communism, worker self-management (instituted in 1950) joined "the brotherhood and unity of the peoples of Yugoslavia" and the idea of worker self-management spread to the organization of amateur folklore groups, KUDs (Kulturno Umjetnicko Drustvo, or Cultural Art Societies). In the excitement of building socialism during this immediate postwar period, party cadres were instructed to encourage and assist in their formation. The first Five Year Plan for Education and Culture was enacted to direct and fund these activities.[12] These amateur ensembles, some based on prewar groups, were sponsored by labor-affiliated organizations such as the Railway Workers (ZKUD), Workers (RKUD),

and University/Academic (U/AKUD) groups. Amateur folklore ensembles had begun to appear in the republics of Yugoslavia by 1945, although political scientist and cultural theoretician Stevan Majstorovic
states that during this period quantitative growth was not equaled by
growth in quality.[13] By the late 1940s, professional folklore groups were
founded on the model of the Moiseyev Ensemble in what was then the
Soviet Union. Some, such as Croatia's LADO, were converted from
amateur ensembles. Slovenia, Bosnia-Herzegovina, and Montenegro
did not support the establishment of a professional ensemble, thus usually the best of the university-affiliated folklore groups acted in that role.
In 1950, the first Smotra Jugoslavie (Gathering of Yugoslavia) was held
in Belgrade, featuring groups from all over the country: eleven choirs,
seven drama groups, seventeen folklore groups, fifteen ethnic art sections, and twenty-two individual singers and other performers. These
large public gatherings later appeared in Zagreb, Croatia, as well as in
other republics and continue today in Zagreb as the Medjunarodna
Smotra Folklora (International Gathering of Folklore).

Typically, the amateur organizations were controlled by a board of
directors, and their activities were divided into areas of interest and age
group. A typical amateur folklore group would be made up of separate
sections. Characteristically, these were a Pioniri (Pioneer) group for
children, "B" and "C" groups that functioned primarily as training
groups, and an "A" group that gave most of the public performances.
These amateur folklore groups competed in public performances that
were judged by visiting choreographers or other approved experts.

A standard requirement for a typical KUD was the performance of
an all-Yugoslav program. This meant that a KUD (as opposed to village
folklore groups, which could perform their local mono-ethnic or national material) had to be able to perform suites of dances and music
from all six republics and the two autonomous provinces. Successful
performance of the all-Yugoslav choreography could result in more
funding being directed to that group through its sponsoring organization, as well as other benefits, such as being authorized to travel and to
represent Yugoslavia in international folklore performances. As an informant remembers this period: "In some places, it was more important
to have a good KUD than a factory, because everybody is happy to
have a big KUD which can perform the all-Yugoslav program."[14]

In many ways KUDs represented a recapitulation of the nineteenth-
century nationalists' search for a symbolism based on peasant culture. A

4.2. Croatian Cultural Association, "Izidor Poljak," Boće-Ravno, Bosnia and Herze-govina, at the 33rd International Folklore Festival, Zagreb, 1999. Photo by Davor Šiftar. Courtesy of Institute of Ethnology and Folklore Research, Zagreb.

few KUDs (the minority) were categorized as *izvorni* KUDs (meaning from the spring or a pure source, that is, traditional) because they performed using traditional instruments and costuming and focused on the preservation and performance of one repertoire, while others (a majority) were *stilizatsia* KUDs (meaning stylized, that is, allowing the use of modern instruments and stage costumes) and performed a two-hour-long, pan-Yugoslav program. Village folklore ensembles, outside the urban-oriented state system, were encouraged to preserve and perform their own folklore, that is, of the nationality of their village.

Given that in the postwar era, villages all over the country were emptying out as young people moved to the city, this sometimes meant that obviously elderly people would be performing dances associated with youth.[15] Village folklore groups were also strongly influenced by KUDs and professional ensembles. This is exemplified by an incident at a *smotra*, or festival, in Bosnia in which a local village ensemble wanted to be taught to perform the suite from Vranje in south Serbia that they had seen performed by KUDs, rather than their own village's traditional material.[16] Ethnic minorities were encouraged to form KUDs of their own, focusing on their own ethno-national repertoire. A Hungarian KUD in Croatia, a Ukrainian KUD in Bosnia (Taras Sevchenko),

4.3 Dance, *korak u četvero* (step in four). A group of Muslim girls, Umoljani, Bosnia, 1955. Photo by Živomir Mladenović. Courtesy of Institute of Ethnology and Folklore Research, Zagreb.

and a Turkish KUD in Macedonia (Jeni Jol) were among this latter type.

During ethnographic research in 1985, the complexity of types of folk dance performance that had arisen was clarified for me by eminent Bosnian choreographer Vaso Popovic. He outlined his view of the traditional-theatrical continuum of folk dance in Bosnia thus:

1. *Izvorni* (pure) folk dancing in the villages.

    This would be the realm of traditional dances done in traditional contexts such as dancing *kolo* after church on Sunday.

2. *Izvorni* dances performed on stage by what he called *seoske grupe* (village groups).

    I have to comment here that "pure" and "on stage" may not always be compatible. In another example from my fieldwork in Bosnia, a village dance group was highly resistant to such elementary stagecraft as modifying their dance so as to not have their backs to the audience. In a sense, they were resisting *scenska kultura* (stage culture). In the living memory of these villagers, this was simply not the way the dance was done.

3. *Izvorni* dance in the city.
   Some urban KUD performances of this material were his example. In other words, urban performers had learned these dances in rehearsal, not in the village.

4. Stylized *izvorni* dances in urban KUDs.
   An example is Popovic's own *Ozrenske Igre* (Dances from Ozren), a choreographed suite of dances from the mountains of north central Bosnia, performed by KUD Veselin Maslesa of Banja Luka.
   In 1999, I witnessed a perfect example of this at the Second International Folklore Festival in Sarajevo. A group from a dance academy in Tirana, Albania, performed a typical Albanian suite of a type familiar to Yugoslavs from suites of dances representing Kosovo. Everything from the dancers' pointing feet to the women's short skirts to the athletic and balletic movement accentuated the fact that this suite of dances was a confection of a stage-oriented choreographer.

5. High style—what Popovic called *balet*, that is, ballet and modern dance.
   I would include in this category some *estrada*, or popular folk dances, that is, those intended as stage entertainments of the type seen on Yugoslav television variety programs.

Popovic's first category represented traditionally contextualized dances. The second represented those dances recontextualized by their traditional performers. The third and fourth represent *izvorni* and *stilizatsia* KUDs of urban folk performing dances they might otherwise never have performed. The fifth, of course, represents state sponsorship of culture. The latter three situations demonstrate, as noted by ethnochoreologist Andriy Nahachewsky, the divorce of professional ensembles from experiential knowledge of traditional folk dance performance.[17] To paraphrase the title of the influential handbook on recontextualizing traditional folk dances to the stage by Croatian choreographer Ivan Ivancan, the connection between *folklor* (traditional participation) and *scena* (stage performance) has been severed.[18] In light of my thesis here, there is an important difference between categories one and two and categories three and four. Categories one and two represent an actual memory of dance as a part of everyday life. The third and fourth categories represent the shaping of the experience of urban folk, giving them a cultural memory of a time and a place (premodern rural life) they may not have personally experienced.

Pleasant memories of the enjoyment of performance inspired a number of members of one Sarajevo KUD from this early era to reconstitute themselves in the 1980s as the Veterani section of U/AKUD Slobodan Princip-Seljo. This was the first such instance that I have found in Bosnia of a 1940–50s "A" section recreating itself decades later. Rather than performing the dances of their own ethno-national group or ancestral/traditional village repertoire, they rehearsed and subsequently performed the dances of the all-Yugoslav repertoire that they had first encountered decades earlier as members of an urban KUD. In this sense, this older generation literally embodied in performance the successful creation of a Yugoslav national identity.

An example of how personal experience and memory shape meaning in dance relates to performances of the *Partizan kolos* (partisan round dances) in various regional and national festival situations. During the Second World War, according to the 1942 Statute of the Proletarian Liberation Brigades, every partisan unit was required to have a culture team.[19] The culture team's mission had a folk dance section, often accompanied by agitprop (agitation-propaganda) theater and the like. The later reenactment of the *Partizan kolos* evoked the brotherhood and unity of the anti-Fascist struggle, and although partisan dances had already been included as a component in other festivals, according to a Sarajevan informant, specific festivals of partisan dances appeared first in Bosnia only in 1984–85.[20] In their original context, partisan dances were often simply traditional round or line dances renamed and thus made ethno-nationally neutral. These ethnically neutral, war-contextualized dances served two functions. On the one hand, they existed in the memory of the postwar audiences as something they may have performed around campfires and under the direction of partisan culture teams as Yugoslavs, not as Serbs, Croats, Slovenes, and so on. Seeing these dances performed, albeit on stage and by dancers too young to have fought together and then to have danced around military campfires, validated this generation's experiences of comradeship and sacrifice. At the same time, partisan *kolos* served to create a memory in audiences too young to have experienced firsthand the unity of the Second World War. Thus, choreographed and recontextualized folk dances contributed to the creation myth of the new Yugoslavia. Croatian musicologist

Naila Ceribasic notes that one folk dance in particular, *Kozaracko Kolo*, was simple enough to be easily recontextualized as the main partisan dance, and this simplicity allowed performers and audiences to make an affective connection.[21] In a way, this process is analogous to the many Second World War movies produced by postwar Yugoslav studios, which simplified the war narrative for a postwar audience of the victors, and which emphasized the comradeship and sacrifice of the participants to create a common social memory for the generation that experienced it.

A Yugoslav Eutopia

If the utopian period considered above is examined as a period during which the new state used existing folklore to create a fresh image, then the eutopian period, painted here with a broad brush as existing from the early 1960s until the outbreak of civil war in 1992, was one in which that image was consolidated both at home and abroad. Tensions, however, existed. In the early 1960s, the attempt to create a unified national Yugoslav culture was abandoned. The Constitution of 1963 replaced "the brotherhood and unity [*bratsvo i jedinstvo*] of the peoples of Yugoslavia" with a pluralist, multinational self-image. It was felt that Titoism and the Yugoslav version of socialism would be enough to hold the state together. Self-management was extended to the role of culture. But who would be the managers in self-managed culture?

In folklore, this eutopian period is best characterized by two themes, commodification and consolidation, and is exemplified by a period known as the KUD *Kriza* (the KUD Crisis). Lasting until the early 1970s, the KUD *Kriza* began in the mid-1950s when socialist realism was abandoned and culture became less "mass" and more concentrated in the hands of culture workers. In the consolidation phase of amateur folklore, tensions arose between being what was described in ethnographic interviews as "a really good, professional-like KUD," where only the best performers were on display, and the ideological need to be open and democratic and so inclusive of all standards. Because of these conflicts, a number of KUDs ceased to function during this era, including some quite distinguished ones, such as KUD Veselin Maslesa of Banja Luka.

Folklore performances also became transformed into more than the *symbolic* commodities of the immediate postwar period.[22] As well as being replaceable units of ideological production and consumption, staged choreographies based on folk themes became *actual* commodities, as performing groups came under pressure to address economic imperatives. KUDs, in order to meet their financial needs, began performing at other venues, taking contracts with tourist hotels, for example. Thus, KUDs also became packaged as part of the value-added segment of a tourist economy, enhancing foreign visitors' memories of their holidays in a romanticized Yugoslavia. In a certain sense, choreographed folk dances may be thought of as particularly "robust" forms of cultural commodities. So long as audiences appreciate them, they can be repeated ad infinitum locally and even be exported internationally, both to make money and to represent the state. Indeed, some suites of dances became iconic representations and would frequently appear in ensembles' repertoires: a Sumadija suite represented Serbia, a Posavina suite represented Croatia, a "silent *kolo*" stood for Bosnia, the *Lindjo* (a couple dance) stood for the coastal region of Dalmatia, and so on.

In comparing utopia (1945 to the early 1960s) and eutopia (the early 1960s to 1992), it is helpful to think of the earlier period as one in which Yugoslav socialism was being built. Dance and music performance was one of its aspects, along with ideologically driven national projects such as railway roadbed projects constructed by idealistic socialist youth. The eutopian period, on the other hand, was one of the consolidation of socialism. A generation had grown up with stage-oriented folklore performance as a normal part of, primarily, urban and modern life. The KUD Crisis represents this process of consolidation of performance under actually existing Yugoslav socialism.

Urban youth were the target of the KUD's primary ideological mission, particularly in Bosnia. Midhat Ridjanovic, a distinguished Bosnian linguist and veteran of Sarajevo's U/AKUD Slobodan Princip-Seljo, used the descriptive phrase *peljovan od* (inoculated against) to indicate the role that amateur folklore groups were assumed to play in creating counterweights to ethno-nationalism. But the youths' principal interest was less in national ideology performance than it was in the opportunity to travel, especially abroad. Bosnian ensembles that had performed at the Eisteddfod (an international festival of traditional folklore, held in Wales) thought it especially ironic, given that festival's particular emphasis on authenticity, that none of them were rural people performing their own traditional material; they were city people from Sarajevo (notably from the RKUD Proleter) from different ethnic backgrounds.

The social memories created for them were much more personal: it was their experience of stage performance as part of a KUD, not as part of a traditional dance context that had meaning for them. When Muslim, Serb, and Croatian Bosnian *Veterani* would gather for a *teferic* (picnic) in the 1980s and 1990s, their memories as a group were of their experience as stage performers. In one sense, the state's attempt to build a nation through performance had some effect. People valued their performance experience, but no "Yugoslav" dance emerged, no dance became "the" dance that represented a unified Yugoslav ideal. Dances of the individual Yugoslav republics, presented as part of the all-Yugoslav program, were always potentially available for nationalist re-appropriation. Attempts were made to continue the supranational dance tradition of *Partisansko Kolo* and *Titovo Kolo* (as some of these recontextualized dances were called) at specific festivals. One such festival I attended in the late 1980s was held in honor of Tito's birthday, with all the KUDs of Sarajevo participating. After the performances of various standard suites, the grand finale took the form of a mass performance of a specially choreographed dance with the dancers remaining in the costumes they had worn during the performances of the various suites that they had performed previously in the program. It should be remembered that the KUDs of Sarajevo were, almost by definition, multi-ethnic. Thus the grand finale mixed both apparent (as indicated by costuming) and actual Serbian, Croatian, and Muslim youth, epitomizing the unity amid diversity that Bosnia, and Yugoslavia, should ideally have represented. This was an interesting parallel to the performance by Sarajevo KUDs at the opening of the Olympic Games in Sarajevo in 1984.[23] Attired in snowsuits, each group in one of the five Olympic colors, they performed a mass, choreographed folk dance representing the submersion, but not the eradication, of national identity in the utopianism of the Olympic movement.

In broader terms, it might be argued that the potential of a socialist utopia had yielded to the actuality of a socialist eutopia. *Utopia*, mostly used to suggest a fantasyland of perfection, in effect, means "no place": the unachievable political and social dream beyond human grasp. *Eutopia*, on the other hand, translates from the Greek as "good place" and arguably, at least, could be perceived as a desirable goal. If not a perfect place, or even a good place, perhaps a good enough place would still be something to be desired in the Yugoslav context. The projected past of a socialist utopia, the projected future of a united but culturally diverse country, was highly visible at staged folk performances. After 1980 and Tito's death, folklore performances became privileged venues for extravagant displays of loyalty to Tito's memory; the slogan "Tito, This We Swear to You, From Your Path We'll Never Deviate" always appeared somewhere near the stage at each performance. The two ideas were thus connected: Tito's vision of a united Yugoslav state and multinational folklore performance. Another popular slogan also appeared, "After Tito—Tito!" presaged not hope but desperation. Again, a social memory of the utopian socialism of the Tito era was evoked, as the country slid far from the goal of eutopian socialism.

By the late 1980s, living standards had declined as a result of hyperinflation and the mistakes of workers self-managing their own failing industries. As some of the constituent peoples of Yugoslavia began to say: it might be better being out than being in. What Marvin Harris has aptly deemed "ethnomania,"[24] an especially aggressive and virulent form of ethnocentrism, began to consume the Serbian imagination, and the country started to collapse in the wars of Yugoslav succession/secession. Yugoslav eutopia for many, especially in Bosnia, soon became quite the reverse: a true distopian nightmare, as Yugoslavia seemed poised to join the ranks of post–Cold War failed states.

(Former) Yugoslavia in E.U.-topia

In the post–Bosnian War era, relationships between folklore performances and political aspiration have continued. Some, indeed most, of the choreographic material from the former periods of utopia and eutopia has been used to represent the contemporary political situation and the projected future of the emergent states from the former Yugoslavia. Not every performer in the various folklore ensembles, however, found a common meaning in the relationship between repertoire and symbolic representation during this postwar period. As I discovered from fieldwork in Bosnia, especially in multi-ethnic, urban KUDs, for many performers their common memory of performance was an important part of their shared memory as Yugoslavs; their interests as folklore performers did not automatically relate to their present and future status as members of the new states or indeed as members of specific ethnic communities. Former war correspondent Steven Erlanger notes the emergence of the phenomenon of "Yugo-nostalgia," of older people remembering when

Yugoslavia was supported by the West as an independent Communist state.[25] This Yugo-nostalgia represents a connection to the utopian future past, a "future history" (a familiar trope in science fiction literature) that was not.

Less nostalgic meanings, however, could be determined in the folklore performances, and these related to the new future signaled by plans for Bosnia-Herzegovina eventually to become a member of the European Union. Since the conclusion of the Yugoslav war with the signing in 1995 of the Dayton Peace Accords, the advantages of economic inclusion and political affiliation with the European Union had became apparent for Bosnia-Herzegovina.[26] Membership in the E.U. requires adherence to criteria for democracy, equality, and respect for minority and human rights. In Bosnia in the early twenty-first century, folk dance is used to illustrate such ideals of fair and tolerant social and cultural inclusion.[27] During the early part of the war against Bosnia, for obvious reasons, KUDs had eliminated almost all local Serbian (and later many Croatian) dances from their repertoires, at least in Sarajevo. They did, nonetheless, continue creating memory through dance. People attended KUD rehearsals and scheduled performances, even during the darkest hours of the Serbian siege of Sarajevo. It was understandable that performers might not want to celebrate the culture of the former Serbian neighbors who were sniping at them on their way to rehearsal, or when Serbian or Croatian ethnic militias were driving their rural relatives from their homes. I remember yet another example of the emotional resonance of dance during times of war, once again captured and broadcast by CNN. As United Nations troops entered a small town east of Sarajevo, the camera focused on a group of women who began dancing a traditional Bosnian dance in celebration.

After the signing of the Dayton Peace Accords, which ended the active military stage of the dismemberment of Bosnia, ensembles began to reintegrate Serbian material into their performances, particularly those performances that might be viewed by foreign dignitaries. In the modern E.U.-topian period, the first step was to perform those national dances that had become iconic standards from before the recent war, dances that many KUD members had performed growing up. Classic choreographies of pre-1992 material filled this need.[28] The next step was to perform integrated dances, that is, those in which the performers were in the costumes of the three main prewar ethnic groups but performed the same dance medley. A medley of dances called *Sarajevo Zavrazlama* was revived and neatly fitted this bill. The final step in the use of folk dances in E.U.-topian Bosnia was to perform a stand-alone suite of Bosnian Serb dances. I witnessed this in 1999, though the organizers were careful to dust off a pre–Bosnian War suite of Serbian dances, *Okolina Sarajeva* (Around Sarajevo) with which audiences were already familiar, as was I. A reference to viewing a performance that included *Okolina Sarajeva* first appears in my field notes in 1985.

Sarajevo, Bosnia's capital, also now plays an active role on the international folk festival circuit. Like its long-established Croatian counterpart, the main festival in July is composed of lectures, costume exhibitions, parades, and performances. I remember one outdoor performance during the festival, in what is certainly a concession to the role of religion in contemporary Bosnia. As a KUD finished one dance in its suite of dances, they stopped, and a pause ensued for several minutes while the dancers and musicians stood idly by on the stage as the muezzin of the nearby mosque began the electronically amplified call to prayer from the minaret.

A Bridge Not Too Far:
The Ethnographic Chrysalis Unfolds

Viewed through the heuristic devices of utopia, eutopia, and E.U.-topia, this consideration of folklore ensembles and their repertoires demonstrates the shifting and situational meanings of dance in relation to political economies. Furthermore, it highlights a key issue in the production of ethnographies and histories of performance. Anthropologists, undoubtedly influenced by Clifford Geertz's elegant and accessible writing style, and certainly stimulated by the appearance of George Marcus and Michael Fischer's *Anthropology as Cultural Critique* in 1986, as well as Derek Freeman's powerful and persuasive critique three years earlier of Margaret Mead's research in Samoa, came face to face with what has come to be a central question of a postmodern ethnology.[29] That is, when we write ethnography, are we writing facts as they appear on the ground, or are we writing fictions, essentially pleasant and entertaining memoirs from our time in the field? Are we recording an ethnographic reality, or is the field a palimpsest upon which we place our own constructions? The answer, of course, is that we are doing something of both. We see the cultures under study through the lens of our experience, our memory, and our theoretical orientations. Emic and etic (insider's view and outsider's view), both past and present, exist in constant interpenetration. In my research work on the folklore performances in various parts of former Yugoslavia, what I am writing about is, in some ways, the conflation and creation of both social and personal memories of the performers and of their audiences. For the performers, there are the formal, culturally created memories of an imagined idyllic past, created on stage for a receptive audience, aided by the individual memories of performers who literally made the performance and who remember, not an idealized rural past nor the creation of a socialist Yugoslav utopia, but rather their own experience of performing the dances and music of the many peoples of former Yugoslavia. For the audience, these dancers and the dances that they perform carry a number of complex and mutable meanings about ethnic and national identity in embodied movement, in bodily habitus. Returning to my original metaphorical moment, during which a curious ethnographer watches CNN, three young women dancing in the dark in Belgrade come to symbolize the complex relationship bridging memory, history, and ethnography.

NOTES

This chapter is based on a paper originally presented at the meetings of the International Council for Traditional Music's (ICTM) Study Group on Ethnochoreology, held on the island of Korcula, Croatia, in the summer of 2000. I am grateful to my colleagues in attendance from Croatia and Slovenia for their insightful comments and useful feedback on that original version of this chapter.

1. NATO was created in 1949 as a military alliance of Western Europe nation-states, the United States, and Canada. Its purpose was to create a common defense against the perceived expansionist designs of the Soviet Union. The period from 1949 to 1989 became known as the Cold War. The Communist state called Yugoslavia was established in the Second World War but has since disappeared from the map of Europe. It consisted of Slovenia, Croatia, Bosnia and Herzegovina, Macedonia, Serbia, and Montenegro.

2. See Benedict Anderson, *Imagined Communities: Reflections on the Origin and Spread of Nationalism* (London: Verso, 1991).

3. Anthony Shay, "Parallel Traditions: State Folk Dance Ensembles and Folk Dance in the Field," *Dance Research Journal* 31, no. 1 (Spring 1999): 29–56, and *Choreographic Politics: State Folk Dance Companies, Representation and Power* (Middletown, Conn.: Wesleyan University Press, 2002).

4. See, for example, the useful paradigms presented by James G. Carrier, *Occidentalism: Images of the West* (Oxford: Oxford University Press, 1995); Yvonne Daniel, *Rumba: Dance and Social Change in Contemporary Cuba* (Bloomington: Indiana University Press, 1995); Jacques Maquet, *Introduction to Aesthetic Anthropology*, 2nd ed., rev. (Malibu, Calif.: Undena, 1979); Zoila Mendoza, *Shaping Society through the Dance* (Chicago: University of Chicago Press, 2000).

5. See Lynn D. Maners, "The Social Lives of Dances in Bosnia and Herzegovina: Cultural Performance and the Anthropology of Aesthetic Phenomena" (Ph.D. diss., University of California, Los Angeles, 1995); Maners, "Clapping for Serbs: Nationalism and Performance in Bosnia and Herzegovina," in *Neighbors at War: Anthropological Perspectives on Yugoslav Ethnicity, Culture and History*, ed. Joel Halpern and David Kideckel (University Park: Pennsylvania State University Press, 2000), 302–15; Maners, "To Dance Is (Not) a Human (Right)," in *Dance and Human Rights*, ed. Naomi Jackson, forthcoming.

6. For an introduction to the history of Yugoslavia, see Misha Glenny, *The Balkans: Nationalism, War and the Great Powers, 1804–1999* (New York: Viking, 2000), and Leslie Benson, *Yugoslavia: A Concise History* (Basingstoke, Hampshire: Palgrave Macmillan, 2004).

7. Eric Hobsbawm, "Introduction: Inventing Traditions," in *The Invention of Tradition*, ed. Eric Hobsbawm and Terence Ranger (Cambridge: Cambridge University Press, 1983), 1.

8. Andrew Baruch Wachtel, *Making a Nation, Breaking a Nation: Literature and Cultural Politics in Yugoslavia* (Stanford, Calif.: Stanford University Press, 1998), 9.

9. See Michael Herzfeld, *Ours Once More: Folklore, Ideology and the Making of Modern Greece* (Austin: University of Texas Press, 1982).

10. Miklos Haraszti, *The Velvet Prison: Artists under State Socialism* (New York: New Republic, 1987).

11. For comparative examples see Anna Ilieva, "Bulgarian Folk Dance in the Past 45 Years," *17th Symposium of the Study Group on Ethnochoreology 1992 Proceedings* (Nafplion, Greece: Peloponnesian Folklore Foundation and the International Council for Traditional Music, 1994), 35–38; Arzu Öztürkmen, "Folk Dance and Nationalism in Turkey," *17th Symposium of the Study Group on Ethnochoreology 1992 Proceedings*, 83–86; Anca Giurchescu, "The Use of Traditional Symbols for Recasting the Present: A Case Study of Tourism in Rumania," *Dance Studies* 14 (1990), 47–63; Tvrtko Zebec, "Dance Events as Political Rituals for the Expression of Identities in Croatia in the 1990s," in *Music, Politics and War: Views from Croatia*, ed. Svanibor Pettan (Zagreb, Croatia: Institute of Ethnology and Folklore Research, 1998), 151–62.

12. Stevan Majstorovic, *Cultural Policy in Yugoslavia* (Paris: UNESCO, 1972), 16–17. Eventually, cultural activities would be funded on a republic level by the *porez kultura*, literally, the culture tax.

13. Majstorovic, *Cultural Policy in Yugoslavia*.

14. "Veteran" of KUD Slobodan Princip-Seljo, informal conversation, Sarajevo, 1987.

15. For a memorable example, see Frank Dubinskas, "Performing Slavonian Folklore: The Politics of Reminiscence and the Recreating of the Past" (Ph.D. diss., Stanford University, 1983), 163.

16. Maners, "Social Lives of Dances in Bosnia and Herzegovina," 155–56.

17. Andriy Nahachewsky, "Searching for Branches, Searching for Roots: Fieldwork in My Grandfather's Village," in *Dance in the Field: Theory, Methods and Issues in Dance Ethnography*, ed. Theresa Jill Buckland (London: Macmillan; New York: St. Martin's Press, 1999), 175–85.

18. Ivan Ivancan, *Folklor I Scena* (Zagreb, Croatia: Muzicka Biblioteka, 1971).

19. Milutin Dedic, "Cultural-Artistic Amateurism," *Yugoslav Survey* (Paris: UNESCO, May 1981): 121–40.

20. Subsequent research has shown this memory to be somewhat faulty. Recently, while searching in the archives of the folk music section of Radio Television–Sarajevo, I found a note referring to the Second Festival of Partisan Songs and Dances, held on 16 April 1978 in the Skenderija venue in Sarajevo. Also mentioned on the same page is a Festival of Partisan Songs and Dances held on 20 April 1980.

21. Naila Ceribasic, "Heritage of the Second World War in Croatia: Identity Imposed upon and by Music," in *Music, Politics and War: Views from Croatia*, 109–30.

22. See Dunja Rihtman-Augustin, "Traditional Culture, Folklore and Mass Culture in Contemporary Yugoslavia," in *Folklore in the Modern World*, ed. Richard M. Dorson (The Hague: Mouton, 1978), 163–72.

23. Sanja Andus L'Hotellier, "The Opening and Closing of the Albertville Olympics: An Invitation to the *Bal Populaire*," in *Proceedings of the 21st Symposium of the ICTM Study Group on Ethnochoreology, 2000 Korcula*, ed. Elsie Ivancic Dunin and Tvrtko Zebec (Zagreb, Croatia: Institute of Ethnology and Folklore Research, 2001), 133–37.

24. Marvin Harris, *Theories of Culture in Postmodern Times* (Walnut Creek, Calif.: AltaMira Press, 1999), 112.

25. Steven Erlanger, "For Yugoslavs, the Past Keeps Getting Better," *New York Times*, 30 April 2000, "Week in Review," 3.

26. For discussion, see Susan L. Woodward, *Balkan Tragedy: Chaos and Dissolution after the Cold War* (Washington, D.C.: Brookings Institution Press, 1995), and David Chandler, *Bosnia: Faking Democracy after Dayton* (London: Pluto Press, 1999).

27. See Maners, "Clapping for Serbs."

28. For a collection of descriptions and choreographies of a number of traditional Bosnian dances, see Hajrudin Hadzic, *Tradicionalne Bosnjacke Igre I Njihova*

Veza sa Obicajima [Traditional Bosnian Dances and Their Connection with Customs] (Sarajevo: Bosanski Kulturni Centar, 1999).

29. See, for example, Clifford Geertz, *Works and Lives: The Anthropologist as Author* (Stanford, Calif.: Stanford University Press, 1988); George E. Marcus and Michael M. J. Fischer, *Anthropology as Cultural Critique: An Experimental Moment in the Human Sciences,* 2nd ed. (Chicago: University of Chicago Press, 1999); Derek Freeman, *Margaret Mead and Samoa: The Making and Unmaking of an Anthropological Myth* (Cambridge, Mass.: Harvard University Press, 1983).

5

Qualities of Memory
Two Dances of the Tortugas Fiesta, New Mexico

DEIDRE SKLAR

Investigating the role of embodiment in practices of knowledge and memory, this chapter considers in particular the felt, somatic aspects of movement knowledge. I argue that thinking itself, including the way we access, organize, retrieve, and present information, is as much a matter of somatic understandings as of semiotic ones. Whereas identity has been considered in terms of ethnicity, race, gender, and class, here I suggest that the way kinetic energy is organized to carry meaning constitutes a "difference" that has yet to be investigated. Drawing on field research with dancers in the annual fiesta of Our Lady of Guadalupe in Tortugas, New Mexico, I review findings resulting from a somatic approach.

Concerning Theory and Method

In the 1970s, Richard Bandler and John Grinder, students of anthropologist Gregory Bateson and originators of the popular therapy Neurolinguistic Programming, showed that different people access memory via different sensory modalities. Further, the sensory mode by which an

individual *accesses* a memory is often different from the one in which he
or she *represents* the memory.[1] All thinking occurs in one or another sensory modality, but the ratios are different for different individuals, and
perhaps for the same individual in different circumstances. At about the
same time Bandler and Grinder were analyzing sensory access to memory, Clifford Geertz, leading the "interpretive turn" in North American
cultural anthropology, wrote that works of art, including dances, are
meaningful because they "connect to a sensibility they joined in creating."[2] Since then, scholars working at the juncture of sensory anthropology, performance studies, and dance ethnography have queried the relationship between the sensual and the ideological in the organization of
cultural knowledge and memory.[3] For many, the goal has been to return sensory modes of knowledge, and bodily consciousness in particular, to a central place in the study of cultural performance. How do we,
in Geertz's terms, "sense with understanding"?[4]

In 1988, James Clifford issued an invitation to assess critically how
participant-observation "obliges its practitioners to experience, at a
bodily as well as an intellectual level, the vicissitudes of translation," in effect opening the door for a "sensory anthropology."[5] Following Marshall
McLuhan, who wrote that "[a]ny culture is an order of sensory preferences," David Howes and Constance Classen suggest, for example, attending to differences in "sensory profiles," the relative emphasis placed
on different sensory modalities in different cultural communities.[6]
"What if," Howes writes, "there exist different forms of reasoning,
memory, and attention for each of the modalities of consciousness (seeing, smelling, speaking, hearing, etc.) instead of reasoning, memory, and
attention being general mental powers?"[7] This is promising, its premise
borne out by the work of Bandler and Grinder cited above. Howes and
Classen, however, omit kinesthesia, the proprioceptive sense of movement within our own bodies.[8] While kinesthesia might be subsumed
under touch, as the changing contours of touch within our own bodies,
omitting it from the sensorium leaves us with no sensory reference point
for addressing movement as a way of knowing. Is kinesthesia, then, excluded from the sensorium because it refers to no external object and can
only be apprehended proprioceptively, that is, within one's own body?

Philosopher Edward Casey distinguishes "body memory" from
"memory of the body," the first working primarily through feelings in
the body, the second through representations of the body as an object of
awareness.[9] For Casey, the first would be properly called *remembering*, the

second *recollecting*.[10] He suggests that whereas remembering manifests in terms of "its own depth," recollection is "projected" at a "quasi-pictorial distance from myself as a voyeur of the remembered."[11] In recollection (as well as in verbal reminiscing), Henri Bergson wrote, we "peer" back toward a past that seems to have independent being distant from the present; in body memory, the past is enacted in the present, as a kind of *immanence*.[12] Casey's distinction is useful for thinking about dance history and memory. One might say that dance can work as either recollection or remembering, or both. Recollection, "seeing" a dance in the mind's eye, is the traditional mode of studying dance history. But, remembering, or "feeling" movement memory as immanent kinesthetic sensation, is essential to dancing itself and to its continuation and transmission over time. It is critical to communication via dance and to the cultural knowledge and values negotiated through dance. We cannot exclude it from attention.

Kinesthetic sensations, much less their meaning, are rarely the focus of everyday awareness. As Marcel Mauss and, after him, Pierre Bourdieu have pointed out, the bodily patterns we master are then enacted outside of conscious awareness.[13] We remember how to drive a car without focusing on the motor skills needed to turn the key in the ignition, depress the clutch, shift into gear, and rev the accelerator. Dancers step up to the barre and begin a daily routine that includes so many brushes, so many pliés, so many relevés, without needing to relearn each day how to do each move. Bourdieu recognized that the very roteness of the "habitus" disguises cultural and historical predispositions, social schemes of perception and thought passed from one generation to the next in patterns of movement. The unconscious braiding of movement practices and ideologies constrains people to perpetuate social structures at the level of the body. For Bourdieu, people are not in possession of the habitus; rather, they are possessed by it.[14]

But the hold of the habitus is not absolute, and we do sometimes transcend its automatic and efficient grip. Performing a plié in the studio, perhaps a dancer has lucid moments of seeing herself, as if from a distance, lined up among the others, holding onto a wooden pole in order to drop and rise "gracefully" over and over again, understanding, in that moment, her complicity with a socioaesthetic system that values "ballet." Her lucid moments may occur in the opposite direction, consciousness diving inward and immersing in the minute sensations of spine extending, wrists softening, breath suspending. In the first kind of lucidity, one calls on visual imagination to project across distances to "see" the larger system; in the second, one calls on proprioception, turning awareness inward to "feel" one's body as a continuum of kinetic sensations. In either case, the hold of the habitus is broken, inviting opening beyond routine.

These two imagined possibilities of transcendence are encapsulated in the polarity of "sensibility and intelligibility," loosely representing, on the one hand, somatic organizations of knowledge and, on the other, the socially sedimented meanings and values embodied in movement systems, especially in their political dimensions.[15] The most succinct elaboration of their complementarity is given by psychological anthropologist Thomas Csordas, who weaves together Maurice Merleau-Ponty's phenomenological analysis of perceptual processes and Pierre Bourdieu's sociopolitical analysis of collective practice.[16] Csordas recognizes that the phenomenologist's "lived experience" is never merely individual and subjective but develops as relational and cultural constructions in social space. He understands that the sociologist's "practice" is not only a collective sedimentation passed on through generations but an opportunity for individuality, agency, and somatic awareness.

Distinguishing between "the body," as biological and material, and "embodiment," as an "indeterminate methodological field defined by perceptual experience and the mode of presence and engagement in the world," Csordas addresses embodiment as "the starting point for analyzing human participation in a cultural world."[17] He coins the term "somatic modes of attention" to refer to "culturally elaborated ways of attending to and with one's body in surroundings that include the embodied presence of others."[18] Following Merleau-Ponty, Csordas suggests that before we come to perceive ourselves as objects, we are first subjects to ourselves in a "pre-objective" world that experiences embodiment but not "the body." Child psychologist Daniel Stern provides clarification of the problematic term *pre-objective* and supports Merleau-Ponty's ontological order.[19] Stern shows that before we are able to differentiate objects, including ourselves as objects, we perceive and organize sensory experience. Stern, like Csordas, considers the processes by which we become objects to ourselves, or, in his terms, how infants begin to have an emergent sense of self. Experiments show that in an infant younger than two months old, a sense of self first develops in relation to its body, "its coherence, its actions, its inner feeling states, and the memory of all these," through the process of organizing sensory experience.[20] This is the framework for his discussion of pre-objective organizations of sensory experience.

Specifically, in the pre-objective phase of development, Stern writes, the senses work in tandem. We are born with the innate capacity to "transfer perceptual experience from one sensory modality to another," translating, for example, between what an object feels like and what it looks like.[21] The same cross-referencing occurs in translating sound intensities (loudness) to visual intensities (brightness) and with recognizing temporal patterns (beat, rhythm, duration) between visual and auditory modes. Before infants recognize that an impression "belongs" to a particular sense or a quality to a particular object, they make global abstractions of shape, temporal pattern, and intensity across the senses. When Csordas says that we are first subjects to ourselves in a "pre-objective" world where we experience embodiment but not "the body," I understand him to be referring to this phase and process.

Philosopher Mark Johnson offers an elegant model for thinking about the pre-objective processes Stern describes.[22] Johnson challenges objectivism, the notion that meaning occurs as objective structures transcendent of human embodiment and independent of human engagement, recognizing meaning to be an *event* of human understanding. For Johnson, both logical and metaphoric thinking are meaning-making processes that depend on imagination, which is, in effect, the capacity to structure experience by organizing perceptions into patterns. Like Stern, he focuses on the prelinguistic and pre-objective phase of ordering bodily experience across sensory modalities. The resulting extrapolations, which he calls "image schemata" or "embodied schemata," are neither perceptions nor reflections, but cross-modal recognitions of pattern, whether of form or of quality, that emerge from and structure perceptions.[23] For example, the spatial embodied schema of "up and down" or the dynamic embodied schema of "rushing" are built cross-modally from movement sensations, seeing, and hearing.

The combination of Stern's concept of amodal perception and Johnson's concept of embodied schema offers a framework for understanding how innate capacities for combining perception and conception are differentially developed in different cultural communities. Although, as anthropologist Brenda Farnell notes, phenomenology carries the danger of positing a "universal bodily experience" that separates "the body from language and culture," here are grounds for a phenomenological approach to knowledge that addresses embodiment as

culturally informed right from the start.[24] Specifically, while the capacity to abstract patterns from sensory experience, via amodal perception, is innate, the metaphoric process of schema-building is indeterminate, open-ended, creative, and continuously active.[25] In other words,
schema-building is inherently open to cultural, as well as individual,
variation. Sensations in the womb, even though they are not organized
objectively, in terms of "my" sensations in "your" womb, are influenced
by a social milieu—the mother's movement patterns, her breathing
rhythms, intrusions from the environment. In Csordas's words, our
bodies, from the beginning, are "in the world," part of "an intersubjec-
tive milieu" that includes others' bodies; thus, it is not subjectivity but
intersubjectivity "that gives rise to sensation."[26] Pre-objective and prelinguistic do not imply pre-cultural. From the womb onward, in different sociocultural and historical circumstances, we learn to emphasize
and value different sensory details of form and quality, different perceptual and expressive media, and different ways of processing somatosen-
sory information.

Concerning the argument for qualitative factors in cultural constructions of meaning and memory, Stern reports that just as infants
extrapolate between quantifiable elements like shape and temporal
pattern, they also cross-modally "yoke together" qualities of feeling.[27]
Stern is emphatic that these feelings are not "categorical affects" like
happiness, anger, surprise, and so on. Rather, they are "vitality affects,"
the complex qualities of kinetic energy inherent in all bodily activity.[28]
An infant can recognize, for example, the similarly lightly caressing
quality of vitality in the way her mother might brush her hair, sing a lul-
laby, and smile at her, before she can distinguish her mother or herself
as objects, and before she can recognize singing, hair brushing, or smil-
ing as discrete actions. Unlike the terminology of emotion, Stern writes,
vitality affects are "better captured by dynamic, *kinetic* terms, such as
'surging,' 'fading away,' 'fleeting,' 'explosive,' or 'crescendo,' 'decre-
scendo,' 'bursting,' 'drawn out,' and so on."[29] Vitality affects are most
revealed, Stern writes, in events like music and dance that have no
"content."[30] Indeed, he acknowledges, they are equivalent to what Suzanne Langer calls the "forms of feeling" embodied in dance.[31] Likewise, if the phenomenologist's "lived experience" is understood to be
the ongoing dynamic changes in vitality affects over time, what Stern
calls the "activation contours of experience," then lived experience is
not, as anthropologist Drid Williams protests, "some mystical bodily

event of shared experience," but the cross-modal apprehension of kinetic dynamics as they are differentially developed in different cultural communities.[32] Until we attend to kinetic dynamics, the way vitality affects are organized in specific movement systems and actions, we lack a crucial dimension in understanding the meaningfulness of movement performance in and as social memory. As Howes calls for "sensory profiles," I am calling for "vitality profiles." The dynamic factors of rhythm, speed, and duration; force; degree of muscular tension or relaxation; and degree of giving in to or resisting gravity (weightiness and lightness) encode cultural dispositions as much as the shapes and spatial patterns of movement do.[33] Labananalysis, as Rudolf von Laban's schema of qualitative factors is now called, offers a systematic way of observing such dynamics. The system focuses on eight core qualities: light or strong use of weight, quick or sustained time, direct or indirect use of space, and bound or free movement flow.[34] As dance critic Marcia Siegel notes, the system has flaws. It is prejudiced toward the extremes, omitting neutral territories that are, for example, neither quick nor sustained.[35] Siegel also recognizes that the Choreometrics system based on Laban's categories is biased toward the Western emphasis on shape and spatial design, with little attention given to rhythm, interaction, continuity, and change.[36] I would add, first, that the eight core qualities do not cover all possible kinds of vitality. Most important, neither Labananalysis nor Choreometrics addresses social interaction or cultural constructions of meaning at all.[37] Although the Laban system is in need of cross-cultural modification and development, it is, for the moment, all we have for guiding observation beyond the shapes and spatial patterns of action toward qualitative factors. If Laban's categories are taken to be aids to observation rather than a catalogue of all possible qualitative factors, they can be useful.[38]

Dance anthropologist Cynthia Cohen Bull's comparison of ballet, contact improvisation, and Ghanaian dance offers a sampling of the possibilities.[39] Working with qualitative factors, she finds that whereas "[b]allet practice and performance hone visual sensibility, giving the dancer an acute awareness of the body's precise placement and shaping in space," contact improvisation, as an oppositional practice to ballet, "seeks to create a sensitivity to touch and to inner sensation."[40] Ghanaian dance emphasizes neither shape and line nor weight and touch, but "the rhythmic dialogue among participants."[41] An early, more detailed comparative study of gesture, conducted in 1941 by anthropologist

David Efron, a student of Franz Boas, went further.[42] Undertaken to refute Nazi notions about the correlation of race and gesture, Efron studied and compared the conversational gestures of two relatively homogenous and stable European communities whose members had migrated to New York. These were Jewish immigrants from the ghettos of Lithuania and Poland, and Neapolitan and Sicilian peasant immigrants.[43] Although he found marked differences between the groups in the immigrant generation, in the following generation, depending on the degree of assimilation, the original gestural patterns had disappeared. Both groups' gestures in the younger generation more closely resembled those of other New Yorkers than those of their immigrant parents. That significant differences in gestural patterns are determined, not by inherent physiological, psychological, or mental differences, but by the interaction between learned traditions and social conditions was predictable even in 1941.

In the course of his study, however, Efron found something less predictable; that differences in gestural systems embody differences in the aesthetic structuring of thought. In short, the Sicilian immigrants employed gestures that depicted the *content* of their thought, like a sign language. Their gestures were largely presentational and connotational, as if they carried "a bundle of pictures" in their hands.[44] They either pointed to objects or referred to the forms of objects, to spatial relationships, or to bodily actions. Gesturing among the Jewish immigrants was neither pictorial nor connotational and referred to the *process* rather than the objects of their thought. The Jewish immigrants used gestures to "link one proposition to another, trace the itinerary of a logical journey, or to beat the tempo of mental locomotion." Their embroideries and zigzags resembled "gestural charts of the 'heights' and 'lows,' 'detours' and 'crossroads' of the ideational route."[45] Where the Sicilians' gesturing emphasized the "what" of thinking, the Jewish Lithuanians' emphasized the "how." Challenging the popular misconception that gestures are a kind of semiotic hieroglyphics that occurs "naturally," Efron concluded that pictorial gesturing occurs among only some cultural groups and that nonpictorial, ideational kinds of gesturing are of equal significance. "We conceive of gestural behavior as an intrinsic part of the thinking process," he writes.[46]

The comment is significant, suggesting that "mind" is as much a matter of kinesthetic as of verbal or visual organization. This organization occurs, Efron's data show, as the aesthetics of thinking, in terms of sensory profiles and formal kinetic elements. For example, a sensory profile of the Italian immigrants' gestural thinking would emphasize the visual shapes of thought content, whereas for the Jewish immigrants, the auditory rhythms of thought process were emphasized. In Labananalysis terms, the Italian immigrants' thinking emphasized continuous flow and direct pathways, whereas the Jewish immigrants' thinking favored interrupted flow and indirect pathways. Efron set out to observe only the spatio-temporal and referential aspects of gesturing;[47] had he been skilled in observing qualities of vitality, we might also have learned about the force of the two kinds of gestural thinking, their changing intensities, and their use of weightiness and lightness. These aesthetic patterns point, in Johnson's terms, toward different embodied schemata of "thinking." What if, then, we conceptualize "thinking" in different cultural communities as different genres of aesthetic, even kinetic, improvisation whose structural rules organize sensory modalities, formal elements, and vitality affects? Thus conceived, we would have a model for thinking about thinking as a matter not only of symbolic representations but also of kin-aesthetic orderings.

If, as Howes has shown, sensory ratios are different for different cultural communities, and, as Efron has shown, different among community members at different historical moments, then the way memory and history are embodied is also different in different cultural communities at different times—not only the content of memory but the aesthetic processes and structures involved in knowing and remembering.

Case Study: The Tortugas Dances

Inevitably, dance and movement researchers, too, have habits of preference among sensory modalities, favoring one or another dynamic and structuring perceptions and conceptualizations according to different embodied schemata of "thinking." Maybe we "see" spatial patterns but are numb to the proprioceptive subtleties of force. Maybe we think in rhythmic processes but are blind to nuances of shape or line, or care nothing about the structures of thought and only about which foot a dancer begins on. We may be trained in either quantitative or qualitative analysis and loyal to our training. Indeed, sometimes I wonder if academic disagreements about methodologies are more a matter of competing pleasures than of conflicts of intellectual conviction. Our sociocultural and personal preferences manifest in choices made about subject matter, theoretical models, and methodological approaches.

Movement, for me, has always been a matter of the pleasures of kinesthetic sensation. Although I was schooled early in modern dance, my studies and performance career were in theater, especially Etienne Decroux's corporeal mime and New York's ensemble movement theater of the 1960s and 1970s, in the mode of Jerzy Grotowski's "poor" or "spiritual" theater and the Open Theatre's improvisational ensemble work. I also grew up folk dancing in a utopian socialist community. Perhaps not coincidentally, when I switched from theater to academic work in dance ethnology and performance studies, I chose to do field research on a communal religious ritual performance, the annual fiesta of Our Lady of Guadalupe in Tortugas, in the southwestern U.S. state of New Mexico.

It was the affects and effects of the fiesta I wanted to understand, what it was to "feel the Virgin's presence," as the people said, and what that presence meant in the fiesta. I hypothesized that religion in Tortugas was as much a matter of somatic as of textual, or liturgical, meanings and that qualitative movement analysis could lead me to appreciation of the fiesta's spiritual work. I did not aim for a structural study of the fiesta's movement events but for a study of the way the meanings of movement comprised a web of sensibility and intelligibility. As I wrote in my ethnographic monograph, *Dancing with the Virgin:*

> "Sensibility" and "intelligibility" imply mutually permeable cultural processes. Sensory perceptions are molded by cultural epistemologies; abstract conceptualizations refer to culturally specific sensory orderings. All our actions in the world are at the same time interpretations of the world. Movement in other words combines felt bodily experience and the culturally based organization of that experience into cognitive patterns. Ways of moving are ways of thinking.[48]

Relying on participant-observation, tacking between movement analysis and extensive verbal exchange, as well as on reviewing the relevant literature, I sought instruction about the weaving of somatic and verbal detail. I brought both my knowledge (academic skills, theater skills, and the multiple accumulations of biography) and my ignorance (about the community, the fiesta, and local processes of making meaning) to learn how to learn. My framework was epistemological, linking bodily sensation with the other senses and with verbalization, and all of these with the processes of coming to know. What follows is the story of my discoveries about the fiesta's two dances. Letting the dances, and people's words about them, lead me, I discovered that they demanded different approaches and pointed to different but complementary aspects of identity. They also demonstrated different ways history and memory can be embodied in the same community.

Unlike the Protestants who killed or "removed" the indigenous people they encountered in New England, the Spanish Catholics required native labor and coveted, in the name of God, indigenous souls. Along the Rio Grande in what is now New Mexico in the southwestern United States, they coerced or convinced many Pueblo people toward religious conversion, while imposing a policy of forced servitude *(encomienda)*.[49] They also banned dancing. Thus, unlike the Jewish and Italian immigrants in Efron's study, for the Puebloans conquered by the Spanish, assimilation was enforced rather than sought. In 1680, the Pueblos revolted and drove the Spanish south, from the Rio Grande Pueblos in northern New Mexico to the Spanish stronghold at El Paso del Norte. Now divided into the U.S. city of El Paso, Texas, and the Mexican city of Juárez, this "pass of the north" was originally settled as a rest stop at the spot where the Camino Real, or "royal road," from Mexico City crossed the Rio Grande on the way to the Pueblos in the north.

In 1692, twelve years after their retreat, the Spanish regrouped and returned north to conquer the Rio Grande Pueblos. The conquered Puebloans chose to continue dancing "underground," in a sense ghettoizing their own corporeal practices to protect them from Spanish, and later American, censorship.

When the Spanish first retreated south after the 1680 Pueblo Revolt, some Puebloans, either by choice or by force, joined the retreat. In El Paso del Norte, they lived in mission communities among the larger Spanish and *mestizo*, or mixed Spanish and indigenous Mexican, population. They embraced Catholicism while sustaining many Puebloan ritual practices, including dance. They also adopted *mestizo* clothing, language, and social practices, somewhat like the "hybrid acculturation" Efron found among some of the second-generation Jewish Lithuanian-Americans.[50] In the mid-1800s, about 150 years after the mission communities were established, a band of El Paso del Norte *indios*, as they called themselves and are still called, again migrated. Responding to internecine Mexican wars, land scams, and Anglo-Texan invasion, they

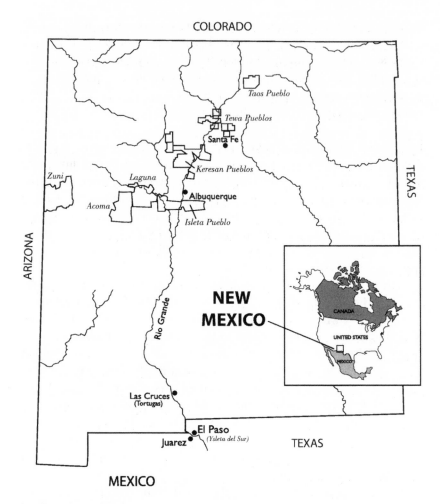

5.1. Locations of Tortugas, Las Cruces, New Mexico and Ysleta del Sur, El Paso, Texas. Map by "Mokey" Lee Davidson.

moved about forty miles northward up the Rio Grande to the area that is now Las Cruces in southern New Mexico. This area was almost immediately ceded to the United States in the 1848 Treaty of Guadalupe Hidalgo, and the immigrants became American citizens. Helping the group to acquire land for a church and ceremonial buildings that would ensure the survival of their religious traditions, an Anglo stagecoach driver who had married "a princess of the tribe" helped the *indios* to incorporate as an American-style benevolent association.[51] Since then, the annual celebration for the Virgin has evolved in the village of Tortugas in Las Cruces, but it is still sponsored by the *Corporación de Nuestra Señora de Guadalupe.*

During the years I participated, between 1984 and 1998, the annual fiesta followed a consistent scenario. On the first night, 10 December, an all-night *velorio*, or wake, honored the Virgin with prayers alternating with rounds of a *matachine* dance that is locally termed *la danza.* Weaving together elements brought to America by the Spaniards with indigenous features, *matachine* dances from Mexico City to the Rio Grande address, in movement elements and meaning, the Hispano-Indian encounter. On the 11th, as many as 250 visitors spent the day in pilgrimage to the top of Tortugas Mountain. On the 12th, a High Mass in the morning preceded a day of dancing in the church plaza. Here the participants of *la danza*, known as *los danzantes*, were joined by other members of the community in the *indio* or "Pueblo dance," similar to the corn or tablita dances performed at all New Mexico's Rio Grande Pueblos.[52] It was also referred to as the "Tigua dance," Tigua being a Spanish spelling of Tiwa, the Rio Grande Pueblo linguistic group from whom many of the El Paso del Norte *indios* claimed ancestry. At midday on the 12th, the *Corporación* offered a feast for several hundred people at the community dining hall, and at dusk, in a climactic procession, the Virgin's image was passed into the care of the next year's *mayordomos*, stewards responsible for the smooth running of the whole event. The fiesta ended with a reception and informal dance when anyone could join in the *danza* or *indio* dance.

When I first looked at the *indio* dance, its general similarity to the Rio Grande Pueblo dances was immediately apparent: a group of approximately ten male singers, one of whom carries the drum; two lines of dancers moving in synchronized unity; the cumulative rather than climactic dance structure; the dance outfits (*mantas*, which are the traditional one-shouldered black dance sheaths worn by Pueblo women; moccasins, shawls, men's decorated dance shirts, downy feathers; see fig. 5.2). As in northern New Mexico, the dancing began with slow songs accompanying a processional choreography. The men in Tortugas used the same basic knee-lifting jogging step and the women the more subdued and flat-footed inching walk as in the north (see fig. 5.3). As in the north, the dance changed to a faster section of choreographic figures. These variations in the north might include turns in place, exchanges of

5.2. Male and female lines in the *indio* dance. Photo by Deidre Sklar.

place between the two lines, or circling in small groups. In Tortugas, there was only one pattern of advance and retreat. During the fast section, both Tortugas and northern dancers performed a duple-beat or accented step; between each footfall they gave a small foot tap forward, or downward against the ground, or against the standing leg, before the foot descended.

People in Tortugas did not discuss either the meaning of the dance or their dancing experience; rather, they talked about the technicalities of performance, debating the fine points of step and music. For the men's basic step, though everyone agreed on the injunction to "lift your knees," there was intense debate about whether the hunting bows they carried in the left hand should be held above or below the gourd rattle, carried in the right. They considered whether the men's body position for shaking the rattles in the fast song's transitional section should be a squat or a lunge, and, most controversial, whether, at the pause when the man has lifted his knee in the duple-beat step, there should or should not be a quick and tiny punctuating forward kick. Qualitative analysis revealed the Tortugas style to be lighter and more direct than the northern styles,

5.3. The female follows her male partner. Photo by Deidre Sklar.

the endpoints of step and gesture more punctuated, giving the dance a sharp and angular quality. "Too sloppy," a Tortugas companion commented as we watched the more lyrical dancing style at Ysleta del Sur in El Paso, Texas. Of the dancing of the northern Pueblos, one woman remarked, "That may be the way they do it up north, but it's not the way we do it here." This kind of scrutiny and commentary suggested to me intentional movement choices that made fine degrees of kinesthetic distinction between an "us" and a "not us."

The distinction referred in part to religion. While many northern Puebloans are Catholic, Pueblo religion and cosmology continue to be their predominant reference system for the dances.[53] Though few Puebloans now farm and hunt for subsistence, the dances occur in an annual cycle corresponding with the growing and hunting seasons, and multiple symbolic elements help dancers harmonize body, thought, and prayer with these cycles.[54] Except for one family, these references were absent in Tortugas. No one spoke any of the Puebloan or other Native American languages, and no one could translate the song texts, except one sung in Spanish honoring the Virgin. At one dance practice, an elder next to me explained that the ubiquitous Pueblo vocables "heya, heya" really mean "for her, for her," the Virgin of Guadalupe.

Movement choices reiterated this orientation. For example, the choreography in the first slow, processional section consisted of following a circular path while changing direction every few steps via a zigzag from side to side. This pattern enabled the dancers to face the four directions in the course of circling, an orientation prevalent throughout the Pueblos. An additional injunction, however, has entered the Tortugas choreography: "Never turn your back on the Virgin." A portrait of Our Lady of Guadalupe hung before the dancers during every rehearsal and performance. The injunction to never turn your back on the Virgin translated choreographically, so that when the dancers neared the portrait, rather than zigzagging to face the four directions, they maintained a single focus forward. The shift was both choreographic and symbolic. The dance had changed from the four-directional spatial and cosmological system of the Pueblos to the one-directional orientation of church architecture and cosmology.

The dance worked as a mnemonic, a way to remember, in the sense of re-embody, a time "before the missionaries came and Christianized us," as one elder put it. In Tortugas, the missionizing process was, for the most part, viewed not as a loss, but as goodness, a gift. The reference to a pre-Christian past was not religious nostalgia but an assertion of ancestry and autobiography. The combination of observation and conversation directed my attention to the problem of biography. The dance, I learned, commemorated a historical link to the northern Pueblos while asserting a differentiation from those same Pueblos. That problem was embodied in the dancing in various ways: in outfits and paraphernalia, in spatial choreography and body shape, and in the qualitative dynamics of movement style.

Where the *indio* dance drew from the north, the *danza* drew from the south, from Mexico. Similar to *matachines* performed throughout northern Mexico and the southwestern United States, its origins lay in Mexico City when the first Spanish missionaries grafted Christian concepts and European dance elements onto Aztec dances to teach the new religion. The dance spread with missionaries and settlers, shaping to local customs and meanings. In Tortugas in the 1980s and 1990s, it was danced by eighteen men, in two parallel lines, accompanied by a violin. Led by a *monarca*, the dance leader, an *abuelo*, his assistant, and a *malinche*, a pre-pubescent girl, in each of ten *sones*, or songs, the dancers unfolded a different *figura*, a choreographic design in space (see fig. 5.4).[55] Except for two of the *sones*, the dancers used a basic repeating step, alternating

5.4. *La danza*. Photo by Deidre Sklar.

initiation between left and right feet: three steps in place punctuated by a stamp and a forward kick. Like the *indio* dance, the *danza* was dedicated to the Virgin. Here, however, talk about dancing did not focus on the correct execution of steps. The *monarca* dismissed my questions about the steps, simply saying they were mostly the same for all the dances. Rather, he drew attention to what the dancers "do" in the changing patterns of the dance, its symbolic action.

While most *matachine* dances refer to the story of the Aztec monarch, Montezuma, and his conversion to Catholicism, the Tortugas version made reference only to Our Lady of Guadalupe. In talking about the *danza*, the men emphasized their devotion to and sacrifice for the Virgin and the personal, transformational effect of the dancing. Both the *indio* dance and the *danza* addressed religion, but where the *indio* dance provided opportunities for negotiations about ancestry, the *danza* provided opportunities for the experience of religious meditation on the Virgin. This was not apparent from a structural analysis of the *figuras* or the step. However, qualitative analysis revealed contradictory movement qualities. The men performed the basic three-steps-in-place, stamp, and kick pattern low to the ground, with a forward-driving momentum: the triplet, a light and tight bounce, followed by the slow, heavy stamp, catching the momentum off the rebound to propel the kick forward, quickly recovering to begin again. Performed in unison, the repetitive stamping and propulsion forward gave the impression of insistent and driving force. In spite of this, however, there was an elusive quality of softness, even vulnerability, in the men's dancing whose source I could not locate in the movement itself.

When I watched the men at rehearsals, dancing without their face-covering *cupiles*, or headpieces, I was struck by their eye focus.[56] Although they occasionally looked around to see where *monarca, malinche,* and *abuelo* were in the choreography, the men's focus was not primarily material. Rather, the gaze was inward directed. The dance leader confirmed this: "When I'm dancing as the *monarca*, I don't see nothing of the people that are standing around. All I see is the dances and the vision to the holy Mary. That's all I see. I don't even know who is around me, if anybody's around me. That's the way I feel. . . . And I never lift my head up. I shouldn't lift my head up. I'm there for one purpose."[57] It was as if the men were already under the *cupiles* that during the fiesta would separate them from their material surroundings.

At rehearsals, the dancers faced a portrait of the Virgin. During the all-night *velorio,* her altar was before them. The *monarca* was adamant that her portrait had to be in front of the men before they would dance. The image the men faced was the image they carried within. The *monarca* clarified further: "When you're dancing it's the same as dancing with the Virgin. It's something like if I were talking to her, expressing our gratitude for what she had done. . . . Every time we're dancing there, it's like we were saying thank you and just talking to her, giving her our thanks."[58] I understood at this point that the elusive quality of softness that contradicted the driving power of the men's dancing was not a structural element of the dancing, but a manifestation of the men's meditation on the Virgin. The *danza* worked somatically, as a meditative space in which conversion could be repeatedly experienced.

Both the *danza* and the *indio* dance were brought from El Paso del Norte, and both commemorated the Virgin and the community's past as a kind of "home." But that home continued to be a home-at-a-crossroads. Where the *indio* dance asserted identity in terms of historical ancestry, the *danza* did so in terms of ongoing religious conversion. Both embodied memory, but the bodily experience of remembering was different for each. The dances offered different profiles of the process of remembering. *Indio* dancers emphasized the look of the dancing, its details of shape and dynamic. The *danzantes* emphasized focus of attention, both somatic and symbolic. Indeed, when I asked one man what made a good dancer, he said, "One that isn't just there for the dance, one that's really there for the sacrifice to dance for the *virgen,* not just to dance because it looks good."[59] Others also specifically directed my attention away from the dance's visual effect.

We cannot ignore the experiential somatic aspects of dancing in favor of the formal, especially if the dancers lead us toward it. Following the *danzantes'* lead, I sought to understand the *danza,* and the fiesta as a whole, in terms of how it enabled the experience of "feeling the Virgin's presence." I found that there was no other way to it than through my own body, sampling, for example, the qualities of time, intensity, and focus of attention I observed. This work demanded a rigorous attention to detail as well as repeatedly checking my understanding with informants, in words. After I left the community I ran headlong into the problem of recuperating the combination of somatic and verbal memories that had been woven in the emergent process of performance. I have written elsewhere about the path of remembering and evoking I followed;[60] here, I will only report that I came to the theory summarized in this chapter by necessity, as it seemed crucial to find models and language with which to talk in ethnographic terms about the somatic dimensions of embodied cultural knowledge and memory.

In the search for theoretical models, I have been led beyond the toolkit of dance, through sensory anthropology, to child psychology and philosophy and back to dance ethnology. The journey of participant-observation, memory recuperation, and analysis has taken me from the visible forms of movement into the phenomenological, cultural particulars of sensory schema and somatic awareness. This is not only a Geertzian quest for social breadth, but a descent into sociosomatic depth. Now, in response to Merleau-Ponty, Csordas, and Stern, I find myself asking, not how we become objects to ourselves, but how we might cease being objects to ourselves. Can we *attend* our bodies, rather than only attending to or with them? Is objectification inevitably simultaneous with sensation, or is this a particular cultural construction? In other words, might we attend, not even "the body" or "the person," but simply sensation, as Buddhist Vipassana meditation instructs? And might such attending open new possibilities for appreciating cultural constructions of embodiment? From the perspective (or the sitting place) of Vipassana, I cannot help but remember that "person" and "self," "body" and "thought," are verbal symbols (embodied schemata) that we come to believe define reality whereas, in effect, they create the territories to which they point. Entering this territory with a "new mind," I offer these thoughts, not as answers, but as openings toward further questions.

NOTES

I am grateful to Olga Najera-Ramirez for giving me the opportunity to present the theoretical section of this paper to the Anthropology Colloquium at the University of California, Santa Cruz, and to the members of that colloquium, Donald Brenneis, Nancy Chen, Daniel Linger, Triloki Pandey, and the graduate students in anthropology, for their helpful comments. I would like to thank "Mokey" Lee Davidson for his computer rendering of the map of New Mexico and Sarah Gamblin at Texas Woman's University for help in clarifying key points.

1. Richard Bandler and John Grinder, *Frogs into Princes* (Moab, Utah: Real People Press, 1979), 14. Bandler and Grinder assert that the "representational

system," the words people use to describe experience or information, is conscious while the "accessing system," the strategies or sequences people use to retrieve it, is not. Within accessing systems, the "lead system" is the one used to "go after" information, and the "reference system" is the one used to check out the information retrieved (14–15).

2. Clifford Geertz, "Art as a Cultural System," in *Local Knowledge: Further Essays in Interpretive Anthropology* (New York: Basic Books, 1983), 101 (originally published in *MLN [Modern Language Notes]* 91, no. 6 [December 1976]: 1473–99).

3. The lineage of these disciplines is too large a topic to summarize here. However, a few key points should be mentioned, including the "experiential turn" of the 1970s and 1980s in North American cultural anthropology led by, among others, Victor Turner and Barbara Myerhoff. Their working relationship with the Department of Performance Studies at New York University was significant in the development of the discipline of performance studies in the United States. Further, the presence of dance critic Marcia Siegel in this department in the late 1980s and early 1990s contributed to graduating a generation of dance scholars schooled in qualitative movement analysis and anthropology-inflected performance theory.

4. Geertz, "Art as a Cultural System," 118.

5. James Clifford, "On Ethnographic Authority," in *The Predicament of Culture: Twentieth-Century Ethnography, Literature, and Art* (Cambridge, Mass.: Harvard University Press, 1988), 23.

6. McLuhan quoted in David Howes, "Sensorial Anthropology," in *The Variety of Sensory Experience: A Sourcebook in the Anthropology of the Senses,* ed. David Howes (Toronto: University of Toronto Press, 1991), 172; David Howes and Constance Classen, "Sounding Sensory Profiles," in Howes, *Variety of Sensory Experience,* 257–88. Howes and Classen write that sensory orders may be gleaned by asking, for example, which senses are emphasized in talk, in performance, in artifacts and body decoration, in child raising, in media of communication, in the natural and built environment, and in mythology and its representations.

7. David Howes, "Introduction: To Summon All the Senses," in Howes, *Variety of Sensory Experience,* 10.

8. While I use the term "somatic sensation" to include all proprioceptive awareness, including, for example, touch, movement, balance, pressure, tension, and temperature, I use "kinesthesia" and "kinesthetic" to refer specifically to proprioception of the joint and muscle action involved in movement. "Kinetic" refers to *any* movement, including but not limited to joint and muscle action.

9. Edward S. Casey, *Remembering: A Phenomenological Study* (Bloomington: Indiana University Press, 1987). "Feelings," here, refers not to emotions but to

somatic sensations. Using the same term for both, the English language blurs the important distinction between complex emotions and somatic sensations, including kinesthetic ones, giving rise to confusion in discussions of feeling in dance. See, for example, philosopher David Best, *Expression in Movement and the Arts: A Philosophical Enquiry* (London: Lepus Books, 1974), on the aesthetics of dance. While kinetic sensations often carry emotional overtones, and emotional states invariably have kinetic components, the two are not the same.

10. For discussions of bodily memory see also Paul Connerton, *How Societies Remember* (Cambridge: Cambridge University Press, 1989); Drew Leder, *The Absent Body* (Chicago: University of Chicago Press, 1990); Elaine Scarry, *The Body in Pain* (New York: Oxford University Press, 1985).

11. Casey, *Remembering*, 167.

12. Ibid., 168 (Bergson's original emphasis).

13. Marcel Mauss, "Body Techniques," in *Sociology and Psychology: Essays*, trans. Ben Brewster (London: Routledge and Kegan Paul, 1979), 97–123; Pierre Bourdieu, *Outline of a Theory of Practice* (Cambridge: Cambridge University Press, 1977).

14. Bourdieu, *Outline of a Theory of Practice*, 18.

15. I have elsewhere reviewed the antecedents of these two approaches, suggesting they are the major trajectories dominating ethnographic studies of dance at the beginning of the twenty-first century; see Deidre Sklar, "Reprise: On Dance Ethnography," *Dance Research Journal* 32, no. 1 (Summer 2000): 70–77. Distinguishing between the political emphasis of dance scholarship derived from cultural studies and the kinesthetic emphasis of studies related to sensory anthropology, I focus on the latter, emphasizing key works such as Cynthia Novack, *Sharing the Dance: Contact Improvisation and American Culture* (Madison: University of Wisconsin Press, 1990) and Sally Ann Ness, *Body, Movement, and Culture: Kinesthetic and Visual Symbolism in a Philippine Community* (Philadelphia: University of Pennsylvania Press, 1992).

16. Thomas J. Csordas, "Embodiment as a Paradigm for Anthropology," *Ethos* 18, no. 1 (March 1990): 5–47; Thomas J. Csordas, "Somatic Modes of Attention," *Cultural Anthropology* 8, no. 2 (May 1993): 135–56. For a discussion of "practice" theory in anthropology, see Sherry B. Ortner, "Theory in Anthropology since the Sixties," *Comparative Studies in Society and History* 26, no. 1 (1984): 126–66. Ortner understands the central problem of a practice orientation to be the relationship between social institutions and structures, on one hand, and people and their actions, on the other. She traces the roots of the concept of practice to the symbolic anthropology of Victor Turner and Clifford Geertz, the cultural ecology of Marshall Sahlins, the structuralism of Claude Lévi-Strauss, and the reintroduction of sociology via Peter Berger and Thomas Luckman into anthropology in the 1970s.

17. Csordas, "Somatic Modes of Attention," 135.

18. Ibid., 138.

19. Daniel N. Stern, *The Interpersonal World of the Infant: A View from Psychoanalysis and Developmental Psychology* (New York: Basic Books, 1985).

20. Ibid., 46.

21. Ibid., 47.

22. Mark Johnson, *The Body in the Mind: The Bodily Basis of Meaning, Imagination, and Reason* (Chicago: University of Chicago Press, 1987).

23. For Johnson, "image" refers not only to visual representations, but also to the full range of sensory modalities through which we apprehend and represent the world; however, "image" carries visual connotations, and I therefore prefer the term "embodied schemata."

24. Brenda Farnell, *Do You See What I Mean? Plains Indian Sign Talk and the Embodiment of Action* (Austin: University of Texas Press, 1995), 300. Farnell criticizes Merleau-Ponty for simply relocating agency away from the mind and "appear[ing] to locate an equally ambiguous notion of agency *in* the body" (12; emphasis in original). She argues persuasively that only a concept of "the person" can resolve the problem of agency, or causality. Her work has informed my discussion here.

25. Unlike Bourdieu, who sees the habitus as composed entirely of sedimented structures, Johnson recognizes that what we regard as fixed meanings are *simply* the sediments of embodied schemata (Johnson, *Body in the Mind*, 175), which are inherently open-ended and therefore variable, depending upon cultural circumstances.

26. Csordas, "Somatic Modes of Attention," 138.

27. Stern, *Interpersonal World of the Infant*, 58.

28. Ibid., 53–59.

29. Ibid., 54; my emphasis.

30. Ibid., 56.

31. Ibid., 57. For Langer these are based on the "sense of vital power" as "our most immediate self-consciousness." See Suzanne Langer, *Feeling and Form: A Theory of Art* (New York: Charles Scribner's Sons, 1953), 30. I understand the "play of powers" Langer took to be the "primary illusion" of dance to be a play with vitality affects.

32. Stern, *Interpersonal World of the Infant*, 57; Drid Williams, *Ten Lectures on Theories of the Dance* (Metuchen, N.J.: Scarecrow Press, 1991), 194.

33. Regarding the importance of temporal factors, see Edward Hall's discussion of rhythm and "synching" in cross-cultural communication. Edward Hall, "Rhythm and Body Movement," in *Beyond Culture* (New York: Anchor, 1977), 71–84.

34. Cecily Dell, *A Primer for Movement Description Using Effort-Shape and Supplementary Concepts* (New York: Dance Notation Bureau, 1977), offers a largely technical encapsulation of Laban's qualitative factors.

35. Marcia Siegel, "Rethinking Movement Analysis" (unpublished ms. in possession of the author, 1991), 5.

36. Ibid., 11. Alan Lomax, Irmgard Bartenieff, and Forrestine Paulay summarize the elements assessed in the Choreometrics project. See "Choreometrics: A Method for the Study of Cross-Cultural Pattern in Film," in *New Dimensions in Dance Research: Anthropology and Dance — The American Indian,* ed. Tamara Comstock, Proceedings of the Third Conference on Research in Dance, *CORD Research Annual VI* (New York: Committee on Research in Dance, 1974), 193–212. The project attempted to correlate qualitative movement factors with subsistence patterns worldwide. Dance anthropologists have criticized the distortion of its oversimplified functionalist organization. See, among others, Joann Kealiinohomoku, "Dance and Human History: A Film by Alan Lomax," *Ethnomusicology* 25, no. 1 (1979): 169–76.

37. For early guidelines addressing dance-in-context from several different perspectives, see Adrienne Kaeppler, "Method and Theory in Analyzing Dance Structure with an Analysis of Tongan Dance," *Ethnomusicology* 16, no. 2 (1974): 173–217; Allegra Fuller Snyder, "Levels of Event Patterns: A Theoretical Model Applied to the Yaqui Easter Ceremonies," in *The Dance Event: A Complex Cultural Phenomenon, ICTM 15th Ethnochoreology Symposium Proceedings 1988,* ed. Lisbet Torp (Copenhagen: International Council for Traditional Music Study Group on Ethnochoreology, 1989), 1–13; Kealiinohomoku, "Field Guides," in Comstock, *New Dimensions in Dance Research (CORD Research Annual VI),* 245–60.

38. Siegel, "Rethinking Movement Analysis," is the only work I know that attempts to extend Labananalysis beyond the eight "core qualities." Derived from a collaborative seminar at New York University with Martha Davis in the mid-1980s, the study advises developing a "lexicon" for each performance event. A lexicon would include *all* the salient features of a dance event, such as eye focus, paraphernalia and costumes, narrative content, and performer-to-performer and performer-to-audience relationships, as well as shape, spatial organization, and qualitative factors. In Siegel's terms, the lexicon is "a list of ingredients out of which the dance is cooked" (12). For observing dance specifically, Siegel attends first to "the beat," or "pulse," on the assumption that the beat is dance's organizing "trope," the source of its energy (16). The beat is conceptualized not merely in terms of fast or slow, syncopated or even, but descriptively. For example, Steven Feld, in *Sound and Sentiment: Birds, Weeping, Poetics and Song in Kaluli Expression* (Philadelphia: University of Pennsylvania Press, 1982), describes the "in-synchrony-yet-out-of-phase" sounding and movement of Kaluli dancing in New Guinea; it is not an even beat, but a series of overlapping waves that organize the energy of the dance. Siegel then turns attention to what she calls the "orchestration" of the beat, including especially the dance's specific rhythmic patterns, phrasing, and transitions, but also the way a dance structures space and choreographic design, unfolds the shape of movement,

and directs interactions between people. If the organization of energy in a dance, its pulse, is the primary trope, then the orchestration is the development of that energy through the dance's structures.

39. Cynthia Jean Cohen Bull (a.k.a. Cynthia Novack), "Sense, Meaning, and Perception in Three Dance Cultures," in *Meaning in Motion: New Cultural Studies of Dance,* ed. Jane Desmond (Durham, N.C.: Duke University Press, 1997), 269–88.

40. Ibid., 282, 283.

41. Ibid., 282.

42. David Efron, *Gesture, Race and Culture: A Tentative Study of Some of the Spatio-Temporal and "Linguistic" Aspects of the Gestural Behavior of Eastern Jews and Southern Italians in New York City, Living under Similar as Well as Different Environmental Conditions* (The Hague: Mouton, [1941] 1972).

43. Efron's methods were fourfold: direct observation; artist's sketches; rough counting of gestural tendencies; and description, graphs, charts, and measurements drawn from film clips. It should be noted that Efron's work preceded the kinesics work of Ray Birdwhistell, Albert Scheflen, and Edward Hall and also preceded Marshall McLuhan's understanding of cultures as orders of sensory preferences.

44. Efron, *Gesture, Race and Culture,* 123.

45. Ibid., 98, 99.

46. Ibid., 95–96, 105 n.48.

47. Ibid., 67.

48. Deidre Sklar, *Dancing with the Virgin: Body and Faith in the Fiesta of Tortugas, New Mexico* (Berkeley: University of California Press, 2001), 4.

49. At the time of the Spanish conquest, there were at least seventy-five Pueblo villages along the Rio Grande, from Socorro in the south to Taos in the north, including Keresan, Tanoan (Tewa, Tiwa, and Towa), Piro, and Tompiro linguistic groups. Hopi and Zuni speakers, linguistically unrelated to the Keresan and Tanoan, were to the east in what is now Arizona. See Fred Eggan, "Pueblos: Introduction," in *Handbook of North American Indians,* vol. 9, *Southwest,* ed. Alfonso Ortiz (Washington D.C.: Smithsonian, 1979): 224–35; and Albert H. Schroeder, "Pueblos Abandoned in Historic Times," in Ortiz, *Handbook of North American Indians,* 9: 236–54.

50. The anthropologist Walter Fewkes, who visited one of the El Paso Pueblo villages in 1901, wrote: "These Indians have practically become 'mexicanized,' and survivals of their old pueblo life which still remain, such as their dances before the church, have long lost the meaning which they once had or that which similar dances still have in the pueblos higher up the Rio Grande. The southern Tiwa and Piros are good Roman Catholics, and their old dances are still kept up not from a lingering belief of the Indians in their old religion, as is the case with certain pueblos in which Christianity is merely a superficial

gloss over aboriginal beliefs, but as survivals that have been worn down into secular customs. They cannot give an intelligible explanation of the meaning of these dances, because they do not know their significance." J. Walter Fewkes, "The Pueblo Settlements near El Paso, Texas," *American Anthropologist* 4, no. 1 (1902), 58.

51. Anon., *History of New Mexico: Its Resources and People*, vol. 1 (Los Angeles: Pacific States, 1907).

52. Two "Azteca" dances, introduced from Mexico in 1923, are also performed by neighborhood groups not sponsored by the Corporación.

53. For discussion of the compartmentalization of Pueblo and Catholic religious systems in the pueblos, see Edward Dozier, "Rio Grande Ceremonial Patterns," *New Mexico Quarterly* 27, nos. 1–2 (Spring/Summer 1957): 27–34.

54. See, for example, Alfonso Ortiz, *The Tewa World: Space, Time, Being, and Becoming in a Pueblo Society* (Chicago: University of Chicago Press, 1969) and Jill Sweet, *Dances of the Tewa Pueblo Indian: Expressions of New Life* (Santa Fe, N.M.: School of American Research, 1985).

55. For an overview of the Tortugas version and a more detailed description of the *danza*'s basic steps, see Sklar, *Dancing with the Virgin*, and Deidre Sklar, "'All the Dances Have a Meaning to That Apparition': Felt Knowledge and the Danzantes of Tortugas, New Mexico," *Dance Research Journal* 31, no. 2 (Fall 1999): 14–33. Deidre Sklar (http://users3.ev1.net/~deidresklar [2003]) gives descriptions, drawings, and video clips of all the figures of the *danza* as well as video clips of the *indio* dance.

56. Siegel, "Rethinking Movement Analysis," suggests attending to focus of attention as an aspect of spatial engagement, in terms of kinesphere, such as outside or inside skin, incorporating other dancers, etc. She distinguishes between five types of gaze: inner focus, functional focus, interpersonal focus, presentational focus, and visionary focus (on imaginary space). Other kinds of eye behavior may include targeting, scanning, probing, flitting, and faking.

57. Rico Bernal (pseudonym), interview with the author (Las Cruces, N.M., 21 October 1987). Pseudonyms are used to protect the privacy of the dancers.

58. Rico Bernal (pseudonym), interview with the author (Las Cruces, N.M., 12 March, 1986).

59. Danny Amador (pseudonym), interview with the author (Las Cruces, N.M., 16 December 1987).

60. Sklar, "Reprise: On Dance Ethnography," and Sklar, *Dancing with the Virgin*.

6

Dancing through History and Ethnography

Indian Classical Dance and the Performance of the Past

JANET O'SHEA

A bharata natyam dancer, clad in a tailored silk sari and bedecked in jewelry, sinks gracefully onto one leg. She smiles as her arm arcs gently and her articulate fingers lead her hand from a high diagonal in toward her torso. Her legs fold out into a rotated, bent-knee position, and her feet beat out a sharp rhythm. With her torso floating gracefully above her dynamic feet, she traces intricate hand shapes that ornament the angular positions of her limbs. She dances in a courtyard, before a temple, a setting that suggests that her solid, graceful movements are as enduring as the pillars and carvings of the temple compound. She is the very emblem of classicism, traditionalism, and the endurance of ancient values in present-day India.[1]

Bharata Natyam and the Production of the Past

Bharata natyam relies upon the choreographic practices of the past.[2] The dancer's movement vocabulary, for instance, derives from *sadir*, the dance practice of *devadasis*, courtesans, and ritual officiants who were associated with the temples and courts of South India until the early twentieth century.[3] The *mudras*, or hand gestures, parallel, in both shape and meaning, those described in the *Natyasastra*, a canonical dramaturgical text written in the ancient, elite lingua franca of Sanskrit. A standardization of concert practice by the nineteenth-century Thanjavur Quartet, a renowned group of musicians, produced the *margam*, or concert order.

Despite these commonalities between bharata natyam and past practice, many elements of present-day performance are new. Dancers transformed the style of rendition of the movements over the twentieth century (in some interpretations more than others), extending lines out into space and augmenting the angularity of positions. Some performers have also broadened the floor patterns of the choreography, covering more ground than *sadir* dancers did, in order to suit the larger, proscenium theaters of the contemporary performance context. Similarly, dancers have amplified and "theatricalized" the facial expressions of the *abhinaya*, or dramatic elements of choreography, again with the aim of rendering the expressions legible to a less proximate audience.

Repertoire also changed during the twentieth century. Even the most "traditional" choreography is not completely fixed. A dance piece consists of a compilation of phrases, set to a piece of music that belongs to a dance style's customary repertoire. A dancer or, most commonly, a dance teacher arranges phrases, learned from her own mentor, but assembled according to her decisions.[4] The amount of decision making increases as a practitioner takes on more responsibility for teaching. Repertoire, therefore, changes in the process of its transmission. Present-day practitioners also commission music and devise new items of repertoire. Likewise, they choreograph pieces outside conventional genres, create works of ensemble choreography, and compose evening-length pieces based on the bharata natyam movement vocabulary.

In addition, many elements that frame the performance are new.[5] The name "bharata natyam," for example, is a twentieth-century appellation.[6] The "traditional" bharata natyam costume developed out of changes to concert attire in the 1930s. Even the temple performance context, despite its suggestion of antiquity, is itself a product of the changes that the dance form underwent in the nineteenth and twentieth centuries. In 1892, activists mobilized against the performance of dance in

Hindu temples and succeeded in banning such events in 1947. Only in the 1980s did dancers return to temple performance, bringing with them the movement vocabulary and repertoire of the concert stage. Present-day temple dance events have therefore developed out of a fractured tradition.[7]

A possible conclusion to draw from this scenario is that the dance form derives solely from an intentional, self-conscious engagement with the past and not from an unbroken oral tradition. One could, in looking at such a situation, call bharata natyam an "invented tradition."[8] An alternative conclusion might be that there is a single authoritative history, which aligns with one set of choreographic choices, while the other versions of history are inaccurate.

I want to suggest, however, that the actual situation is more complex than such assertions would indicate. Bharata natyam is neither entirely "ancient" nor is it solely a product of the twentieth century. Furthermore, none of the histories that practitioners put forth is spurious: dancers describe different versions of the past through the selection of competing sources, each of which constitutes a potentially valid historical "truth." Twentieth-century dancers, through their choices in repertoire, choreographic themes, and movement vocabulary, connected their performance work to practices of the past. This explicit and intentional use of historical sources separates their practice from that of nineteenth- and early-twentieth-century dancers.[9] They have selected a wider range of influential materials, using them in divergent ways and making their engagement with the past more apparent in choreography and pedagogy than it had been previously.

Most dancers who define their work as classical bharata natyam agree that a sense of continuity should undergird choreographic endeavors. Nonetheless, individual dancers disagree as to what the most important aspect of the dance form's history is, what elements should be maintained or revivified, and how best to express allegiance to that history. Concepts of authenticity, tradition, classicism, and history do not necessarily invoke agreement; rather, they form the bases of diverse points of view. Such a situation raises several questions. Why are notions of tradition and classicism, rooted as they are in ideas of consensus, points of departure for different interpretations?[10] Why does this dance form appear to need history at the same time that its practitioners vary in their approach to that history?

Ethnography, Performance Praxis, and
Anthropological Concerns

These questions developed out of my personal experience, as a performer and scholar, with bharata natyam. At present, I write primarily
as a dancer and cultural historian who has investigated choreographic
and political strategies of the past as they inform current practice. My
study of bharata natyam since 1988 has, however, used methodologies
from anthropology and history as well as from choreographic analysis,
critical theory, and cultural studies. A dual attention to social significance and change over time has enabled me to investigate transformations in bharata natyam's form and content over the twentieth century.
Each approach, however, especially coupled with my own performance
practice of bharata natyam, has complicated and challenged the other
methodologies.

Despite these changes in interpretative strategies, I have returned, on
several occasions, to ethnographic field methods. For my initial study, I
undertook ethnographic fieldwork in 1989. During subsequent trips to
India in 1995–96 and 1999 (at the same time as researching diasporic
practice in Toronto in 1998 and 1999), I conducted formal and informal
interviews, viewed performances, and researched written accounts. I
have moved into and out of ethnography, valuing immediate experience
but questioning some of the anthropological assumptions that undergird
ethnographic practice and drawing upon historical methods.

My inquiry into bharata natyam's twentieth-century history has
negotiated the concerns of performance, historiography, critical theory,
dance analysis, and ethnography.[11] Because I have drawn on a blend of
methodologies, I cannot identify myself as solely a performer, historian,
ethnographer, or dance analyst. This shifting methodology reflects not
only my changing interests but also, and more importantly, the complexity of the field of study itself. Therefore, the pages that follow trace
the phases of my study of bharata natyam as they deploy ethnographic,
historical, and analytical methods. I do this to comment on these methodologies as they engage with the study of dance, generally, but also to
illuminate why bharata natyam has required such theoretical maneu-
vers. In doing so, I hope to indicate how ethnography and history have
served this study and how, in themselves, they remained incomplete.

I entered this field in 1988 as an undergraduate student in dance and
anthropology at Wesleyan University in Connecticut. I began training

6.1. T. Balasaraswati at Veterans Auditorium, San Francisco, 1972. Photo by Jan Steward © 1985.

in the Thanjavur Court style of bharata natyam, from the South Indian state of Tamil Nadu, a style associated with the legendary *devadasi* practitioner T. Balasaraswati. My initial study (1989–90) followed an ethnographic pattern of immersion in a situation—the study of bharata natyam—and the generation of interpretations from that experience. The dance study itself and my interactions with other dancers yielded insights about how a bharata natyam performer develops a characteristic way of moving and how she learns to think about her body. This period of research hinged on questions about choreographic priorities, repertoire, format of performances, training methods, criteria for the evaluation of student and professional dancers, and the "worldview" of the dance field.

This inquiry relied upon on my experience with anthropological thought and raised questions about the cultural relativism of dance aesthetics, dance technique, and therefore the dancing body itself. Using an anthropological model proposed by Adrienne Kaeppler and further developed by Cynthia Novack, I argued for a complex and multifaceted relationship between dance and other social practices. I relied upon anthropologists Marcel Mauss and Pierre Bourdieu in order to suggest that corporeal techniques created the dancing body as much as they relied upon it.[12] Initially, I was more interested in the anthropological construction of a bodily subject than in the production of historical narratives in dance practice. The study, therefore, attended to technical requirements, especially as put forth in dance pedagogy. My research focused on the specific muscular strengths and postural stances developed through dance training; on culturally specific notions of what is beautiful, virtuoso, feminine or masculine, and age appropriate; and on the selection or nonselection of different body types.

Yet, from the beginning, some aspects of bharata natyam urged my study out into other methodological fields. Bharata natyam already had a long history of representation and, thus, unlike a traditional fieldworker, I could supplement my interpretations with the writings of others, including Indian musicologists, dancers, dance critics, and literary and religious studies scholars. My teacher Nandini Ramani's father, the distinguished Sanskritist and musicologist V. Raghavan, had written extensively on bharata natyam. An archive of his work was made available to me during my stay in India. The Music Academy, Madras's renowned dance and music venue, has its own library. The city also houses dance and music archives such as Sampradaya and features publications, like *Sruti* and *Kalakshetra Quarterly*, dedicated to classical dance and music.

The use of such materials began to align my project with historiography. As the study progressed, the theorizing behind it also intersected with questions of history. The social construction of the body, I argued, occurred through a worldview that surrounded the dance, as well as through studio practices. This argument led into historical concerns as the study contended with bharata natyam's recontextualization. Originally, courtesans and ritual practitioners had performed *sadir*. Dance reformers recrafted the form in the 1930s and renamed it "bharata natyam." On the one hand, the present-day social significance of bharata natyam hinged on the religious and courtly function of its predecessor.

On the other hand, present-day dancers diverge in their approaches to the dance form's complex history.

My interest in the form itself, rather than with dance practice as a marker of broader social values, also shifted my interest away from anthropological concerns and toward historical ones. My project was ethnographic and informed by anthropological thought and not a work of dance anthropology *per se*. In Adrienne Kaeppler's terms, because of the emphasis on dance works and a concern with geographic-political alignment, gender identity, and class status, my study might be classified as more "ethnological" than "anthropological."[13] As the form became more familiar to me, I also noted its multiple interpretations. This inquiry, then, moved from generality to increasing specificity, focusing on individual strategies rather than providing an authoritative account of what bharata natyam is or was. The more I wanted to address these competing versions of the dance practice's identity, history, and social meanings, the less useful I found the traditional anthropological concept of culture.[14] My inquiry shifted away from traditional anthropology when I realized that the cultural meanings of the form had changed dramatically over the twentieth century.

As I became more closely involved with bharata natyam, I became increasingly uncomfortable with some of the underpinnings of conventional anthropology. Traditional anthropology relies upon cultural difference as its basic premise. The global circulation of bharata natyam, including my own practice of it, complicates the notion of cultures as discrete, bounded entities.[15] Moreover, I am not the first foreigner to cross into the realm of bharata natyam performance. The bharata natyam revival hinged upon the inclusion of those hitherto outside the form, including South Indian brahmans, non-Tamils, non-Hindus, and dancers from countries other than India. The extension of bharata natyam into a global performance milieu through an internationalization of pedagogy draws dancers from North and South America, Europe, Africa, and other parts of Asia to the form. Bharata natyam's twentieth-century history has, therefore, shifted the constitution of belonging within the form.

My participation in dance study and performance may have worn away boundaries of inside and outside more quickly than other ethnographic situations. The people who would, in a traditional ethnographic model, be "other" to me are my colleagues and mentors; I interact with them as part of my quotidian, nonfieldwork experience. Bharata natyam thus became less a foreign form to be understood and more an integral part of my life. This transition challenged assumptions about the distinction between scholar and "informants."

I am likewise not the first to straddle performance and scholarship. Numerous bharata natyam dancers have pursued their study of the form through both performance and scholarly avenues. Kapila Vatsyayan, whose groundbreaking studies initiated the critical history of Indian dance, pursued extensive training in Indian classical dance forms.[16] Dance theorist Avanthi Meduri began her career as a bharata natyam and *kuchipudi* performer and subsequently turned to scholarship and theater direction. Dutch scholar Saskia Kersenboom-Story and Canadian sociologist Anne-Marie Gaston have integrated their study of bharata natyam into their research. Choreographer Padma Subrahmanyam trained in dance before turning to scholarship in order to further her inquiry into the form. She has brought her intellectual investigations back into performance by proposing a new dance form, *bharata nritya*, based on the reconstruction of material from Sanskrit texts.[17] For many of these dancers, scholarship underwrites a particular interpretation of bharata natyam.

Here, too, traditional anthropology provided an uneasy fit with this subject matter. Traditional anthropology assumes an imbalance between an articulate scholar and a largely inchoate "other," as Lila Abu-Lughod has argued from within the discipline.[18] Joann Kealiinohomoku's influential essay of 1970 on the cultural investments of ballet represents a significant exception to the then existing trend of anthropologists studying others abroad and the disempowered at home.[19] The imperative to represent an other group was challenged in the 1980s by disciplinary critiques like native anthropology and minority discourse. A field like bharata natyam, populated by articulate artist-scholars, each with her or his own version of history, provides a further challenge to an attempt to represent the field as a whole.

My own studies of anthropology (1986–90) had occurred at a time when the inclusion of history in anthropological studies was not typical. One way of addressing my concerns about the traditional culture concept could have involved a deeper inquiry into postmodern and experimental anthropology, by following the subdisciplinary critiques of native anthropology, dialogic anthropology, feminist anthropology, and transnational anthropology.[20] I elected instead to employ historical approaches because I found useful the attention that the discipline of history conventionally gives to individual action. In addition, historical perspectives informed my inquiry because dancers articulate their competing understandings of bharata natyam through reference to the past. Historical narratives legitimize particular choices, and, therefore, comprehending such decisions required knowledge of history. Furthermore, many practitioners, even those with divergent choreographic projects, agree on the importance of the bharata natyam revival from 1923 to 1950.[21] Therefore, I found it necessary to gain an understanding of these events, which I developed through historical inquiry, stimulated by my interest in the work of individual artists. This latter concern shares an emphasis with the focus of traditional aesthetics but, as I detail below, also diverges from it in the attention I give to social context.

Critical Historiography and Constructs of Tradition

If my first study borrowed from ethnography, then the second relied on critical historiography. This investigation began with a simple but productive theory: if several practitioners claim that their approaches are classical, traditional, and "authentic," and yet these approaches vary, the practitioners must define classicism and tradition in different ways. In revisiting the material I gathered in India, I realized that most performers and viewers agreed on the importance of tradition. They offered contrasting opinions as to what constituted tradition and what lay outside the boundaries of a classical performance.

The source of this discrepancy lay in bharata natyam's recontextualization, during the period from 1923 to 1950. The debate about what constituted tradition emerged out of questions raised during that time regarding the dance form's "disreputable past" and how to contend with it. Drawing on political studies, especially those of Benedict Anderson and Partha Chatterjee, I argued that the "revived" version of bharata natyam, represented most clearly by choreographer and dance reformer Rukmini Devi, addressed the concerns of the emergent nation-state.[22] It, like the nation, contended with a paradox in which indigenous identity articulated itself in negotiation with Western-defined systems and structures. So, for example, Devi referenced Western theatrical protocol and ballet technique as a model for the recrafting of bharata natyam. In addition, Devi mobilized the orientalist nationalism of the Theosophical Society that supported her efforts by looking to the distant past and

6.2. Rukmini Devi ca. 1940s. Photo courtesy of Jerome Robbins Dance Division, The New York Public Library for the Performing Arts, Astor, Lennox and Tilden Foundations. Used with permission.

to Sanskrit theoretical texts as an indicator of bharata natyam's true identity. *Devadasi* practitioner Balasaraswati, by contrast, responded to this nationalist reconstruction by emphasizing regional, Tamil origins for the form, highlighted the recent historical past, and privileged praxis over aesthetic theory. As such, she provided a counter-discourse to the shifts bharata natyam underwent in the 1930s and 1940s.[23]

This project focused on two influential figures from the past, Rukmini Devi and Balasaraswati. The study framed areas of debate key to early- and mid-twentieth-century bharata natyam, focusing on the dominant history and one major counter-discourse. I returned to material, mostly published, that I had gathered in India and supplemented it with further research into textual sources, focusing on the plethora of writing that surrounded both Devi and Balasaraswati. Each produced her own body of literature, through lectures, essays, and debates, that commented on her choreographic practice. I augmented this material with the accounts of those in the present who were closely linked to these dancers, such as Kalakshetra exponents V. N. and Shanta Dhananjayan and Balasaraswati's disciples Nandini Ramani and Kay Poursine.[24]

My interest lay largely in understanding how each dancer defined bharata natyam and in highlighting that each identified the form in strikingly different ways. Both used historical narratives to authorize her version of bharata natyam. Each dancer also expressed a different politics of representation through her understanding of the form, offering competing opinions on regionalism, nationalism, caste, class, and gender identity. How Devi and Balasaraswati portrayed their choices discursively held as much significance to this inquiry as the choreographic decisions themselves. As such, their public representation of such points factored into the investigation more than how they thought about them privately or how they had approached them in a class context.

Devi maintained that bharata natyam descended from a pan-Indian high culture rooted in the classical language Sanskrit. She privileged ancient Sanskrit aesthetic theory texts and Sanskrit drama as the origins of bharata natyam and claimed to access their spirit, if not precisely their form. She maintained that dance and theater were once, and should rightfully be again, the domain of "women of good families." She therefore drew on the tactics of anti-colonial nationalism by "rewriting the script" for bharata natyam and finding in it the glories of a shared tradition that could unite a diverse subcontinent.[25]

For Balasaraswati, by contrast, bharata natyam derived from the literary, religious, and musical heritage of the courts of the South Indian state of Tamil Nadu. She located the sources for bharata natyam in ancient Tamil poetry, local temple rituals, and the cultural traditions of the Thanjavur Court. Nonetheless, she acknowledged parallels with pan-Indian Sanskrit sources such as the Vedas, the Upanishads, and the Puranas and upper-caste practices like yoga.[26] She rejected attempts to

6.3. Rukmini Devi ca. 1940s. She is wearing the modified dance costume introduced during the revival. Photo courtesy of Jerome Robbins Dance Division, The New York Public Library for the Performing Arts, Astor, Lennox and Tilden Foundations. Used with permission.

6.4. T. Balasaraswati performing *abhinaya* (dramatic dance) at Mills College, Oakland, California, 1984. Photo by Jan Steward © 1985.

"improve" bharata natyam by aligning it with the tenets of Sanskrit aesthetic theory texts. The dance form, she maintained, found its proponents in the hereditary community of *devadasis*. She traced an unbroken chain from the artistic practices of the eighteenth- and nineteenth-century Tamil courts to twentieth-century bharata natyam. For Balasaraswati, attempts in the present to improve, purify, or modernize bharata natyam threatened to sever this connection. A profound sense of loss accompanied her version of history.

Devi thus eschewed the very past that Balasaraswati celebrated. Devi located bharata natyam's authenticating history not in the nineteenth-century *devadasi* temple and court traditions of South India but in ancient Sanskrit drama, the values of which could be reconstructed in the present. For Devi, the *devadasi* were subject to a system that restricted and degraded them. She thus maintained that the twentieth century was a time of rejuvenation, not of a threatened destruction.

Their two perspectives lined up into sets of binary oppositions. Devi privileged a Sanskrit tradition, Balasaraswati a Tamil one. Thus, Devi identified bharata natyam as a national form; for Balasaraswati, its roots were regional. Devi celebrated the new generation of brahman (upper-caste) practitioners, while Balasaraswati maintained that the form rightfully belonged with the relatively lower-caste *devadasi* practitioners who had nurtured it for centuries. Devi saw herself as purifying and revitalizing a form in decline, whereas Balasaraswati saw herself as upholding a threatened tradition.

This historical and discursive paradigm yielded important insights, as, through it, I was able to analyze a dominant narrative of bharata natyam's "revivification" and to begin to theorize resistance to this narrative. This model indicated how choreographic projects yielded particular sociopolitical strategies. The distinction between these two practitioners indicated a split at the roots of present-day bharata natyam. This approach, therefore, opened up a means of investigating discrepancy as well as consensus within Indian classical dance.

At the same time, this study encountered limitations, some of which point out the boundaries of a historical discourse analysis. For example, the history that this inquiry built did not address choreographic practice directly. Traditional historical methods offered a means of understanding only those choreographic decisions that had already been documented, leaving, in this case, more of an emphasis on how dancers represented their decisions than on how these two versions of history articulated themselves in theatrical form. In addition, my study of bharata natyam began with, and continues to hinge upon, the practices of the present. Classical historiography became less useful as I returned to present-day choreography from the reconstruction of the past. The aim of this study was also to understand and to highlight the nondominant narratives about the form. Despite significant challenges issued from the subdisciplines of social history and cultural history, traditional history privileges the actions of a few, luminary individuals over those pushed to the margins.[27]

Because of such limitations of conventional historical approaches, my resulting argument rested on a binary model that featured one hegemonic and one resistant narrative, providing for two positions:

brahman-nationalist-Sanskritic or *devadasi*-regionalist-Tamil. Because Balasaraswati was always cast in the responsive role in this binary, it was difficult to theorize her position. My continued investment in Balasaraswati's historical narrative was even more difficult to contend with. In this regard, my role as dancer carried over into my entry into historiography. I was less able to theorize Balasaraswati's history simply because, in part, I still thought of it as "true." It took a return to immediate experience and, thus, to an ethnographically based inquiry to challenge these assumptions further.

Ethnography and the Politics of Culture: History as Strategy

I returned to India in 1995 for nine months' intensive technique and repertoire training, having applied for admission to the Ph.D. program in Dance History and Theory at the University of California, Riverside. My aim in going to India was twofold: to immerse myself in performance practice, while supplementing this with preliminary "fieldwork" that would prepare me for further academic study. I arrived in India retaining my Devi-Balasaraswati focus and, largely unwittingly, my investment in the Balasaraswati version of the past. Contemporaneous choreographic practice and verbal accounts pushed me to contend with the present and to problematize Balasaraswati's version of the past.

In early 1996, I met artists and scholars who identified themselves as activists and who aligned their positions with the early Dravidianist movements, combining a class critique with an embrace of Tamil identity.[28] They questioned what they called the "brahman" version of bharata natyam's history, critiquing the Madras arts milieu from a socioeconomic position as well as from a large-scale political one. These colleagues encouraged me to extend my critique by pointing out that most *devadasis* had been more marginalized than Balasaraswati and that my research should address the position of those outside the elite, urban sphere.

My response to such a challenge was to embark on a project that bridged oral history and ethnographic methods. I traveled from Madras to towns and villages of Tamil Nadu and met artists from these communities, seeking out *devadasis* and men of their community—now collectively known as the *icai vellala* caste—who participated in the dance field as dancers, musicians, and teachers. This project drew on the methods of oral history in its emphasis on change over time. I spoke with people who had a direct connection to pre-revival dance and who could address it through their own memory and through what they recalled of their older relatives' experiences.[29] My aim was to reconstruct *devadasi* practice of the past as it contrasted with the stage performance of the present.

One of my main concerns in these discussions pertained to the use of aesthetic theory texts as the source of and basis for dance practice. My inquiry into Devi's project suggested that the revival initiated an integration of theoretical study into dance training. I wanted to find out if *icai vellala* practitioners shared Balasaraswati's suspicion toward reconstruction. Rather than simply corroborating the Balasaraswati version of history, these conversations provided a third version of history, one that drew on the same sources as Balasaraswati but interpreted them differently. Like Balasaraswati, these practitioners maintained that the arts of Tamil Nadu had always been the domain of the *devadasis* and their male counterparts, the *nattuvanars*. (A *nattuvanar* conducts the musical orchestra that accompanies a dance performance and is traditionally also the dancer's mentor.) Indeed, the *icai vellala* practitioners suggested that their communities were the true authors of Tamil tradition. Several of these practitioners rejected the Sanskrit language and texts in a way that Balasaraswati did not.

These artists, however, did not accordingly distance themselves from theory; instead they gave aesthetic theory a South Indian past. Some practitioners like violinist T. S. Ulaganathan spoke in overtly politicized terms when he maintained that "this is a Tamil tradition. They [brahmans] destroyed it in Tamil and re-created it in their own language [Sanskrit]."[30] By contrast, T. R. Navaneetam, a musician, replied to a question about the current interest in Sanskrit texts, as follows: "[T]here was more of that then than there is now. Like if present now, today's dancers were to dance in front of them [*devadasi* dancers], they could quote the text and say where these people are going wrong. They didn't have books as they have now, but still they knew." She then went on, however, to say that "they learned most of these things through Telegu [the language of the state of Andhra Pradesh and a major literary and musical language of Tamil Nadu]."[31]

Comments like this revealed several insights. At first, the political implications of dance had seemed to me to hinge upon nationalist politics.

The perspective of those marginal to the Madras milieu, combined with the politicization of linguistic and caste identity in the daily life in Tamil Nadu, indicated how regional and linguistic affiliation, alongside caste and class issues, intersected with and, in some cases, interrupted projects of nation making. At the same time, such overtly political interpretations of history indicated that the nonhegemonic history was just as constructed and just as ideologically based as that of middle-class dancers like Devi and her students. Such encounters indicated that bharata natyam provided for the crafting of multiple affiliations and multiple histories. They also suggested that identity, whether established through caste, class, or training lineage, did not yield predictable responses to questions about past and present practice.

Multiple, competing versions of the past replaced a dialogue between one dominant and one resistant history. It now seemed impossible to locate—and write—a singular, "accurate" history. I therefore became concerned less with uncovering the authoritative history and more with the divergence within these inquiries into the past. My inquiry developed into a history of the competing histories created from different perspectives within the bharata natyam field. I decided then to approach bharata natyam not through metaphors that emphasize wholeness and social cohesion but through those that foreground individual action.[32] On my return to academic study in September 1996, I sought out methods for understanding how individuals politicized aesthetic practice through history.[33]

Another encounter, earlier in 1996, fostered my shift toward competing versions of history: witnessing a performance of Lakshmi Viswanathan's *Vata Vriksha,* or *The Banyan Tree,* on 1 January 1996.[34] The piece has a Sanskrit title, and its choreographer is a middle-class brahman woman who followed in the footsteps of Devi, receiving her training as a result of the events of the revival. Viswanathan has not followed the still-conventional pattern of training in dance with one teacher. She began studying as a child but learned with several different teachers as "at that time, no one wanted a career as a dancer, it was part of [her] education." It was only following her university study that she trained under Ellappa Pillai, a mentor of the Thanjavur style of bharata natyam. In addition to this dance education, Viswanathan has conducted ethnographic fieldwork and textual research on bharata natyam's history, which she has then channeled into both written and choreographed works.[35]

6.5. *The Banyan Tree*. Lakshmi Viswanathan in attire re-created after the costume of Rukmini Devi. Photo courtesy of V K Rajamani.

6.6. *The Banyan Tree.* Lakshmi Viswanathan as Rukmini Devi observing the dance of young *devadasis* at the Music Academy in 1935. Photo courtesy of V K Rajamani.

Vata Vriksha opens with the choreographer's onstage introduction of "the story of the dance of my people." It soon becomes apparent, through depictions of the folk dances of the Kaveri River delta, possession rituals, and the accomplishments of the temples and courts, that the people to whom she refers are not Indians generally but Tamils. Like Balasaraswati, Viswanathan celebrates the early *devadasi* legacy, draws from Tamil poetry, and foregrounds the accomplishments of the Thanjavur courts. Yet, like Devi, she treats the nineteenth century as a period of decline and distances her vision of bharata natyam from remaining twentieth-century *devadasi* practice. The piece concludes with a celebration of the efforts of Devi and of the revival.

This piece provided a history that, to me, was unexpected. Viswanathan draws upon similar sources as Balasaraswati when she invokes the

6.7. *The Banyan Tree*. Rukmini Devi's encounter with Pavlova as *The Dying Swan*. Photo courtesy of V K Rajamani.

Tamil literary canon.[36] Like Devi, she references the *Natyasastra* as "the basis of all Indian performing arts."[37] She also, however, highlights the importance of praxis over aesthetic theory, stating, "I don't think dance grows out of text. It grows out of the life of the people."[38] She foregrounds the temple and court dance traditions but, like Devi, celebrates a distant past, albeit a Tamil, not pan-Indian, one. As did Devi, she represents the mid-twentieth century as a time of restoration, not of threatened disintegration. Although Viswanathan acknowledges the significant difference between her view of history and Devi's, she nonetheless credits the revival-period choreographer for her efforts to "make [dance] credible." Unlike either of the early-twentieth-century practitioners, Viswanathan also explicitly acknowledges the globality of the revival when she refers to Devi's "inspiration during colonial times from seeing [Anna] Pavlova."[39]

Vata Vriksha developed out of an extended period of research in which Viswanathan investigated local and regional origins for bharata natyam, producing written works that emphasize bharata natyam's origins in Tamil Nadu. She embarked on this research in order to uncover "the multiple influences over centuries" on dance in South India.[40] Like Balasaraswati, she highlights the importance of the mentor-disciple tradition and the contributions of the Thanjavur Quartet musicians to the present-day repertoire.[41] In her monograph *Bharatanatyam: The Tamil Heritage*, Viswanathan also acknowledges the influence of Sanskrit sources on the dance, when she maintains that "[i]nfluences, both Vedic and Aryan, bringing with them the richness of Sanskrit scholarship were absorbed, adapted, and modified by an already fully developed Tamil Culture."[42] She uses the *Natyasastra*, however, as a source not that prescribes the form that bharata natyam should take now, but that describes the nature of an early South Indian dance form.

Her history draws together the divergent sources that Balasaraswati and Devi used to different ends. Upon encountering this, and other equally complex narratives, I could no longer fix bharata natyam even as a site of contestation. The writing that followed this research emphasized individual decisions and specific strategies.[43] Pieces like *Vata Vriksha* also encouraged me to locate these projects not only in a dancer's discursive representations but also in choreography. I thus deployed the idea that choreography operates as a strategy for negotiating a multifaceted field of social and political concerns. I defined choreography as the planned and intentional selection of movement that includes the arrangement of conventional items of repertoire, material generated through improvisation, and the composition of entirely new work. All of these forums offered dancers opportunities to express their perspectives on history, politics, and the social meanings of bharata natyam. The concept of choreography-as-strategy suggests that through their choices individuals negotiate a field of discourse not of their own making.[44] The metaphor of strategy rather than, for instance, that of "creation" acknowledges that although broader concerns—social, political, cultural, and economic— inform a dance practice, they do not determine it.[45] As such, the concept of choreography acknowledges the interplay of social, political, and historical concerns, while foregrounding a circumscribed agency.

Although anthropology and sociology have, in recent years, attended to individual agency, critical, especially poststructuralist, history has contested the idea of individual action. The anti-humanist critique pushed scholars to look at social context as determinative of individual actions; anthropologists, by contrast, have already traditionally privileged context over individual decisions.[46] Thus, while poststructuralist historians have treated the notion of agency with skepticism, contemporary social scientists now include individual decision making in their inquiries. For those concerned with non-Western forms the situation is made still more complex by the endurance of an orientalist framework that identifies practitioners of such forms as constrained by "tradition."[47] With their practices rendered fixed, such artists have been denied agency in traditional scholarship. In such a situation, a wholehearted anti-humanism can replicate the orientalist assumption of a static, unselfconscious culture that simply reiterates itself through its practitioners. My discussion of choreography represents an attempt to negotiate between these two disciplinary perspectives by suggesting that practitioners select from a set of possible options and, in doing so, creatively respond to larger social and political discourses.

This interest in individual interpretations also urged a return to ethnographic methods. While historiography emphasizes individual action, ethnography can provide a means of uncovering and understanding such strategies. Upon returning to India in 1999, I conducted formal interviews with dancers, dance teachers, and promoters, ranging across generations and levels in their careers. This involved raising questions about individual perspectives and particular experiences rather than general insights. I wanted to understand how dancers articulated their point of view within a professional sphere and, thus, how they spoke about their work in a relatively formal setting. I also selected formal interviews because I preferred interviewees to know when they were speaking on and off the record. Likewise, I intended for this choice to respect the difference between public and private selves. The dancers interviewed spoke about their procedures for performance, choreography, and research as well as about their understanding of history, their perspective on the revival, and their sense of the current dance milieu, including its economic conditions.[48]

Conclusion: Ethnography, Methods, and Practice

In my study of bharata natyam since 1988, I have drawn on ethnography, history, performance practice, and choreographic analysis. These methods have come into play less as a means of ascertaining the "truth" about this dance form and its past, and more as a way of tracing different choreographic strategies and their politics of representation. Through these inquiries I have realized that twentieth-century bharata natyam challenges boundaries between the disciplines of history, ethnography, and cultural studies.

When dancers participate in projects of intentional cultural production, they present "culture" as a site not of implicit consensus but of divergence.[49] This suggests that culture as articulated in bharata natyam choreography is not seamless, organic, or implicit. Culture is not a single identity that dance reflects or contributes to. Rather, culture is a set of politicized "belongings" that shift in relationship to concerns that are local and contemporaneous. This phenomenon challenges older anthropological notions of generality. While traditional forms of anthropology continue to seek out commonalities among members of a community, ethnography can be used for other ends. The ethnographic method of participant-observation, through its emphasis on immediate experience, generates a personal involvement that can challenge dichotomies and problematize assumptions of unity within a form. It also produces a familiarity with a practice that can highlight difference in practice and interpretation. Interviewing, too, although perhaps originally used to glean insights about a shared culture, provides a vehicle for soliciting individual perspectives and understanding how the approaches of individuals differ from those of their peers, as well as how they are in accord.

Choreographic practice within bharata natyam likewise complicates an academic inquiry into history as practitioners deploy historical sources to divergent political and aesthetic ends. Practitioners produce social and political affiliations through historical narratives. This challenges a search for historical "truth." At the same time, however, because bharata natyam choreography produces social meanings through historical narratives, such strategies can only be understood through attention to the practices of the past.

This proliferation of social meanings and historical narratives, with their accompanying multiple truths, can be freeing for dancers, choreographers, historians, and for those who bridge these categories. Since the early twentieth century, this dance genre has looked back into the past in order to find its rightful place. Inquiries into the past have legitimized different interpretations of form and history. These divergent notions of past-ness have, in turn, fostered the emergence of different choreographic visions. The very presence of these multiple historical narratives, then, provides bharata natyam practitioners with a means of looking forward.

This study has also offered me an opportunity to look forward. I began this study as a dancer who wanted to unravel the complex narratives that I encountered through my participation in the Thanjavur Court style of bharata natyam. Through this inquiry, I have ended up, literally, dancing through and between ethnography and history. The process of writing these multiple histories has illuminated both the validity and the constructed nature of all of them. As such, it has shaken— and ultimately challenged—the faith I had invested in one particular version of history. Although productive, this left me temporarily without a place for my dancing in this field. As I wrote this chapter, however, I returned to performing bharata natyam after a three-year hiatus.[50] The traditional repertoire of the Thanjavur Court style will, I trust, continue to undergird my danced inquiries of the future, but perhaps I will not be constrained by a particular version of history and aesthetic quality. I hope that through performing in and writing about such projects, I, too, can consider bharata natyam's future as well as its past.

NOTES

1. This description is drawn from a filmed sequence of bharata natyam included in the JVC World Music and Dance video anthology. As I suggest, this representation of bharata natyam is not specific to this footage. Rather, it forms part of a general portrayal of bharata natyam as ancient and timeless. Kunihiko Nakagawa, dir., "Bharata Natyam: A Devotional Dance to Shiva," vol. 11, South Asia I, India 1, track 11.1, *The JVC Video Anthology of World Music and Dance* (Tokyo: Victor Company of Japan, n.d.).

2. U.K. choreographer-scholar Vena Ramphal comments on the continuity between bharata natyam and forms that preceded it while also challenging claims, based on this continuity, for bharata natyam's antiquity (personal correspondence 2001, 2003). Choreographer Shobana Jeyasingh also comments on the confusion of origins with form: "[I]t is one thing to say that it has roots that go back two thousand years and quite another to say it hasn't changed over that period of time. Roots go back a long way, every dance has roots." Shobana Jeyasingh, transcript of untitled presentation, in *"Traditions on the Move" Open Forum 1993* (London: Academy of Indian Dance, 1994), 7.

3. For more information on the *devadasi* system in South India, see Amrit Srinivasan, "Reform and Revival: The Devadasi and Her Dance," *Economic and Political Weekly* 20, no. 44 (1985): 1869–76.

4. I use the feminine pronoun to indicate that the majority of bharata natyam dancers are female and also to reflect the changing demographics of the teaching field.

5. I draw the idea of framing devices from Susan Foster, *Reading Dancing: Bodies and Subjects in Contemporary American Dance* (Berkeley: University of California Press, 1986).

6. For further discussion of the change in nomenclature from "sadir" to "bharata natyam," see Arudra, "The Renaming of an Old Dance: A Whodunit Tale of Mystery," *Sruti* 27/28 (1986/87): 30–31; Matthew Allen, "Rewriting the Script for South Indian Dance," *The Drama Review* 41, no. 3 (1997): 63–100.

7. The present-day concert repertoire derives from the court, not temple, tradition of *sadir.* As part of a separate project, also beginning in the 1980s, dancers reconstructed items from the temple repertoire. For a detailed discussion of the reintroduction of bharata natyam to temples, see Anne-Marie Gaston, *Bharata Natyam: From Temple to Theatre* (New Delhi: Manohar, 1996), 39–40, 335–37; Janet O'Shea, "At Home in the World: Bharata Natyam's Transnational Traditions" (Ph.D. diss., University of California, Riverside, 2001), 190–92.

8. Anne-Marie Gaston argues that the repetition of the "historical pedigree of the dance . . . qualifies bharata natyam to some extent as an invented tradition." A panel called "Invented Traditions" (South Bank Centre, London, 26 August 2001) debated the antiquity versus inventedness of classical Indian dance and proposed other models for identifying these forms' engagement with the past. The term "invented tradition" is drawn from Eric Hobsbawm, "Introduction: Inventing Traditions," in *The Invention of Tradition,* ed. Eric Hobsbawm and Terence Ranger (New York: Cambridge University Press, 1983), 1–14.

Early critical accounts of the bharata natyam revival represent the form as an "invented tradition." Joan Erdman comments on dancers' frustration with the revivalist rescue narrative. Avanthi Meduri invokes this narrative in order to critique it. Amrit Srinivasan researched the *devadasi* system as a corrective to the revival's meta-narrative. Anne-Marie Gaston, *Bharata Natyam,* 283; Joan Erdman, "Dance Discourses: Rethinking the History of the 'Oriental Dance,'" in *Moving Words: Re-Writing Dance,* ed. Gay Morris (London: Routledge, 1996), 288–305; Avanthi Meduri, "Bharatha Natyam: What Are You?" *Asian Theatre Journal* 5, no. 1 (1988): 1–22; Amrit Srinivasan, "The Hindu Temple Dancer: Prostitute or Nun?" *Cambridge Anthropology* 8, no. 1 (1983), 73–99, and "Reform and Revival."

9. For this reason, Kapila Vatsyayan identifies bharata natyam as both reflecting a modern sensibility and engaging actively with "fragments of antiquity." Joan Erdman identifies this phenomenon as "retronymic histories" that are "created to respond to questions asked after the fact." Anne-Marie Gaston likewise argues, "No secure and unmodified custom would need to reiterate its claims to antiquity so frequently." Amrit Srinivasan makes a similar point when she says, "All revivals . . . present a view of the past which is usually an interpretation fitting in with a changed contemporary situation." Kapila Vatsyayan, *Indian Classical Dance* (New Delhi: Publications Division, Ministry of Information and Broadcasting, Government of India, 1992), 8; Erdman, "Dance Discourses," 301, n.13; Gaston, *Bharata Natyam*, 283; Srinivasan, "Hindu Temple Dancer," 90.

10. I draw this idea of "tradition" as determined by consensus from Jeyasingh, transcript of untitled presentation, 6.

11. Here, I use the term "historiography" in the sense deployed by critical historians like de Certeau: the writing of history in contrast to "history," the past that is manufactured through this practice. Michel de Certeau, *The Writing of History*, trans. Tom Conley (New York: Columbia University Press, 1988), 87.

12. Adrienne Kaeppler, "Dance in Anthropological Perspective," *Annual Review of Anthropology* 7 (1978): 34–47; Cynthia J. Novack, *Sharing the Dance: Contact Improvisation and American Culture* (Madison: University of Wisconsin Press, 1990); Marcel Mauss, "Techniques of the Body," in *Sociology and Psychology* (London: Routledge and Kegan Paul, 1979); Pierre Bourdieu, *Outline of a Theory of Practice* (Cambridge: Cambridge University Press, 1977).

13. Adrienne Kaeppler, "Dance Ethnology and the Anthropology of Dance," *Dance Research Journal* 32, no. 1 (2000): 116–21.

14. Scholars within the field of anthropology had also shifted away from an assumption that equates "culture" with coherence and agreement. For an outline of anthropology's self-critique, see Lila Abu-Lughod, "Writing against Culture," in *Recapturing Anthropology: Working in the Present,* ed. Richard G. Fox (Santa Fe, N.M.: School of American Research Press, 1991); Sally A. Ness, "Observing the Evidence Fail: Difference Arising from Objectification in Cross-Cultural Dance," in *Moving Words: Re-Writing Dance,* ed. Gay Morris (London: Routledge, 1996), 245–69.

15. As I discuss below, anthropologists have attended to transnationalism. See, for instance, Vered Amit, ed., *Constructing the Field: Ethnographic Fieldwork in the Contemporary World* (London: Routledge, 2000); Arjun Appadurai, *Modernity at Large: Cultural Dimensions of Globalization* (Minneapolis: University of Minnesota Press, 1996); Carol A. Breckenridge, ed., *Consuming Modernity: Public Culture in a South Asian World* (Minneapolis: University of Minnesota Press, 1995).

16. For more on Kapila Vatsyayan, see Uttara Asha Coorlawala, "Kapila Vatsyayan: Formative Influences—an Interview," *Dance Research Journal* 32, no. 1 (2000), 103–9; Joan L. Erdman, "Circling the Square: A Choreographed

Approach to the Work of Dr. Kapila Vatsyayan and Western Dance Studies," *Dance Research Journal* 32, no. 1 (2000), 87–94; Mohd Anis Md Nor, "Kapila Vatsyayan and Dance Scholarship: India and Beyond," *Dance Research Journal* 32, no. 1 (2000), 95–102; Janet O'Shea, "Technique and Theory in the Work of Kapila Vatsyayan," *Dance Research Journal* 32, no. 1 (2000), 82–86; Vatsyayan, *Indian Classical Dance;* and Kapila Vatsyayan, *Classical Indian Dance in Literature and the Arts,* 2nd ed. (New Delhi: Sangeet Natak Academy, 1977).

17. Indira Viswanathan Peterson also comments on this phenomenon of "dancer-scholars" in her article "The Evolution of the Kuruvanji Dance Drama in Tamil Nadu: Negotiating the 'Folk' and the 'Classical' in the Bharata Natyam Canon," *South Asia Research* 18, no. 1 (1998): 67.

18. Abu-Lughod, "Writing against Culture," 139.

19. Joann W Kealiinohomoku, "An Anthropologist Looks at Ballet as a Form of Ethnic Dance," in *Anthropology and Human Movement,* 1, ed. Drid Williams (Lanham, Md.: Scarecrow Press, 1997; originally published in *Impulse* [1969–70]: 24–33).

20. See Abu-Lughod, "Writing against Culture"; Kamala Visweswaran's *Fictions of Feminist Ethnography* (Minneapolis: University of Minnesota Press, 1994); James Clifford and George E. Marcus, ed., *Writing Culture: The Politics and Poetics of Ethnography* (Berkeley: University of California Press, 1986).

21. Matthew Allen critiques the use of the term "revival," identifying this process as a "re-population," "re-construction," "re-naming," "re-situation," and "re-storation" as well as a "re-vivification" ("Rewriting the Script for Indian Dance," 63). I posit the date of the revival's beginning as 1931, as that year saw the Music Academy's first performance of bharata natyam by the Kalyani Daughters. These dates are debatable: brahman lawyer E. Krishna Iyer began his training in *sadir* in 1923, and therefore the revival's beginnings could be linked to his first forays into the field. Alternatively, since disinterest and ambivalence met the first Music Academy dance performance, the revival could be dated later. Arudra makes this argument when he suggests that the revival began in 1933 with the Music Academy's presentation of the Kalyani Daughters, Balasaraswati, and the American Ragini Devi. Arudra, "The Transfiguration of a Traditional Dance: The Academy and the Dance Events of the First Decade," *Sruti* 27/28 (1986/87): 20.

The end of the revival is harder to determine. I set it at 1950 because the 1940s were a pivotal time for bharata natyam with the entry of young, middle-class women into the field, ensuring its respectability. See, for instance, Allen, "Rewriting the Script for Indian Dance," 80–81; N. Pattabhi Raman, "The Trinity of Bharatanatyam: Bala, Rukmini Devi, and Kamala," *Sruti* 48 (1988): 24.

22. Benedict Anderson, *Imagined Communities: Reflections on the Origin and Spread of Nationalism* (New York: Routledge, 1991); Partha Chatterjee, *Nationalist*

Thought and the Colonial World: A Derivative Discourse (Minneapolis: University of Minnesota Press, 1986).

23. For a fuller articulation of this argument, see my "'Traditional' Indian Dance and the Making of Interpretative Communities," *Asian Theatre Journal* 1, no. 1 (1998): 45–63.

24. As source material, see, for example, a lecture demonstration by V. N. Dhananjayan at University of California, Berkeley, on 28 October 1993; V. N. Dhananjayan, *A Dancer on Dance* (Madras: Bharata Kalanjali, 1984); V. N. Dhananjayan and Shanta Dhananjayan, "Rukmini Devi the Choreographer," *Kalakshetra Quarterly* 8, no. 3–4 (1986): 30–34; Gowri Ramnayaran, "Bala: My Guru," *Sruti* 5 (1984): 35–39; Kay Poursine, "Hasta as Discourse on Music: T. Balasaraswati and Her Art," *Dance Research Journal* 23, no. 2 (1991): 17–20; Nandini Ramani, artist biography and publicity information, received by author October 1989 and in her possession.

25. I draw the phrase "rewriting the script" from Allen's "Rewriting the Script for Indian Dance."

26. It is not surprising, then, that she found support from the Madras Music Academy, which supported nationalist claims through the propagation of regional forms and from the Tamil Isai Sangam, an organization founded in order to foster the development of classical music in the Tamil language.

27. Dance historian Linda Tomko identifies social history as a subdiscipline that attends to immediate, lived experience as "indexes of people's identities, beliefs, and agencies" and cultural history as a method that addresses "the ways and means by which people make meanings for and about themselves in society." Linda J. Tomko, *Dancing Class: Gender, Ethnicity, and Social Divides in American Dance, 1890–1920* (Bloomington: Indiana University Press, 1999), xiv–xv.

28. Dravidianism includes several reform movements that celebrated Tamil identity and culture as a separate entity from North India, Sanskrit, and Indo-Aryan traditions. The early Dravidianist movements were egalitarian in nature, atheistic, and strongly influenced by Marxism. For more on Dravidianism and other Tamil regional movements, see Sumathi Ramaswamy, *Passions of the Tongue: Language Devotion in Tamil India, 1891–1970* (Berkeley: University of California Press, 1997) and Eugene F. Irschick, *Tamil Revivalism in the 1930s* (Madras: Cre-A, 1986).

29. S. Ravindran assisted me with translation and in identifying research leads.

30. T. S. Ulaganathan, interview with author, Tiruchipalli, India, 24 May 1996.

31. T. R. Navaneetam, interview with author, Chennai, India, May 1996.

32. See Margaret Trawick, *Notes on Love in a Tamil Family* (Berkeley: University of California Press, 1992), xvii; Abu-Lughod, "Writing against Culture,"

146. Timothy Rice likewise urges a subject-centered approach to ethnography in his "Time, Place, and Metaphor in Musical Experience and Ethnography," *Ethnomusicology* 47, no. 2 (2003): 151–79. My approach aligns with the "tactical humanism" urged by Abu-Lughod and the "pragmatic humanism" promoted by Paul Gilroy, *Between Camps: Nations, Cultures, and the Allure of Race* (London: Penguin Books, 2000). I also base this emphasis on strategy, rather than individuality, on the work of Michel de Certeau, *The Practice of Everyday Life*, trans. Steven Rendall (Berkeley: University of California Press, 1984), xi.

33. For instance, Hayden White, *The Content of the Form: Narrative Discourse and Historical Representation* (Baltimore: Johns Hopkins University Press, 1987).

34. Viswanathan with Deborah Dunthorn as associate director, Gitanjali Kolanad as co-choreographer, and Ambika Buch and Raju for bharata natyam and kalaripayattu choreography, respectively.

35. L. Viswanathan, interview with the author, Chennai, India, 31 August 1999.

36. Viswanathan refers to her sources for the work as "ancient literature, epigraphy and historical accounts, as well as folklore, newspaper articles, and personal encounters." She also identifies the musical and poetic text as from "'Silappadikaram,' an epic of the 3rd century, hymns of the Shiva worshippers—the saints of the 7th and 8th century, composers of the Thanjavur Court of the 17th century." Lakshmi Viswanathan, "In the Words of the Choreographer" (program notes), *Vata Vriksha*, January 1996.

37. Viswanathan also states in the program notes, however, that "[t]he theatrical impulses are based on my own perceptions in 25 years of performing in India and countries around the world."

38. Viswanathan interview.

39. Ibid.

40. Ibid.

41. By contrast, Devi, writing in the same volume, refers to bharata natyam as "the root and origin of all dance in India," connecting the dance form to a pan-Indian, rather than local, heritage. Lakshmi Viswanathan, "Bharatanatyam: The Thanjavur Heritage," *Kalakshetra Quarterly* 9, no. 3 (n.d.): 2; Rukmini Devi, untitled entry, *Kalakshetra Quarterly* 9, no. 3 (n.d.): 22.

42. Viswanathan uses Manmohan Ghosh's translation of a stanza from chapter fourteen of the *Natyasastra*: "The Southern (countries) favour various kind of dances, songs, and instrumental music, an abundance of the graceful. . . . Style and clever and graceful gestures." In Lakshmi Viswanathan, *Bharatanatyam: The Tamil Heritage* (Madras: Sri Kala Mandir Trust, 1984), 8.

43. O'Shea, "At Home in the World."

44. I draw the idea of choreography as methodology from Susan Leigh Foster's theorization of the semiotics of choreography in *Reading Dancing* and of bodily practice as thought process in "Choreographing History," in

Choreographing History, ed. Susan Leigh Foster (Bloomington: Indiana University Press, 1995), 3–21. Cynthia Novack also comments on the ability of dance to negotiate between individual decision-making and social inscription, see *Sharing the Dance*, 141.

45. Anthropologist Pierre Bourdieu's notion of the habitus in his *Outline of a Theory of Practice* has also influenced this idea.

46. Appadurai, in *Modernity at Large*, notes this intersection between the concerns of anthropology and poststructuralism. This phenomenon parallels a shift in research methods and methodologies as historians have raised questions about contemporaneous social life and quotidian experience and used oral history as a supplement or alternative to traditional historiography. Meanwhile, anthropologists have moved toward questions of change over time. Examples of this cross-disciplinary exchange within South Asian Studies include Piya Chatterjee, *A Time for Tea: Women, Labor, and Post/Colonial Politics on an Indian Plantation* (Durham, N.C.: Duke University Press, 2001); Bernard Cohen, *An Anthropologist among the Historians and Other Essays* (Delhi: Oxford University Press, 1987); Nicholas B. Dirks, *The Hollow Crown: Ethnohistory of an Indian Kingdom* (Ann Arbor: University of Michigan Press, 1993).

47. John Blacking makes a similar point in "Making Artistic Popular Music: The Goal of True Folk," *Popular Music* 1 (1981): 9–14. Kamala Visweswaran also argues for erring on the side of agency in *Fictions of Feminist Ethnography* (1994).

48. Intending to account for the global circulation of bharata natyam and its production of meaning in different contexts, I took this method of inquiry to research on bharata natyam in other countries, especially Canada and the U.K. See Janet O'Shea, "At Home in the World? The Bharata Natyam Dancer as Transnational Interpreter," *The Drama Review* 47, no. 1 (2003): 176–86. The successful practice of bharata natyam now requires a global orientation of its practitioners. See O'Shea, "At Home in the World" (2001), 188–89; Gaston, *Bharata Natyam*, 129. Thus, while non-Indian viewers may initially see the dance form as culturally distinct, they would also find, in the dancers, a group of people who inhabit the same kind of globalized sphere they do.

49. I draw the term "intentional cultural production" from Appadurai, *Modernity at Large*.

50. With the British bharata natyam–based dance company Angika (led by Mayuri Boonham and Subathra Subramaniam) in *Urban Temple* (Royal Festival Hall Ballroom, London, 8 August 2003) and in a workshop demonstration presented by neoclassical choreographer Mavin Khoo (The Nehru Centre, London, 19 August 2003).

7

Interpreting the Historical Record

Using Images of Korean Dance
for Understanding the Past

JUDY VAN ZILE

When I began field research on Korean dance, I made a conscious decision to focus on the analysis of contemporary performances of older dances. As a dance ethnologist, I planned to use my specialized movement analysis skills as an entrée, and then branch out and deepen my understandings by digging into history and by learning about such other cultural manifestations and belief systems as religion, music, and philosophy. My research in Korea began in 1979 and since then has involved four extended periods of residence and numerous short visits.[1] While learning to perform a number of dances, transcribing the dances into Labanotation, and trying to understand better the nature of the movements and choreography, I began to see how intricately interwoven were the ethnography of the present and the historical records of the past. Documenting the dances of the present was important, but a real understanding of the present could not ignore the impact of the past and a careful examination of its records.

As I sought to understand contemporary performances, Korean colleagues and consultants continually referred me to the past.[2] They identified events they believed contributed to the present, pointed me to historical documents, and justified current practices on the basis of records of the past. When I began to study some of the historical records that were repeatedly referenced, however, I often became puzzled. I could not always see in them the validation of the present that my Korean associates espoused.[3]

My purpose here is to examine selected iconographic representations of Korean dance, one particular type of historical record, to show the interface between history and ethnography in researching the dances of this country.[4] Along the way I comment on my discoveries and dilemmas, as well as on the responses of Korean colleagues and consultants to things that struck me as of particular significance. In doing so, I call into question the assumption that Korea's iconographic representations of dance, even when commissioned by the royal court for the explicit purpose of documenting events, represent actual dance moments. This resonates with contemporary thinking on historical dance research. For example, Susan Manning tells us: "An event bound in space and time, a performance can be read only through its traces— on the page, in memory, on film, in the archive. Each of these traces marks, indeed, distorts, the event of performance, and so the scholar pursues what remains elusive as if moving through an endless series of distorting reflections. But this pursuit leaves its own sort of illumination, and that illumination is what the scholar records, in effect penning a journal of the process of inquiry."[5]

Georgiana Gore states the belief that the "discovery of historical knowledge or disclosure of historical truth are no longer tenable research objectives," but what is possible is "the mapping of a multiplicity of authorial voices through the deployment of interpretive strategies which acknowledge that all writing is situated."[6] And Joan Erdman advocates contextualizing historical events, examining them in relation to contemporaneous occurrences, in order to obtain the clearest understanding of them.[7] The emphasis of these authors on the situatedness of writing, the use of interpretive strategies, and the value of establishing multiple "truths" applies equally to iconographic records and points to the importance of examining historical records, regardless of their format, from many points of view. I offer selected examples from my studies of Korean dance that reinforce the necessity of fully embracing multiple perspectives in order to comprehend historical documents and the relationship between history and ethnography.

Ch'ŏyongmu: Realistic Depiction of Performance Moments?

The primary focus of my early research was *Ch'ŏyongmu*.[8] The dance is performed today by five masked dancers, usually men, each wearing a different colored tunic. Written historical documents tell us the dance began in ritual contexts, and contemporary Korean dancers and scholars acknowledge this origin. The dance is now generally described by Koreans as a court dance, since that is the primary context in which it was performed for countless centuries prior to the demise of the court in the early 1900s.[9]

As I began to explore the history of *Ch'ŏyongmu* in order to understand the nature of today's version of the dance, colleagues referred me to paintings and woodblock prints of the dance in addition to textual manuscripts. Fully cognizant of the many challenges involved in using iconographic representations of dance in historical research, I became particularly interested in the paintings and prints for two reasons.[10] First, I thought their visual nature might yield more information than such instructions as "do the poking the sky gesture," one example of the kind of description contained in manuscripts.[11] Second, because many of these images were commissioned by, and done under the supervision of, the royal court to record, for posterity, important events, I assumed considerable attention would be paid to accuracy of detail.

I encountered a number of fascinating images of *Ch'ŏyongmu*. They portrayed various settings in which the dance was previously done and costumes and suggestions of choreographic moments that appear in today's dance. The latter often took the form of circular or diamond formations through which the dancers pass, and displayed a sense of liveliness, which characterizes certain portions of the dance. I found one painting especially intriguing because of its direct relationship to a sequence in today's dance. Figure 7.1 documents the entertainment at a banquet honoring elderly gentlemen. When I juxtaposed this image against the contemporary choreography of *Ch'ŏyongmu*, I realized that while the artist appeared to have captured a moment in the dance, this moment was both similar to and different from one in today's performances. At one point in contemporary presentations the dancers place themselves in a diamond formation, as shown here, with one dancer in the center. The central dancer then faces and performs with each of the other dancers in a canon (a movement sequence in which the remaining

7.1. Detail of King Sukjong's Private Party for Elder Ministers, from *Kisa kyechŏp* (Album of Gathering for Officials Over the Age of 70), 1719–20. Color on silk, original 44.0 x 67.7 cm. Photo by Kim Chin-yo et al., Ho-Am Art Museum.

dancers each join in succession). The moment suggested here could easily be a canon, with the dancer at the bottom awaiting his turn to join the others, but the order in which the dancers appear to join the canon is different from the order followed in today's performances. The original image from which this detail is extracted is in vibrant color, and the order in which the dancers join the canon, based on the tunic color of the figure who appears to be waiting for his turn, suggests a difference from current performance practice.

Another difference between this painting and contemporary performances is the way the dancers' movements relate to each other. Today, once the dancers have joined the canon, they all perform exactly the same movement. While the central dancer and the one to our right are shown doing identical movements here, the dancers at the top and to our left, although animated and apparently dancing, are doing something different: they do not have one leg lifted so high nor one arm thrust upward.

In this image the formation shown and the suggestion of a movement canon parallel things seen in contemporary performances. Details of the canon portrayed here, however, are different. This raises at least two important questions. First, did the artist intend to record a realistic moment, or take artistic license in using the techniques allowed by his medium to capture only the flavor of a particular moment and the fact that the dance was performed? This latter possibility is suggested by Korean art historian Pak Chŏng-hye when she says that painters "could not easily represent all details . . . on a picture plane. Sometimes a painter's discretion or ability yielded changes in the paintings."[12]

Because today's version of the dance has been reconstructed on several occasions (see discussion below), the second question is posed by turning the first question around: is the painting an accurate representation of what transpired, while reconstructors of today's version of the dance took liberties in modifying movements and choreographic sequences as they brought the dance to life again?

Ch'ŏyongmu: Who Is the Choreographer?

As I continued to seek out images of *Ch'ŏyongmu* I encountered a number that puzzled me in a different way.[13] Figure 7.2 is representative of these kinds of images. Here we see five masked dancers as well as four additional unmasked dancers. (In this case, based on the costumes worn, the additional dancers are likely to be men. In some similar images, again based on costumes, the unmasked dancers are likely to be women.) Performances of *Ch'ŏyongmu* today rarely include more than the five masked dancers, and my Korean colleagues never referred to additional dancers. As I showed some of these images to them and asked about the additional performers, they seemed surprised. If they had seen the images before, they never bothered either to look closely at them or to question the presence of additional performers. Some simply stated they did not know why the additional performers were included; some speculated they were ceremonial attendants, who were often present during court dances. I turned to textual manuscripts for possible clues to the extra performers.

7.2. *Ch'ŏyongmu* illustration from *Sunjo muja chinjak ŭigwe* (1828). Courtesy of Kyujanggak, Seoul National University.

The *Akhak kwebŏm* (Guide to the Study of Music), an important fifteenth-century court manual, contains verbal descriptions of two versions of *Ch'ŏyongmu*, one performed as part of New Year rituals to expel evil spirits and that is described as elegant *(Chŏndo Ch'ŏyongmu)*, and one that was done for entertainment and that is described as lively *(Hudo Ch'ŏyongmu)*. The dance done for entertainment was part of a suite *(Hak yŏnhwadae Ch'ŏyongmu hapsŏl)* consisting of three dances—the Crane Dance *(Hangmu)*, the Lotus Pavilion Dance *(Yŏnwadaemu)*, and *Ch'ŏyongmu*. Because of a number of textual references that translate as "spirit," as well as text included directly on some of the pictorial images that contain the additional figures, it is possible the extra dancers were used when the dance was part of New Year rituals. Does this mean all images that include more than five dancers record ritualistic performances?

Or did some artists include the additional dancers because of the elaboration, or ornamentation, they contributed to the painted image? Once again the issue of realistic depiction as opposed to artistic license emerges. And again, the question can be turned around: did such images contribute to today's performances?

Ch'ŏyongmu is first described in a late-thirteenth-century document (*Samguk yusa*—Memorabilia of the Three Kingdoms) and subsequently in numerous records up through the twentieth century. Despite this long history, there have been at least two breaks in the tradition of performing *Ch'ŏyongmu*, both caused by the country's engagement in political battles. Each time, however, the dance was reconstructed, either from the memories of living dancers or on the basis of extant documents such as those described here.

The dance performed most often today is said to replicate a version reconstructed in 1923. Following a hiatus in court performances during the early days of the Japanese occupation (1910–45), *Ch'ŏyongmu* was reconstructed by members of the court music academy (Yiwangjik Aakpu). Because of a belief that the nature of the movements made *Ch'ŏyongmu* more suitable for men than women, and because there were no men alive who had previously performed the dance, young boy musicians were given several months of dance lessons so that they could perform. At that time, only *Ch'ŏyongmu* was restaged, not the set of three dances constituting the suite described above. Thus, claims of "authenticity" regarding the dance performed today are based on the belief that it is essentially a continuation of the dance reconstructed in 1923, which, in turn, is considered "authentic" and "accurate" because it was based on information in historical documents.[14] In subsequent years, other extant documents were consulted to refine performance details as well as to reconstruct the other two dances of the suite, but with only two exceptions, no effort was made to perform the dances as a suite.

A major departure from the independent performance of *Ch'ŏyongmu* with five masked dancers was staged in 1983. At that time *Ch'ŏyongmu* authority Kim Ch'ŏn-hŭng decided to reconstruct the entire suite.[15] Although several textual records attempted movement descriptions of each of the three dances, none described how they were linked to create the suite. Based, in part, on some of the same pictorial representations described here, Kim Ch'ŏn-hŭng staged the full suite of dances. Following the three dances in the suite, all performers joined together in a kind of grand finale. During this culminating section, women performers joined the men *Ch'ŏyongmu* performers to dance, at one point, in between each of the masked dancers and, at another point, in a circle surrounding the masked dancers. In mixing the masked male and unmasked female dancers, Kim replicated the configuration shown in a number of iconographic representations of *Ch'ŏyongmu*. Interspersing unmasked female dancers with the five masked dancers in this 1983 performance was consciously based, at least in part, on iconographic representations in historical documents, documents assumed to represent a historical reality. In addition, since no masks from former times could be located for the 1923 reconstruction, an illustration in the *Akhak kwebŏm* was used to create new ones, an image that continues to serve as the model for today's masks.[16]

The mixing of masked and unmasked dancers in a series of configurations similar to those in the 1983 reconstruction was used in 2001 when staff of the National Center for Korean Traditional Performing Arts (Kungnip Kugagwŏn) presented a reconstruction of an abbreviated version of a 1795 banquet at which documents indicate the full suite was performed.[17]

Since we know that there have been several breaks in the continuity of *Ch'ŏyongmu* performances and that the dance has been reconstructed several times specifically based on various historical documents, do we know who choreographed today's *Ch'ŏyongmu*? Although many of these documents were commissioned by the court to record actual events and are assumed to be accurate in detail, we also know that movement is extremely difficult to represent in a two-dimensional medium, either textual or pictorial. Once again, it is possible that while documenters, particularly those creating pictorial records, sought to represent the actuality of individual events, they also took artistic license. Although based on reality, they in fact may have created a kind of mythical performance moment. When people tried to reconstruct *Ch'ŏyongmu* after periods of inactivity and turned to pictorial documentation for inspiration, they developed a performance based on artistic license taken by the documents' creators—ultimately establishing a new reality based on a mythical reality. When contemporary dancers and scholars use such documents as the basis for reconstructing dances as they believe them to have been performed in the past, artists may, unwittingly, become contributors to the choreography.

Chinju kŏmmu: Court Dance or Folk Dance?

A second dance that has been the focal point of some of my research is *Chinju kŏmmu*, a knife dance from the city of Chinju that is performed by women.[18] My interest in this dance grew from curiosity relating to several distinctive movement patterns, patterns not typically found in other "traditional" dances performed today, and which are the antithesis of stereotypically appropriate Korean female deportment.[19] Among these movements are a displaying of the palms and a sequence in which the dancers tilt their torsos slightly backward and open their arms sideward, "presenting" the front surface of the torso in an explicitly open fashion (see fig. 7.3).

While virtually all sources, both written and living, trace the origin of the dance to a likely legendary story of a young boy dancer, significant debate revolves around whether today's dance is a folk dance or a court dance: whether it originated in entertainment for royalty and their guests in the central court, or among women entertainers in outlying districts.[20] In fact, there are now three quite different categories of knife

7.3. The torso-display movement of *Chinju kŏmmu*, in a performance by dancers from the National Center for Korean Traditional Performing Arts. Courtesy of Kungnip Kugagwŏn.

7.4. *Kŏmmu* (Sword Dance) illustration from *Kyobang Kayo* (Text Collection of Court Entertainers' Training Institute), 1872. Courtesy of National Library of Korea.

dances: one that retains many of the movement features of other court dances and that is classified as a "court dance" *(kungjung muyong)*; several that are quite lively, acknowledged as having been created toward the middle of the twentieth century and which are categorized as "folk dance" *(minsok muyong)* or "new dance" *(shin muyong)*;[21] and several regional variations, including *Chinju kŏmmu*. In discussing these diverse versions with colleagues, various historical documents were again cited, but this time no one ever referred to countless woodblock prints and court paintings I was discovering of knife dances. (Fig. 7.4 is one such example.)

As I tried to sort out the court/folk origin of *Chinju kŏmmu* I found myself increasingly returning to these iconographic images. With such distinctive movements in *Chinju kŏmmu* and the absence of even hints of these movements in the images, why had my Korean colleagues not used these records to point out the distinct differences between the court version of the dance and *Chinju kŏmmu?* Other images, such as those discussed here of *Ch'ŏyongmu*, captured predominant features of individual dances even though not precisely aligning with today's performance realities. Could the iconographic images of court versions of knife dances be used to support the argument that the origin of *Chinju kŏmmu* might lie elsewhere? Why were existing sources not being mined to the fullest extent to approach answers to acknowledged questions?

Were Many Dances Really So Similar?

As my interest in iconographic images grew I began to look increasingly at different representations of the same dance from different time periods.[22] What struck me was the similarity of many of the group formations in these images as well as the similarity in positions of many dancers. Why had so many artists chosen to record the same moment in the dance? And why were the positions of individual dancers identical — sometimes within the same image and sometimes in images from different time periods?

Most of these images, such as those in Figure 7.2, are woodblock prints, in some instances with color added during the initial rendering, a format used for many other contexts besides dance. Korean art historian Yi Sŏng-mi has carefully scrutinized images that record formal processional activities, such as that in the detail of Figure 7.5.[23] She believes that many of the figures were produced by multiple stampings from a single woodblock, and that after the woodblock was stamped the image was sometimes modified by hand to create *seemingly* new figures, as in Figure 7.5; discretely backgrounded beneath the layer of paint that forms the skirt of each of the women in the upper portion of this image is a pair of legs with knee breeches identical to those of the men just beneath her. This exemplifies Yi's conviction that the creator used a single block to produce all of these images and, when appropriate, transformed individual figures by hand-painting details. The similarity

7.5. Detail from the 1696 Record of the Superintendency of Royal Weddings' Painting of the Wedding of Crown Prince Kyŏngjong *(Wangsaejo Kyŏngjong karyae togam ŭigwe panch'ado)*. Photo by Yi Sŏng-mi. Courtesy of Han'guk Chŏngshin Munhwa Yŏn'guwŏn (The Academy of Korean Studies).

between individuals in a single representation of a dance suggests the possibility of a parallel technique.

Another explanation for similarities in images from different time periods lies in the training of painters. It was common practice to copy earlier images when learning requisite skills.[24] Thus, whether intentional or not, details of images created by predecessors may have found their way into the works of later artists.

I propose that in some instances the dance images were stamped out by an artist using a woodblock created by an earlier artist, and then occasionally modified by hand, and in other instances training practices contributed to the inadvertent replication of images created at another time. The implication, then, is that these images simply serve as a printed program that makes the statement "This dance was done," rather than representing an actual moment from the performance of the dance on a specific occasion. This then means that assuming such images are a kind of realistic photograph of a historical moment and relying on them for accuracy in reconstructing past choreographic details are questionable practices.

Simultaneous Performance of Different Dances?

Many court paintings, such as those in Figure 7.6, raise an issue relating to time. In these images several dances are depicted in a single "frame." If read literally, the images suggest the dances were all performed simultaneously. Is it likely this would have been the case? Would there have been a sufficiently large number of dancers available to engage so many performers at one time? Would accompanying music have been the same for all the dances shown? Would there have been a grand finale in which portions of several dances were, indeed, performed simultaneously, as in the suite reconstructed by Kim Ch'ŏn-hŭng? Or do these images show us the creations of painters who took artistic liberty with the element of time? Did they simply combine, in one frame, all or many of the dances done over a period of time at a particular event?

Did painters try to suggest the elaborateness and full content of the event in a single image rather than create separate illustrations for each dance? Does the painting, once again, serve as a kind of printed program that tells us which dances were done rather than suggest an actual moment from the event? That such images were composite renderings

7.6. Detail of hand scroll, Inaugural Celebrations Welcoming the New Governor of P'yŏngyang, attributed to Kim Hong-do, late-eighteenth/early-nineteenth century. Courtesy of National Museum of Korea.

rather than temporally realistic moments is suggested by Song Hye-jin in her analysis of a nine-panel folding screen when she states that one panel of the screen includes dances performed in 1902 at a morning banquet as well as those danced at an evening banquet.[25] In her analysis of a number of images in relation to textual descriptions of the events they record, Kim Eun-hee suggests that vertical alignment in a single frame represents the order in which dances were presented.[26]

Conclusion

Korea's history of iconographic representations of dance extends back at least as far as the sixth or seventh century A.D. to the now-famous paintings on the walls of the Dance Tomb *(Muyong ch'ong)*. Because of this long history, because in many instances court painters were officially commissioned either to document events after they transpired or to create manuals that could be used as scripts to plan and stage events, and because both dance and iconographic images are visual media, I was tempted to rely on such images as accurate depictions of a past reality. This temptation was, I believe, the same as that to which many of my Korean colleagues had succumbed. Their reliance on the veracity of the content of historical documents, however, is also attributable to a long-standing Confucian tradition of the unquestionable authority of history and the historical record.[27] Despite my colleagues' references to these documents, close examination of them to determine what they did or did not reveal was not a research concern for them. This acceptance of historical records was exemplified when, in the late 1990s, I gave a public presentation in Korea on several of the aspects of iconographic representations of *Ch'ŏyongmu* discussed here. Instead of reiterating the validity of the historical records that I was calling into question, a validity they took for granted, several individuals expressed surprise and disappointment that I had not magically discovered some new historical documents.

Korean historian Choe Yong-ho stresses the Confucian use of historical records, by their creators, to teach moral lessons. He points out that contemporary scholars believe this intent may have contributed to the distortion of reality in order to justify a particular point.[28] I do not suggest here that the creators of iconographic representations of dance sought intentionally to distort a truth. Rather, I consider that the nature of dance and the iconographic medium may have contributed to a fictionalized reality and that, until recently, adequate attention has not been paid to interpreting the documentary veracity of these records and their possible contributions to the present.

The unquestioning acceptance, or unscrutinizing examination, of iconographic records of dance is changing. Several examples of recent research point to the kinds of analysis and interpretation that have now begun, such as that mentioned above by Song Hye-jin.[29] Because of her background as a musicologist and specific interests, she pays particular attention to representations of music, but she also offers occasional comments on dance. In 1990 she shared with me a database she had developed that catalogued court paintings and the individual dances depicted in each of them. The database is an extremely valuable approach to ascertaining when different dances were performed. It includes records of more than a dozen events and information on the location of each event, gender of the audience and performers, person in whose honor the event was presented, and names of dances performed. In 1997 art historian Pak Chŏng-hye published an article in which she briefly discussed the sociocultural context in which many court paintings of the Chosŏn era (1392–1910) that included dance were created, as well as details relating to some of the events they recorded.[30] This was followed in 2000 by her book, based on her doctoral dissertation, which elaborated on the topic in significant detail.[31] In 1999 Sŏng Ki-suk, a dance researcher and writer, authored a chapter in which she examined one important image from the Dance Tomb.[32] Besides the fact that it was written by an individual trained in dance, this chapter is noteworthy because its analysis of the relationships between figures in the image is based on information contained in archaeological reports about the site as well as on Sŏng's own reasoned interpretation.[33] In 2002 graduate student Kim Eun-hee compared movements represented in sixteen images of *Ch'ŏyongmu* to movements in the dance performed today.[34] Her work is important because it is the first by a Korean researcher that is rooted in movement analysis, and it points out the anatomical impossibility of positions shown in some images.

Growing concern with understanding more fully how to interpret historical iconographic records in the context of Korean dance, as well as an interest in the views of someone not native to the culture, is reflected in attention to some of my own work. This has taken the form of an invitation to contribute an article on the topic to a Korean dance journal, and to contribute an essay on related ideas to a book, published by the National Center for Korean Traditional Performing Arts (Kungnip Kugagwŏn), of court paintings of music and dance.[35] In both instances the material is published in Korean as well as English, and the content focuses on broad issues relating to the interpretation of images specifically in the context of Korean dance; analysis of individual images serves to exemplify points raised rather than to treat any individual one in depth.

Although some issues described here are unique to Korean dance and artists who represent it, they are of broader concern. Thomas Heck tells us that "art usually imitates *art* more than it imitates life" (emphasis in original), and cites an example from theater that points to paintings as commodities: replication resulting from the selling of wares rather than the recording of actual events.[36] And French painter Edgar Degas expresses his belief in the importance of artistic license: "A painting is above all a product of the artist's imagination, it must never be a copy. . . . the air one sees in the paintings of the masters is not the air one breathes."[37] In another statement he remarks, "a painting requires a little mystery, some vagueness . . . the fantastic; when the i's are always dotted and the t's crossed, it gets boring in the end."[38]

It could be argued that these points are irrelevant to Korean court painting, in which artists were specifically tasked with accuracy. Indeed one Korean writer describes court images as "photo-journalistic," commenting on the dispatch of court painters to areas struck by natural disasters so that their paintings could assist officials in assessing damages, and to the imposition, in 1431, of punishment on painters "who failed to draw an exact representation of a dragon for the box of a diplomatic letter which was to be sent to China."[39] But because dance exists in time as well as in three dimensions of space and is not a physical object, representations of it have unique problems of interpretation, and they must be evaluated especially carefully.

At the beginning of the twenty-first century, issues such as those raised here, as well as others, were being addressed from multiple geographic perspectives by members of the substudy group on dance iconography of the Ethnochoreology Study Group of the International Council for Traditional Music. At meetings in 2002, 2003, and 2004, participants focused on issues relating to dances in Poland, Greece, Italy, Hungary, Tonga, and Malaysia.[40]

That events of the past contribute to the present is widely acknowledged. That historical documents represent *the* truth is increasingly being questioned. And that iconographic representations of dance in Korea, or elsewhere, can be assumed to be any more valid than verbal documents is now an issue. It is important that the extraordinary quantity of iconographic representations of dance in Korea be critically analyzed for how they relate to other forms of documentation, realistic feasibility of human movement, and relationships to contemporary practices.[41] In Korea the tension between history and ethnography plays itself out not only in coming to grips with trying to understand events of the past, but with interpreting the historical records of that past, regardless of their format, and ultimately in understanding how the past and its records contribute to the present.

NOTES

For Korean authors who have published in English and used alternate roman-
izations for their names, the spelling used in the original publication is retained.
In these instances, McCune-Reischauer spellings are provided in brackets.
When such authors have published in both Korean and English, the McCune-
Reischauer spelling is used for Korean-language publications.

1. I am grateful for research funding assistance at various times to the Ko-
rean Culture and Arts Foundation (Han'guk Yesul Munhwa Chinhǔngwǒn),
Academy for Korean Studies (Han'guk Chǒngshin Munhwa Yǒn'guwǒn),
Korean-American Educational Foundation (Fulbright Program), International
Cultural Society of Korea (Han'guk Kukche Munhwa Hyŏphoe), and the Uni-
versity of Hawai'i at Manoa's Center for Korean Studies.

2. I use the terms "colleagues" and "consultants" to refer to the many different kinds of people with whom I came into contact during my research. In
some instances these individuals were peers: dance teachers, professional performers, and university professors. In other instances they were senior to me:
established scholars of various aspects of Korean culture or master teachers of
specific Korean dances. All of these kinds of people contributed in meaningful
ways to my knowledge and understanding of Korean dance. Hence, I use the
terms interchangeably here.

3. I refer here only to Korean associates because scholarly research on Korean dance by non-Koreans is extremely minimal, and to my knowledge none
of it deals with issues of interpreting the past and its records.

4. My use of "iconography" and "iconographic representations" is based
on issues presented here indicating that such things as paintings, sculptures,
and other "pictorial" images constitute symbolic representations, even if the
meanings of these symbols are debatable.

Korea was once a unified country; hence early documents come from a period in which there was a single nation. In 1953, however, the peninsula was divided. References to contemporary performances reflect practices in the Republic of Korea, or what is often referred to as South Korea.

5. Susan A. Manning, *Ecstasy and the Demon: Feminism and Nationalism in the
Dance of Mary Wigman* (Berkeley: University of California Press, 1993), 12.

6. Georgiana Gore, "Present Texts, Past Voices: The Formation of Contemporary Representations of West African Dance," in *20th Symposium Proceedings, August 19–26 1998, Istanbul, Turkey, International Council for Traditional Music,
Study Group on Ethnochoreology,* ed. Frank Hall and Irene Loutzaki. Special edition
of *Dans Müzik Kültür Folklora Doğru* (Istanbul: Boğaziçi University Folklore Club,
2000), 56.

7. Joan L. Erdman, "Dance Discourses: Rethinking the History of the 'Oriental Dance,'" in *Moving Words: Re-writing Dance*, ed. Gay Morris (London: Routledge, 1996), 288–305.

8. The discussion in this section is based on Judy Van Zile, "Resources for Knowing the Past: Issues in Interpreting Iconographic Representations of Korean Dance," in In-hwa Sŏ, Pak Chŏng-hye, and Judy Van Zile, *Chosŏn shidae chinyŏn chinch'an chinhapyŏngp'ung / Folding Screens of Court Banquets and Congratulatory Ceremonies in the Joseon Dynasty* (Seoul, Korea: National Center for Korean Traditional Performing Arts, 2000), 267–78; Judy Van Zile, *Perspectives on Korean Dance* (Middletown, Conn.: Wesleyan University Press, 2001), 65–109. "Ch'ŏyong" is the name of an individual upon whom the dance is based. "Mu" simply means "dance." Hence, the dance's title is "The Dance of Ch'ŏyong."

9. The royal court officially ended with the beginning of the Japanese occupation of Korea in 1910.

10. A concise summary of selected research in this area and some of the major issues can be found in Thomas Heck, with contributions from Robert Erenstein, M. A. Katritzky, Frank Peeters, A. William Smith, and Lyckle de Vries, *Picturing Performance: The Iconography of the Performing Arts in Concept and Practice* (New York: University of Rochester Press, 1999). Literature dealing specifically with dance includes, for example, Lillian Lawler, *The Dance in Ancient Greece* (Middletown, Conn.: Wesleyan University Press, 1964); Tilman Seebass, "Iconography and Dance Research," *Yearbook for Traditional Music* 23 (1991): 33–51; Kapila Vatsyayan, *Classical Indian Dance in Literature and the Arts* (New Delhi: Sangeet Natak, 1968); and Kapila Vatsyayan, *Dance in Indian Painting* (New Delhi: Abhinav, 1982). A related work dealing in depth with music is Bonnie C. Wade, *Imaging Sound: An Ethnomusicological Study of Music, Art, and Culture in Mughal India* (Chicago: University of Chicago Press, 1998).

11. This description is found in the *Akhak kwebŏm* (Guide to the Study of Music), an important fifteenth-century court treatise dealing with both dance and music.

12. Jeong-hye Park [Chŏng-hye Pak], "The Court Music and Dance in the Royal Banquet Paintings of the Chosŏn Dynasty," *Korea Journal* 37, no. 3 (Autumn 1997): 140.

13. Portions of the discussion in this section are based on Judy Van Zile, "Nuga Ch'ŏyongmutŭl Mandŭlŏnga?" [Who Choreographed *Ch'ŏyongmu?*], *Ch'um Chisŏng: Thoughts on Dance Theory and Criticism* 2 (2005): 146–158, and Van Zile, *Perspectives on Korean Dance*, 98–109.

14. Authenticity, which in Korea is most often equated with age and an adherence to something assumed to be correct, is an important issue because of Korea's National Treasure System; the government officially recognizes what it considers to be important cultural manifestations and provides funding to

contribute to their perpetuation. For discussions of this system see Keith Howard, "Preservation or Change? The Sponsorship of Folk Music in Chindo within the Intangible Cultural Asset System," in *Papers of the 5th International Conference on Korean Studies: Korean Studies, Its Tasks and Perspectives*, vol. 2 (Unjungdong, Korea: Academy of Korean Studies, 1988), 935–58; Keith Howard, "Preservation and Presentation of Korean Intangible Cultural Assets," in *Methodologies for the Preservation of Intangible Heritage* (Seoul: Korean National Commission for UNESCO and the Office of the Cultural Properties of the Republic of Korea, 1996), 85–114; Judy Van Zile, "How the Korean Government Preserves Its Cultural Heritage," *Korean Culture* 8, no. 2 (Summer 1987): 18–19; Judy Van Zile, "From Ritual to Entertainment and Back Again: The Case of *Ch'ŏyongmu*, a Korean Dance," in *Dance, Ritual and Music*, Proceedings of the 18th Symposium of the Study Group on Ethnochoreology, the International Council for Traditional Music (Warsaw, Poland: Polish Society for Ethnochoreology Institute of Art—Polish Academy of Sciences, 1995): 133–40; and Van Zile, *Perspectives on Korean Dance*, 110–47.

15. Kim Ch'ŏn-hŭng is one of the individuals recognized through the government's National Treasure System to perpetuate *Ch'ŏyongmu*.

16. Ch'ŏn-hŭng Kim, interview with author, 21 October 1990.

17. This performance is preserved in the videotape *Music of Peace, Dream of Dynasty: Royal Court Banquet Music* (Seoul: National Center for Korean Traditional Performing Arts in conjunction with Arirang Television, 2001).

18. For a discussion of *Chinju kŏmmu* see Van Zile, *Perspectives on Korean Dance*, 110–47.

19. I use the term "traditional" here because, although it is vague and debated in scholarly dance circles, it is used in Korea *(chŏnt'ong)* to identify older dances that evolved before significant Western influence and that clearly bear a Korean identity. For a discussion of Korean dance terminology see Van Zile, *Perspectives on Korean Dance*, 30–50. For a discussion of stereotypically Korean female movements and their manifestation in *Chinju kŏmmu* see Judy Van Zile, "For Men or Women: The Case of *Chinju Kŏmmu*, a Sword Dance from South Korea," *Choreography and Dance* 5, no. 1 (1998): 53–70, and Van Zile, *Perspectives on Korean Dance*, 143–47.

20. The term "folk dance" is considerably debated in scholarly dance circles. See, for example, Theresa J. Buckland, "Definitions of Folk Dance: Some Explorations," *Folk Music Journal* 4, no. 3 (1983): 315–32. I retain the term here because it is the translation of a term *(minsok muyong)* commonly used by Korean dance researchers.

21. For a discussion of "new dance" *(shin muyong)* see Van Zile, *Perspectives on Korean Dance*, 39–41; Haeree Choi, "*Ch'angjak Ch'um*: History and Nature of a Contemporary Korean Dance Genre" (M.A. thesis, University of Hawai'i, 1995), 18–21, 32–38.

22. Portions of the discussion in this and the following section are based on Van Zile, "Resources for Knowing the Past."

23. Sŏng-mi Yi in Sŏng-mi Yi, Shin-hang Kang, and Song-ok Yu, *Changsŏgak sojang karye togam ŭigwe* [Official Documents, in the Royal Library of the Chosŏn Dynasty, of the Department of Royal Weddings] (Kyŏnggi-do: Han'guk Chŏngshin Munhwa Yŏn'guwŏn [Academy of Korean Studies], 1994), 34–116. See especially plate 201.

24. Keith Pratt, *Korean Painting* (Hong Kong: Oxford University Press, 1995), 21.

25. Hye-jin Song, "Iminnyŏn 'chinyŏn pyŏngp'ung' 9-p'ok ŭi kŭrim" [Paintings from the Nine-Panel Folding Screen Created in the Year of Imin], *Kugagwŏn nonmunjip* [Journal of the National Center for Korean Traditional Performing Arts], December 1989, 18.

26. Eun-hee Kim, "An Iconographical Study of Korean Dance: The Pictorial Representation of *Ch'ŏyongmu* in the Eighteenth Century Chosŏn Dynasty" (M.A. thesis, University of Hawai'i, 2002), 67–68.

27. Robert C. Provine comments on this with regard to music: "[E]arly Chosŏn writings on rites and music often quote from Chinese texts of earlier times, in line with the traditional Confucian method of compilation with reference to authoritative precedent." *Essays on Sino-Korean Musicology* (Seoul: Il Ji Sa, 1988), 105.

28. Yong-ho Choe, telephone conversation with author, 11 November 2000.

29. Song, "Iminnyŏn 'chinyŏn pyŏngp'ung' 9-p'ok ŭi kŭrim," 93–119.

30. Park, "Court Music and Dance."

31. Chŏng-hye Pak, *Chosŏn sidae kungjung kirokhwa yŏn'gu* [A Study of Court Documentary Paintings in the Chosŏn Dynasty] (Seoul: Iljisa, 2000).

32. Ki-suk Sŏng, *Han'guk chŏnt'ong ch'um yŏn'gu* [A Study of Traditional Korean Dance] (Seoul: Hyŏndae Mihaksa, 1999).

33. For an English-language summary of Sŏng's analysis and a slightly different interpretation of a portion of one image see Van Zile, "Resources for Knowing the Past."

34. Kim, "An Iconographical Study of Korean Dance."

35. Van Zile, "Nuga Ch'ŏyongmutŭl Mandŭlŏnga?"; Van Zile, "Resources for Knowing the Past."

36. Heck, *Picturing Performance*, 5, 79–80.

37. Edgar Degas quoted in Paul-André Lemoisne, *Degas et son œuvre*, 5 vols. (New York: Garland, 1984), 1:100. Originally published in 4 vols. in Paris, 1946–49. Translation here provided by Jill De Vonyar.

38. Edgar Degas quoted in Georges Jeanniot, "Souvenirs sur Degas" (part 2), *Revue Universelle* 55, no. 15 (1 November 1933): 281. Translation here provided by Jill De Vonyar.

39. Sung-jin Yang, "Hwawons Composed Realistic Works," *Hangookilbo* (12 October 1998).

40. In the early years of the group, discussions focused on methods for cataloguing images. Beginning in 2002 discussions shifted to issues in interpreting images.

41. A well-known image in the Dance Tomb shows what are assumed to be performers in an anatomically impossible position (see Van Zile, "Resources for Knowing the Past"). Colleagues have continually expressed surprise when I pointed this out, never having considered this detail. And Eun-hee Kim ("An Iconographical Study of Korean Dance") is, I believe, the first to raise questions of anatomical possibility in images of court dances.

8

Romani Dance Event in Skopje, Macedonia

Research Strategies, Cultural Identities, and Technologies

ELSIE IVANCICH DUNIN

The longitudinal study described in this chapter presents an ideal opportunity to examine ethnographic and historical dimensions in relation to a specific dance event, and also to reflect upon the context of the pioneering academic development of dance ethnology at the University of California, Los Angeles (UCLA) in which the research was pursued. Several histories intersect in this personalized narrative: influences upon research, such as the changing means of documentation available to the dance ethnographer, the emergence of a sociopolitical Romani cultural identity during the years in which the study was conducted, and generational interpretations of a continuing annual dance event. My initial purpose was to document dance events in their social contexts among the Roms living in Skopje, Macedonia, in 1967.[1] This became a foundation for a methodology with multilevel contacts in multiple time frames. Tangible visual data provided a comparative view in continuities and changes of a dance event within the continuities and changes of the social, cultural, and political fabric of an otherwise marginally recognized population. The study became a historical record, but given the involvement of dancing bodies in particular spaces, it also provided a basis for uncovering layers of social history that had been implicit through the dancing occasions.

Dance Ethnology as a University Discipline

"Dance ethnology," "ethnochoreology," or "dance anthropology" had not yet appeared as a university academic subject within a dance curriculum when I was a graduate student in the early 1960s. The founding of the Department of Dance at UCLA in 1962 under the umbrella of a College of Fine Arts with three other departments—music, theater, and art—was in itself an innovative curricular development. The college within the university environment provided a major step toward recognizing dance as an arts discipline, with its own body of knowledge. Prior to 1962, various dancing classes (folk dance, social and square dance, modern dance, tap dance) were offered as "body activity" classes within the Department of Physical Education, which trained students as teachers for sports programs. Within the newly established Department of Dance under the leadership of Dr. Alma Hawkins, a visionary in dance education, an undergraduate or graduate student could focus on dance and dancing (albeit creative dancing) and earn a Bachelor of Arts and then a Master of Arts in dance. The emphasis in the curriculum was to produce a broadly educated dancer/performer/choreographer/teacher who could pursue a profession in dance or in advanced dance education. One of the required courses of all dance students was the history of dance, but the emphasis here was on a survey of "art" dance seeped in Western cultures of Ancient Greece, medieval, Renaissance, and Baroque dance styles leading to dance as a performance art in contemporary times. Also in the earliest years of the 1960s only a beginning and advanced "folk dance" class offered a preliminary experience of "social" dances from an international array of countries, but mainly examples from northwestern Europe.

I entered this new Department of Dance as an older graduate student with a set of experiences differing from that of most American-born dance students: first as a child in Los Angeles growing up in South Slavic "ethnic" communities (Croatian, Serbian, and Slovenian) that offered dancing and music at most every community- or family-sponsored social event (almost a weekly occurrence), and then as a young adult performing in Skopje, Macedonia (then part of Yugoslavia), with the professional Tanec Folk Dance and Music Ensemble.[2] After a period of looking after my two young children, I returned to academia into the newly formed graduate dance program of UCLA, to expand my knowledge about dance and to prepare myself for teaching dance in higher education. I realized with Allegra Fuller Snyder, a colleague who had also just returned to academia, that there was a major lack in the literature about dance beyond ballet, modern dance, and Western history of dance. We were seeking a broader knowledge about dance in other parts of the world and to learn about the social and ritual contexts of dancing.[3] Among readings, the most satisfying was in a newly published and seminal article by Gertrude Prokosch Kurath.[4] I was inspired, for Kurath had recognized the Yugoslav-based Janković sisters and their contributions to the description of dances, their creation of a dance notation system, and their attempts at structural analysis. Kurath's article expanded my thinking toward possible studies among populations located in Slavic areas of southeastern Europe, where I had already had personal experiences. I began to consider the possibility of recording and describing dancing events rather than recording only the dances as found in many field collections and publications of dance, such as those collated for use by teachers of "folk dance" classes in physical education curricula. Philosophically within the Department of Dance, all dancing was considered an art form. I began to be strongly aware of a difference in that "art" dance was "formally organized" and intended to be performed for an audience, whereas the social forms that I encountered as a child within the South Slavic community events were unrehearsed and spontaneous in participation. Were these dances art? The kind of dancing that I performed with the professional dance ensemble in Macedonia was "art," but the dances were derived from spontaneous social forms. The extent of their adaptation for the staged performance was dependent upon the "choreographer," who was not of the community from where the dances were taken. The dances were out of their social context and became crafted as "art."

Seminal writings for studying or understanding dance learned through field participation and observation had not yet appeared. Thinking about dance in social contexts came later.[5] My models in the 1960s came empirically by way of UCLA graduate courses in folklore and ethnomusicology and readings in anthropology. "Going into the field" was a method of study in all three disciplines. Anthropological ethnography recognized dancing within a culture, but there was no

mention of dancing characteristics, structural form, the body movement, numbers of dancers, and so on. "People danced." Furthermore,
the anthropological fieldwork tended to be within Native American,
African, or Asian groups of peoples who were unfamiliar to my own
living experiences and to the search for understandings of my own experiences. Folklorists, such as the head of the Program of Folklore at
UCLA, Wayland Hand, conducted fieldwork in Western-based cultures, but these folklorists were principally interested in the "oral traditions" and made extensive comparative studies of oral texts independent of their social contexts. The texts as products were analyzed and
compared with each other. Ethnomusicology at UCLA (a fledgling field
of study under the leadership of Mantle Hood) was the closest model to
my dance interests: the music was recorded within a cultural context, as
far away as Indonesia, but also closer to Los Angeles, in northern Mexico and southwestern United States. The dancing that was accompanied by the music, however, was usually not considered by the young
graduate ethnomusicologists. They too were not prepared to understand the body movement or interrelationship of the music to the dancing. With dance at UCLA as a newly recognized field of study, there
was clearly a need to conduct our own fieldwork with a focus on dance
within its social and cultural contexts.

Who are the people who do the dancing? When? Where? How?
Why? At the time of my graduate studies at UCLA, ethnographic descriptions answering these questions for peoples from southeastern Europe were rare. Joel Halpern, a young anthropologist who was at UCLA
before me and who had done fieldwork in Yugoslavia for a doctoral dissertation, published *A Serbian Village* but like most other anthropologists,
he did not include dancing in any of his analysis of lifestyle.[6] As a result
of my childhood experiences in Los Angeles and those as an adult performing in Macedonia, I knew that dancing was a vital expressive activity in the geographical area of his studies. There was, however, another
unexpected and important outcome of Halpern's time in Yugoslavia in
the 1950s. The chancellor of UCLA had assigned Halpern to acquire
publications for the university during his fieldwork in Yugoslavia. Halpern with his anthropological background collected all forms of publications, old and new, and created the largest and fullest collection of publications in humanities, history, and folklore from that part of Europe. I
had at my disposal an unequalled fund of written materials from pre-
Yugoslavia and the then current Yugoslavia, a collection not available

anywhere else outside Yugoslavia. At the time of my graduate studies, I was not aware of this wealth but learned of its significance in following years.

Also owing to the new program in dance at the university, there was a policy of enriching the collection of dance literature for the UCLA Research Library.[7] Available at the time were early-twentieth-century published collections of "folk dances" particularly from northwestern and western Europe; the 1950s international handbook series of folk dances from many countries in Europe;[8] the International Folk Dance and Song Society yearbooks that happened to include Felix Hoerburger's folk dance survey and his suggestion of first and second existence of "folk dance."[9] His survey reinforced existing emphasis on the dance product, rather than the ethnographic information about the dancing contexts. The models for "folk dance" study were limited to the "product" and not the context of the dancing. In the geographical area of the South Slavs,[10] eight volumes of "folk dances" *(narodne igre)* were published by sisters Ljubica and Danica Janković between 1934 and 1962, a full set not available anywhere else in the United States at that time (thanks to Halpern's collection).[11] Their and other descriptions of dances from all parts of Yugoslavia through the 1950s produced an extensive resource, but I was interested in understanding the social context of the dancing of these dances and not just the described dance product. Another area of unique expansion in the library supplemented the course on the folklore of the Gypsies taught by Visiting Professor Walter Starkie. The UCLA Research Library added readings and studies on the Romani peoples, also not equaled at any other university. In an assignment for his class, I used this collection in a bibliographic search on dancing of the Roms, and I saw that almost nothing was written about their dancing or their dancing contexts, even though the "Gypsies" were reputed to be a dancing culture.

New recording technology had become available at this time, which facilitated understanding of how dancing forms continue or change over time.[12] Portable reel-to-reel audio tape recorders and hand-held 16-millimeter film cameras with portable battery packs revolutionized the ability to make tangible the study of a whole dancing context, rather than needing to extract and describe the dances (the product) independently of the context. Even a single person could record spontaneous dancing during social events. No longer was a multiperson crew necessary to invade the context for recording purposes. Furthermore, there

8.1. Republic of Macedonia in southeastern Europe after 1991.

was less dependence upon the vagrancies of memory and less drilling native dancers to perform their dances repeatedly (and out of context) with the objective of notating the dance.

With the personal experience of growing up dancing in "ethnic" events in the United States, I was particularly sensitized to immigrant groups and their descendants. My questions became polarized toward a comparative view of emigrant and immigrant dancing customs. Both the South Slavic and Gypsy communities in Los Angeles sparked my inquiries into comparative continuities and changes in dances and their dancing. Serbian Gypsy families happened to live nearby the part of the city where my family lived, so that I had an awareness of their mixed Serbian-Romani language and familiar customs. Then while a university student, I had the opportunity to attend their family events, which included open-circle chain *kolo* dancing and solo dancing.[13] Eventually, funded by the United States Department of Health, Welfare and Education, in 1967 I traveled to southeastern Europe for several months, supplied with a 16-millimeter film camera, rolls of film, a reel-to-reel tape recorder, and a still camera with an attachable telephoto lens. Little did I realize that this first professional dance ethnology project would become a basis for a longitudinal study. The tantalizing excitement of my first experience at a massive social event with dancing and music motivated me to "revisit" the community and its multiday celebration of St. George's Day (Gjurgjevden in Macedonian), also known as Coming of Summer (Erdelezi in Turkish), in Skopje, Macedonia. This annual festivity (hereafter referred to as St. George's Day) was celebrated exclusively by the Roms in Skopje and offered an ongoing base from which to note selected markers of continuities and changes. I conducted an audiovisual documentation of the multiday event (5–9 May) six times over a thirty-year period: ten-year intervals in 1967, 1977, 1987, 1997, with two interim years, 1995 and 1996. The hundreds of still photographs along with movement documentation on film and videotape of this single event over a span of years provides a tangible means to study this event against a background of sociocultural and sociopolitical changes.

Documenting Romani Events in 1967

Because of my memories of many Gypsies in Skopje during the time I spent with the Tanec professional dance and music ensemble, I had decided to begin my documentation of dancing within social events in Skopje. I knew that I could "find" Gypsies in that area even though I did not know very much about this particular community. Although I had planned to arrive in time for a national holiday (1–2 May), with the expectation that there might be dance and music, followed by the celebration of Macedonian Orthodox Easter (discouraged during the Communist regime, nevertheless observed on a limited basis), I was not aware of the overlapping of the St. George holiday dates that these Gypsies celebrate. After watching dancing at the crossroads in a Gypsy neighborhood and making visits to several other neighborhoods in the city during early May, I was told that I should go especially to the hill adjacent to the old Gypsy quarter, Topaana, on Tuesday afternoon, 9 May. I did and was awed by what I witnessed. Imagine a mass of about 10,000 Gypsies on a green and wooded hillside, dressed in their finest—the women in pantaloons made of twelve meters of colorful lightweight fabric with matching billowing sleeves and delicately decorated headscarves—and at least twelve bands of musicians scattered throughout the hillside,

8.2. Women dancing in holiday dress of *čintiani* (pantaloons), 9 May 1967. Photo by Elsie Ivancich Dunin.

each accompanying from twenty to seventy dancers. The sounds of *zurla* (double-reed wind instruments) and *tapan* (large but portable double-headed drums struck on one side by a stick and on the other with a type of twig), saxophones, tambourines, violins, accordions, and bagpipes all intermingled into a din of rhythmic sounds. This was an extraordinary participatory social dance event. Families feasted on foods brought from home, while sitting on brightly woven rugs spread out along the hillside, and with hundreds of musicians and dancers, negotiating their space between these family groupings. Furthermore, based on the manner of dress and body behaviors, I noted that there were almost no "outsiders" (non-Gypsies) at the event. By sunset, the hillside was empty; the families had returned to their homes to continue socializing among themselves. Unknown to me at the time, I had observed the most significant annual event of the Gypsies in Skopje.

Over the next months, I filmed and recorded dancing at several social events, mainly family celebrations of weddings, circumcisions, and naming of babies. There were basically three types of dancing—two in public, that is, outside of the home, in the streets, or in another public setting, and one that was restricted to private contexts. One public type of dancing was performed by people, linked by a handhold either at shoulder height or down at the sides, moving in open circles that progressed in a counterclockwise direction. The other public type was performed in linked handholds as the dancers paraded frontally, using a repetitive step, through the streets in forward-moving lines. Such public open-circle dancing might have included anywhere from three or four to thirty or forty dancers performing a repetitive step pattern. The music accompaniment consisted of *tapan* and *zurla* or a small band in some combination of clarinet, accordion, *darabuka* (clay-based hourglass-shaped hand drum), trumpet, or saxophone (electrified instruments had not yet been introduced). The rhythmic meter was usually an uneven pattern, identifiable by a combination of slow and quick beats: slow, quick, quick ($\frac{7}{8}$), or quick, quick, quick, slow ($\frac{9}{8}$). Dancing to one melody could last several minutes, and a medley of tunes might last up to a half hour or more. The tempo of the music was usually moderate, but quickened when the musicians warned the dancers that the piece would soon end. At the right end of the chain, the leader could be female or male.

The other type of dancing took place at gender-exclusive parties in private settings where dancers took turns performing the solo form known as *čoček*. The solo was danced only during private segregated occasions, such as part of the five-day wedding cycle, or a three-day cycle for the circumcision of a son, or at the naming of a newborn child. During the event, every female at the party was expected to rise up from her floor-seated position to dance a type of "belly-dance" producing a vertical up-and-down movement of the abdomen (in Labanotation terms this is a somersaulting movement of the pelvis); the arms are moved in an improvised range at about shoulder level, with snapping fingers, while the feet are stepped in place to the rhythm of the music — usually in a $\frac{9}{8}$ meter. The music accompaniment was by a hired Romani woman, who sang and held a tambourine in an upright position with her left hand, while tapping the skin with her right hand; more affluent families used a phonograph player for 45-rpm records of Turkish melodies in $\frac{9}{8}$ meter. This type of solo dancing tended to occur at all-night parties, involving light drinking (sweet liquor and beer) and feasting. Men and women partied in separate rooms, and each with their own musicians or phonograph players. Young children, who would also be encouraged to dance the *čoček*, joined the female members of the family.

Because of the large numbers of Gypsy families in Skopje, there were multiple events most every week. Since the dancing during these events tended to be "public" (that is, in the streets), there was ample opportunity to watch along with local Gypsy spectators and, when I had been given permission, to record with still photographs or film footage. In addition, whenever I was invited to join the dancing line, I took advantage of dancing next to other females and tried to emulate their style. I did not feel that it would be appropriate to dance next to a male or to lead a chain of dancers. Although nonfamily members could participate in the public dancing, it was, of course, noticed when this "Amerikanka" participated. Although I loved dancing with them, I only participated when invited. While attending the private events with *čoček* dancing, however, I was expected—and even urged—to dance, because every female at the event danced. No excuse was valid. If one did not feel well enough to dance, then one did not go to the party.

Wherever I learned of an event in Skopje and later elsewhere in the Balkans, I brought my cameras and tape recorder. Since I had use of a car, it was possible to be mobile. As a result, I experienced and recorded an overview of Gypsy dancing in southeastern Europe preceding the arrival of "Rom" advocates (particularly from England) to Gypsy suburbs and communities. This was still a time when Gypsies had not yet been sensitized to a "Rom" identity in place of the degrading identity of "Cigan." In most countries, sizeable Gypsy populations were not even included in official census statistics; this was the case in Yugoslavia until 1971. The Gypsies had no political representation, no literature, and very few studies had been done about them. The events that I attended and the contacts that I made were all achieved through personal references.

Although this was a very fulfilling learning experience, with exposure to various styles of dancing among the Gypsy populations in much of southeastern Europe, I was not able to proceed with my underlying interest of comparative continuity and change of immigrant and emigrant contexts owing to my lack of proficiency in the various dialects of Romani. My focus then shifted to Croatian communities with whose language and traditions I was more familiar. It was this latter study that brought me back to southeastern Europe for an extended time of research during a university sabbatical leave in 1976–77. Remembering

8.3. Women dancing in holiday dress of skirts, 8 May 1977. Photo by Elsie Ivancich Dunin.

my 1967 experience of the extraordinary St. George's Day in Skopje, however, I planned to revisit Skopje in May (but now with portable video equipment) to observe and record this event again. So it was not until ten years later that I realized it would be possible to take an event such as St. George's Day and compare it with itself. Although I continued with the Croatian research, the St. George's Day event turned out to be a long-term field study.

Romani History and Identity in Skopje

Although the population of the Skopje-based Roms is one of the largest in Europe, there is scant written information about their history in Skopje or in Macedonia. The chronicling of Roms into Europe begins in Constantinople (Istanbul) in the tenth century. The earliest record of "Egipchani" (Egyptians) in former Yugoslav lands is in Dubrovnik (Ragusa) in 1362.[14] By the middle of the sixteenth century there are more numerous records, including a count of Cigan (Gypsy) households in Skopje.[15] During the Ottoman Turkish advances into Europe, there are notings of Gypsies who provided blacksmith and music services for the Turkish army garrisons in Skopje, Beograd (Belgrade), and other centers.[16] In Skopje, the Romani presence began at least by the fourteenth century. The Roms in Skopje are not nomads, but "settled" peoples with traditional occupations. Itinerant Roms *(čergari)* do come and go through Yugoslavia, but in the twentieth century at least, they did not integrate or intermarry with the sedentary Skopje Romani population.

Two sets of census records, almost a hundred years apart, are significant markers of the count of Roms in Skopje. Statistics gathered in 1891 list 1,920 Cigani (240 houses) in Skopje, making the Roms the third largest population in Skopje at the end of the nineteenth century.[17] A hundred years later, the official 1994 census shows that the Roms continued to be the third largest population in Skopje, with 20,070 (4.5 percent of Skopje population), while in 1997 they were the fourth largest population in the Republic of Macedonia, following the Macedonian, Albanian, and Turkish language groups.[18] Although there have been shifts in the size of other nationalities, the Roms have maintained their proportionate numbers since the late nineteenth century.

When I went to Skopje in 1967 to document dances of the Gypsies during their social events, the old Gypsy quarter, known generally as Topaana, was in a state of flux. Due to the disastrous earthquake four years earlier, when many families had suffered damage to their homes, they were placed in temporary housing on the safer outskirts of the city. Within four years a new suburb, Šuto Orizari, was under construction north of the city, and families were given plots of land and financial credit toward building new homes. Hundreds of Romani families began to resettle in this suburb, and although the St. George's event began to be observed in both Romani settlements of Topaana and Šuto Orizari, the height of the event on 9 May, with its music and dancing, continued to take place on the hillside near the older community in Topaana.

During the early 1970s advocates of human rights for Roms initiated changes in self-identity. The First Romany Congress held in London in 1971, and the Second Romany Congress in Geneva in 1978, firmly established the shift in self-identity terms from "Cigan," "Gypsy," and "Gitano," considered to be degrading terms, to Rom or Roma, a word taken from their Romani language; a tri-colored (red, blue, and green) flag with a centered wagon wheel was designed to represent the

8.4. Holiday dress—only one dance leader in pantaloons, 5 May 1987. Photo by Elsie Ivancich Dunin.

Rom; and a popular song "Gjelem Gjelem" was selected as an anthem.[19] The 1971 census added "Roma" (instead of "cigani") as one of the multinational categories in Yugoslavia. The growth of Skopje's industries after the earthquake provided opportunities for employment, resulting in scheduled work hours and scheduled public transportation, which in turn influenced the timing in the celebration of family events that included music and dancing. Greater educational opportunities were provided, leading to developing professionals and political leaders, who became influential in later decades.

Beginning in the 1980s the community in Šuto Orizari became more involved politically, both internationally and locally. Romani leadership and performing artists from Skopje were invited to participate in the next World Congress (held in Sweden), and a Romani festival and scholarly meeting was held in Chandigar, India, where Prime Minister Indira Gandhi embraced the Roms as peoples from India. In the late 1970s and 1980s, the newly composed Romani music in Skopje included Indian music themes (taken from Indian-produced films shown in Skopje).

Macedonia became independent from the "former" Yugoslavia in 1991, but the political and economic situation was tense owing to border closings caused by Greece in the south and Serbia in the north, followed by tensions with Kosovo Albanians. The seeds of education that had been sown in the 1970s, however, provided a growth of leadership from within the Romani community. For the first time there was Romani representation in the democratic state of the Republic of Macedonia, with political parties and political self-determination in the government. Romani television and radio stations were established by and directed by Roms, with dissemination of Romani news in Romany language causing language standardization and programming that provided affirmation of Romani identity.

The entire Romani population, however, continued to be involved with the St. George's Day celebration. There were changes in the melodies (more Indian themes), the addition of electrified instrumentation, and less use of the "traditional" dress in public. Dancing and music continued all five days.[20] As music bands became more and more dependent upon electricity, only *tapan* and *zurla* instruments continued to accompany dancing during the St. George's Day event in the next two decades. Dancing and costuming (festive dress of the past) have become identity markers of their community. The pantaloons and colorful headscarves that were once worn daily, only to be embellished with "new" outfits for St. George's Day celebration, weddings, and other family events, now are reserved for wear during a part of the wedding or for special occasions that display a "Romani" identity to non-Roms, such as political rallies and stage performances. *Čoček* solo dancing has become a staged identity for Roms. In 1967 the *čoček* was a "behind closed doors" dance, which by 1997 had become a public performance dance as an identity marker with amateur organized dance ensembles. Young people see their "costumes" as making a statement or symbolic show of the past, but their dancing continues to be a reality of the present. The "public" open circle chain dancing is still a community-wide social form, and everyone still knows how to participate in the dancing. The solo *čoček* dancing has become more specialized. It is acceptable for this dancing to be done in public, and it is this dance that is the Romani identity marker for music and dance ensembles who give professional staged performances—now an "art" dance rather than a spontaneous social form.

Against the background of these major sociopolitical changes among the Skopje Roms since my recording of their events in 1967, the five-day holiday continued to be celebrated as the most important event in a year's cycle of social activities. "We must celebrate St. George's Day . . . if we have the means—but for St. George's Day, if we cannot or can, we must. Spring comes only once a year."[21]

Time, Technology, and Documentation

Reflecting upon the continuities and changes within this community has led me to consider how technology may provide a means of revealing and reflecting upon the past. Regardless of the advances in recording live dance events and my care to take advantage of the very latest equipment available, it was an already established technological means for documentation—the still photograph—that unexpectedly provided insight into the past. What had been the capturing of an ethnographic moment in 1967 became, in the late 1990s, itself a historical source that enabled older members of the community to communicate a hidden knowledge to myself and to younger generations of their own people.

Unknown to me as a researcher at the time, I had happened to document my first St. George's Day in one of the early years of transition after the catastrophic earthquake of 1963, which had its epicenter in Skopje. Dancing in Topaana in 1967 occurred on each of the three days, 6–8 May, at the crossroads *kod česma* ("by the water fountain"), while on 9 May, the height of the event, most of the Romani population gathered on a hillside adjacent to Topaana. My documentation of ten, twenty, and thirty years later showed that the dancing no longer took place at the crossroads, nor anywhere else in Topaana, for the St. George's Days, although 9 May, the last day of the holiday, continued to be held on the spacious hillside adjacent to Topaana. I was curious why the dancing on 6–8 May 1967 took place in the narrow streets near the crossroads, with cars, trucks, or buses frequently honking their way through the thick lines of dancers, when there were other more spacious areas nearby with no passing vehicles. My understanding of the dancing on the street at this particular intersection developed indirectly, thirty years later, after tracing genealogies of musician families, and through discussion with the participants I had recorded in 1967.

In 1996, I took an album of photographs from 1967 to elicit comments from those participants. The 3x5-inch photographs seemed easily viewable to me, but an unexpected problem surfaced. The people in the photos were, in 1996, aged in their late forties, fifties, or sixties and had poor eyesight, with no access to eyeglasses. In 1997 I returned to the same families with the same photos, which had been scanned to large-size paper and placed into a binder. Also I supplied a magnifying glass to help those with very poor eyesight, and I paid particular attention to visiting them during good daylight hours. Conversations about the dancers represented in the photographs and about the *tapan* and *zurla* musicians revealed information about the neighborhoods prior to 1963. These discussions brought to light a Romani self-identity that was based on a territorial distribution of the Roms in Skopje, which hitherto had not been mapped or studied.

When I came to Skopje in 1967, the rebuilding of the city following the earthquake and the partial removal of the *ciganska maala* (the old Gypsy quarter), a part of Topaana, were in their early stages. Many Romani families had suffered damage to their homes and had been placed in temporary housing on the safer outskirts of the city. By 1967, a new suburb, Šuto Orizari, was under construction north of the city, where hundreds of Romani families had begun to resettle. In 1967 the St. George's event was split in its celebration between the old Romani district of Topaana and the new suburb of Šuto Orizari.

There was a notable distinction in the musical accompaniment provided for the celebrations in each of these districts. Music for the celebrations on the hillside was and has continued to be provided by sets of musicians playing *tapan* and *zurla*. The *tapan* and *zurla* musicians did not play for the dancing at the crossroads. The traditional *tapan* and *zurla* were played only within musician families who passed on the skill of constructing and playing their instruments. These musicians supplied the accompaniment for family events (such as weddings) only in their own neighborhoods. The event that took them to the Topaana hillside was 9 May, where all neighborhoods converged for feasting and dancing. But even on the hillside, the musicians tended to play for those families who knew them in their own neighborhoods. Music for the dancing at the crossroads in 1967, on the other hand, was provided by "modern instruments" such as clarinet, trumpet, hand drum, and accordion, played by musicians who did not come from a long family tradition.

Not until I began to trace genealogies of musicians did I uncover that there were distinct neighborhoods prior to the 1963 earthquake. The *tapan* and *zurla* musician families came from two of the oldest parts of the *ciganska maala* that had been erased as a result of the earthquake and subsequent urban renewal. These changes had also brought about intermarriage between the families of these two old neighborhoods. The adjacent neighborhoods were considered to be of "newcomers." The presence of these different families and their residence patterns were the result of new Rom migration into the area following the withdrawal of the Ottoman Turkish Empire from its northern territory during the nineteenth and early twentieth centuries. Those Roms who were not Christian found haven in the Skopje "Turkish" Romani quarter, and each major migration seems to have settled on the fringes of the older neighborhoods.

Before the earthquake, marriages were controlled by the families and did not integrate the groups of Roms from different migrations. In 1967, although I noted that many marriages had been brokered between families, a large proportion of the marriages appeared to be "love" marriages—that is, the young people knew each other before the marriage (which, I was told, in the days of their grandparents and great-grandparents was not the case). Most of my informants in 1967, in fact, had been married after the earthquake and lived in either Topaana or Šuto Orizari, where their own neighbors were of "mixed" marriages— that is, between families from different (although contiguous) neighborhoods. My photographic record on 7 and 8 May happened to document two late afternoons when there was dancing at the crossroads, and which did not happen in later years, because most of the homes in Topaana had been demolished for apartment buildings, and families had moved into the new Šuto Orizari suburb, where the prior distinctions of migrations had become erased physically and eliminated in the dancing events. Those who were dancing at the crossroads in my 1967 documentation thus represented a mixture of neighborhood populations. The year was part of a transition when there was a physical breakdown of the neighborhoods, and families from these neighborhoods were becoming integrated by marriage. The St. George's Day in 1967 was the only event in the year when dancing was the key means for once separate groups to have social mixing, and this was at the margin of the old and new neighborhoods. The crossroads marked the nonverbalized, unmarked neutral space dividing the older and newer migrations into Skopje, representing the territorial division between the Romani neighborhoods and distinct identities.[22]

As a result of combining my own past documentation with present interpretations from the local people depicted in the photographs, a shift in residence and marital patterns was thus revealed to me, an aspect that was manifested in the manner in which St. George's Day had been celebrated over the thirty-year period and before. This historical perspective was revealed only through my previous documentation of the event.

Such collaboration with local people, using technology as a research tool beyond its immediate function of documentation, has similarly led to fresh insights into the continuity of the celebration. Advances in technological capabilities over the years have facilitated my understanding of local implicit interpretations. For the dance researcher, developments in the long-play capability in both audio and visual recordings to allow for "real time" and whole dance sequences rather than "selected" moments have been of undoubted benefit for analysis. Also, it is now easier to be unobtrusive in the field, both because the equipment is smaller and capable of operating in low light levels and because the equipment itself is no longer particularly novel and hence distracting. Indeed, it has now been possible to hire local videographers to document those moments that are not possible for a dance ethnologist to access as a result of being an outsider to the community. It is never possible, of course, to make a "complete record," but supplementary tangible visual data is helpful to the understanding and interpreting of the context.

By the 1990s, videographers other than me were common at Romani events. Professionals with their own video cameras were hired by families to record whole events just as still-camera photographers were once engaged to take photographs. These video images are used in a manner similar to that of home movies or as photo albums for the event. With the advent of Romani-produced television programs, freelance or station videographers were also employed to cover events in the community for broadcast purposes. In 1997 I hired local videographers who had experience in recording events for local Romani television stations. I explained that I wanted their perspective of the St. George's Day event. In looking at their first tapes, I realized that they were accustomed to taping short takes, and I could not understand a sequence without their verbal input. They were so familiar with the context that a short take was all that was necessary. But as an outsider, I needed more explanatory footage. I then directed them to do nonstop video "scenes." They went on to document aspects of the holiday that I, as an outsider, could not or would not. Especially useful was their videotaping of private family aspects of the holiday, such as the bathing of the children (placing herbs and gold jewelry in the bath water) and dressing the children in new clothing, preparation of special foods for the holiday, neighborhood and family visitations, at-home spontaneous dancing to audiocassette music, multiple recordings of lamb sacrifices over a two-day period in neighborhoods of varying economic strata. Although they had freedom to record events, we discussed ahead of time their suggestions and ideas for recording. My interests in the ethnographic purpose behind video-recording do not, however, seem to have left any long-term influence upon them. There was no sense that the videographers were recording for posterity; rather, they were simply recording as paid professionals.

Given this change in the nature and profile of technological docu-mentation, to what extent has this influenced kinetic transmission of the dances? The dances occur mainly during wedding and circumcision events at which musicians (now with electronic music) are hired, and space is consciously provided for participatory dancing. As large family events, these parties are partially "public" so that children and young-sters are frequently exposed to the dancing in their homes and in their neighborhood streets. In the Romani community there are no teachers or demonstrators. Dancing in close proximity, with a handhold contact with dancers on either side of oneself, one may easily blend into the group body action with the repetitive dance steps. Technology does not play a direct role in the transmission of these dances. Since the early 1990s, however, dancing has been regularly viewed on the Romani-produced television programs and videocassettes produced by Romani music groups, both of which regularly show the *čoček* dancing in cos-tume. Although the rapid advances in technology for consumer use are incredibly useful for the documentation, preservation, and analysis of dance movement, the dancing within the Skopje Romani community has, nonetheless, continued to be transmitted through imitation learn-ing or teaching (I prefer the term "body movement transmission" rather than "oral tradition").

In the thirty-plus years of my tracing of their lifestyle and dance events in Skopje, the dancing repertoire and style of dancing during

8.5. Dancing to *tapan* and *zurla* music on Topaana hillside, 9 May 1997. Photo by Elsie Ivancich Dunin.

group dancing in open chains has not, however, been influenced directly by television and video intervention into their lives. So long as the dancing has continued to fulfill social needs within the communities and there are musicians (such as *tapan* and *zurla*) who still accompany the outdoor dancing, specific technology has not changed the manner of transmitting the dances. The dance repertoire of the "public" dancing during weddings and circumcision celebrations has continued. There are changes in the music accompaniment, clothing, and frequency of dancing, but the basic dance repertoire, the manner of dancing, and the acquisition of knowledge of dancing have remained. The repertoire that was danced in 1967 accompanied by such "outdoor" music instruments as the *zurla* and *tapan* was danced in 1997 accompanied by a younger generation of *zurla* and *tapan* musicians.

Conclusion

The Romani population in Skopje has come a long way since 1967 in terms of educational levels, political self-determination, media communication, introduction of social services, and living conditions, and has set a model for Romani communities elsewhere in Europe. Family support for education has produced professionals within the community and for the Macedonian state at large, such as community leaders, journalists, attorneys, medical personnel, educators, theater directors, internationally esteemed professional entertainers, and more. The five-day St. George event with its dancing continues to be a major annual celebration, and dancing remains a vital ingredient within life-cycle events. No one, however, in the community or in the country of Macedonia has ventured into an ethnographic documentation of these festivities. Consequently, my own thirty-year study of a contemporary dancing event has now become their historical record.

Initiated prior to the development of a dance ethnology curriculum in the United States, this study, using the latest technology as a means of documentation, became the first dance ethnology project at UCLA to emphasize the importance of experiencing, observing, and recording dance in its context over a long-term period. It demonstrates that a dance ethnology study is not based upon one-time contact but upon multilevel contacts in multiple time frames providing a continuity of data making for a historical record. This longitudinal ethnographic investigation developed into a model for future research projects that commence with contemporary forms of dancing, with understandings of continuities and changes not otherwise possible, except through tangible images and through direct observation, participation, and interviews with the living. Such ethnographic strategies, as evidenced above, may offer unexpected opportunities to uncover hidden historical dimensions and to celebrate the rich rewards that may be gained through moving across past and present.

NOTES

1. Rom refers to a singular person, Roms a collective plural, and Romani is used as an adjective. Romany or Romani (in English usage) has also become standardized as a reference to the language of the Roms. Gypsies or Cigani is a term used to identify the population during early stages of this research. After 1971, the terms Rom, Roma, Romi, Roms, and Romani creep into usage. My own mixed usage of the terms Gypsy, Rom, and Roma in prior publications in essence shows the state of flux in the Romani language and writings about them. For English language usage I currently follow the model suggested by Victor Friedman of the University of Chicago, linguistic specialist in the

Romani language. See Friedman, "A Note on Usage," in *Identity Formation among Minorities in the Balkans: The Case of Roms, Egyptians and Ashkali in Kosovo* (Sofia, Bulgaria: Minority Studies Society Studii Romani, 2001), 6.

2. In this chapter, "Yugoslavia" or "former Yugoslavia" has varying identities based upon the political time period. In 1918, after the First World War, a country with South Slavic language groups was formed as the Kingdom of the Serbs, Croats, and Slovenes, later to be named the Kingdom of Yugoslavia (the term Yugoslavia [Jugoslavija] literally means the country of the South Slavs). At the end of the Second World War, in 1945, a Communist state was established as the Federated People's Republic of Yugoslavia with six republics: Slovenia, Croatia, Bosnia and Herzegovina, Montenegro, Serbia, and Macedonia. In 1991 the Communist state broke into separate democratic countries: Slovenia, Croatia, Bosnia and Herzegovina, and Macedonia. The republics of Serbia and Montenegro chose to stay united and continued to refer to themselves as Yugoslavia, causing confusion on the international scene. Therefore, former Yugoslavia refers to the pre-1991 country with all six republics. During 2003, the partial Yugoslavia was changed to a country named Serbia and Montenegro. In 2006 Montenegro voted to become an independent country.

3. While still graduate students under the leadership of Dr. Alma Hawkins, Allegra Fuller Snyder and I were encouraged to create new courses that became a pioneer dance ethnology curriculum in a university program. In 1974 Snyder followed Hawkins as the chair of the Department of Dance.

4. Gertrude Prokosch Kurath, "Panorama of Dance Ethnology," *Current Anthropology* 1, no. 3 (1960): 233–54.

5. Joann Kealiinohomoku, "An Anthropologist Looks at Ballet as a Form of Ethnic Dance," in *Impulse 1969–1970*, ed. Marian Van Tuyl (San Francisco: Impulse, 1970), 24–33; Alan P. Merriam, "The Arts and Anthropology," in *Anthropology and Art*, ed. Charlotte M. Otten (New York: Natural History Press, 1971); Adrienne Kaeppler, "Method and Theory in Analyzing Dance Structure with an Analysis of Tongan Dance," *Ethnomusicology* 16, no. 2 (1972): 173–217; Suzanne Youngerman, "Method and Theory in Dance Research: An Anthropological Approach," *Yearbook of the International Folk Music Council* 7 (1975): 116–33; Anya Peterson Royce, *The Anthropology of Dance* (Bloomington: Indiana University Press, 1977); Judith Lynne Hanna, *To Dance Is Human: A Theory of Nonverbal Communication* (Austin: University of Texas Press, 1979).

6. Joel Martin Halpern, *A Serbian Village* (New York: Columbia University Press, 1958).

7. The UCLA Research Library was later named the Charles E. Young Research Library.

8. Early-twentieth-century folk dance collections were compiled in Finland, Sweden, Denmark, and England. They became the model for "folk dance" collections in the United States and the basis for dances taught in schools. From

1950 to 1952 collections of "folk dances" from most of Europe became available with translations into English in a series called *Handbook of European National Dances*, published in both New York (Chanticleer Press) and London (Parrish), under the auspices of the Royal Academy of Dancing and the Ling Physical Education Association. Countries included Bulgaria, France, Germany, Hungary, Italy, Norway, Poland, Romania, Scotland, Spain, and Yugoslavia.

9. Felix Hoerburger produced a folk dance survey for the International Folk Dance and Music Council ("Folk Dance Survey," *Journal of the International Folk Music Council* 17 [1965]: 7–8) and provided a theoretical basis for first and second existence of "folk dance" ("Once Again: On the Concept of Folk Dance," *Journal of the International Folk Music Council* 20 [1968]: 30–31). This theory initiated further discussions and analysis, such as by Andriy Nahachewsky ("Once Again: On the Concept of 'Second Existence Folk Dance,'" *ICTM Study Group on Ethnochoreology 20th Symposium Proceedings, August 19–26 1998, Istanbul, Turkey* [Istanbul, Turkey: Dans Müzik Kültür Folklora Doğru, 2000], 125–43).

10. South Slavic in this chapter refers to the Slavic languages spoken in southeastern Europe: Slovene, Croatian, Serbian, Macedonian, and Bulgarian. The Slovene and Croatian languages use the Latin-based alphabet, while the Serbian, Macedonian, and Bulgarian languages utilize the Cyrillic-based alphabets. But for the difference in the alphabets and dialects, Croatian and Serbian might be considered one language; prior to the breakup of former Yugoslavia, the two languages were referred to as Serbo-Croatian, or Croat-Serbian. Macedonian and Bulgarian are also closely related, but each utilizes its own Cyrillic alphabet. The Slovene, Croatian, Serbian, and Macedonian languages were all part of the former Yugoslavia, while Bulgarian is spoken in Bulgaria. Other Slavic and non-Slavic languages were spoken in former Yugoslav lands (1918–91), such as Albanian, Turkish, Romani, Italian, German, Hungarian, Czech, Slovak, and Romanian—representing the "minority" populations.

11. Ljubica Janković and Danica Janković, *Narodne igre*, vols. 1–3 (Belgrade: authors, 1934–39), vols. 4–8 (Belgrade: Prosveta, 1948–64; in Cyrillic).

12. By the mid-1960s, twenty-pound reel-to-reel half-inch tape recorders were being used in the field. Some quality hand-held 16-millimeter cameras with three-minute reels of film had sound-syncing generators to be connected by cable to reel-to-reel audiotape machines. All this equipment was battery powered with at least a half-hour time. Not until the mid-1970s were battery-powered portable video recorders (also reel-to-reel tape) available for single-person fieldwork.

13. *Kolo* is a term meaning "dance" in both the Serbian and Croatian languages. Serbian dancers implicitly identify this as dancing in an open-circle formation with dancers holding hands; the path of the dancing usually progresses in a counterclockwise direction. The step pattern is usually in an even rhythm of three to eight measures in length and repeated until the musicians stop playing.

The Roms in Los Angeles danced in this *kolo* formation in a counterclockwise path with a simple stepping pattern.

14. Djurdjica Petrović, "Cigani u srednjovekovnom Dubrovniku" [Gypsies in Medieval Ragusa], *Zbornik Filozofskog Fakulteta* 13, no. 1 (1976): 124 (Belgrade: Filozofski Fakultet; summary in English).

15. Olga Zirojević, "Romi na području današnje Jugoslavije u vreme Turkske vladavine" [Roms during the Period of Turkish Rule on the Territory of Today's Yugoslavia], *Glasnik etnografskog muzeja* 45 (1981): 232 (Belgrade: Etnografski Muzej; in Cyrillic).

16. Andrijana Gojković, "Cigani i muzika" [Gypsies and Music], *Narodno stvaralštvo folklor 9–10* (January 1983): 722–28 (Belgrade: Organ saveza udružnja folklorista Jugoslavije; in Cyrillic).

17. Vasil K'nčov, *Izbrani Proizvedenia 2 grad Skopie* (Sofia: Nauka i Izkustvo, [1900] 1970; in Cyrillic).

18. Statistical Office of the Republic of Macedonia (1997): 55.

19. *Gjelem Gjelem* (I Am Traveling) is a Romani song popularized through a motion picture about Gypsies produced in 1967 in Belgrade by Avala Films, directed by Aleksandar Petrović. The film's title, *Skupljači perja* (Feather Gatherers), was converted into an unrelated title in English, *I Even Met a Happy Gypsy*, and distributed internationally after the film won two awards in the 1967 Cannes Film Festival. The film is a derogatory story about Gypsy feather gatherers from the Vojvodina area of Yugoslavia. This was the first Yugoslav film that focused upon this marginal population and was one of the first films about the Gypsy population, using mixed Romani and Serbian languages. It featured some Romani actors (most of the lead characters were Serbian). The Romani melodies and lyrics from the film were produced on 45 rpm and LP phonograph recordings and were distributed internationally. The song *Gjelem Gjelem* began to be sung by Roms in many countries (including the United States, such as by the Los Angeles–based Roms) and thus by 1971 was so popular and widely enough known to be selected as an anthem at the First Romany Congress.

20. See Elsie Ivancich Dunin, "Dance Change in Context of the Gypsy St. George's Day, Skopje, Yugoslavia, 1967–1977," in *Papers from the Fourth and Fifth Annual Meetings of the Gypsy Lore Society, North American Chapter*, 2, ed. Joanne Grumet (New York: Gypsy Lore Society, North American Chapter, 1985), 110–20.

21. Translated quote from Skopje Roms, 1997.

22. This section is based on my earlier paper "Dancing in the Crossroads by the Skopje Roma during St. George's Day," *ICTM Study Group on Ethnochoreology, 20th Symposium Proceedings, August 19–26, 1998, Istanbul, Turkey* (Istanbul, Turkey: Dans Müzik Kültür Folklolra Dogru, 2000), 244–54.

9

Being Traditional

Authentic Selves and Others in Researching Late-Twentieth-Century Northwest English Morris Dancing

THERESA JILL BUCKLAND

Neat divisions into traditional and revival practices of dance frequently obscure often complex relationships to the past and present. A particular case is English morris dancing, a dance type that boasts six hundred years of recorded history, although in some quarters it is believed to date from prehistoric times.[1] In serious decline by the end of the nineteenth century, morris dancing underwent documentation and revivification in the early 1900s, within the framework of the national English Folk Revival. This movement included song, music, drama, and other dance forms that were designated by the collectors as authentic folk practices worthy of being recorded for revival.[2] A handful of the older teams of morris dancers that had not disbanded by the early 1900s performed throughout the twentieth century, continuing to the present day.

Such long-established morris teams, together with those that had died out, and other pre-twentieth-century folk performance arts, became collectively categorized as the Tradition. In order for a dance to be judged traditional, a key criterion was an origin that predated the folk revival movement of the early twentieth century. The oppositional category of the Revival was used to designate those folk activities, including

teams of morris dancers, that largely owed their inception and existence
to the program of national recovery. These constructs of the Tradition
and the Revival were thus created by the collectors of folk material and
employed by those who took up performance of the nationally delineated folk repertoire to distinguish between the existing practitioners
and contexts of performance and those inspired by a national, self-
conscious movement of revivalism.

The concepts of the Tradition and the Revival exist through mutual
and exclusive definition, signaling dichotomies of old versus new, authentic versus invented, and genuine versus spurious.[3] They also signal
different aspects of the past. The Tradition is usually accorded a mythic
past, as the origins of most customary practices are deemed to lie beyond
living memory and written and iconographic records. The Revival, on
the other hand, demonstrates a documented past, since the origins of revival practices, deriving their inspiration from the folk collections of the
early twentieth century, are demonstrably retrievable through the typical written and oral memory-type source material of history.

The late twentieth century witnessed some revisionism of this once
accepted distinction, however. Scholarly investigation of nineteenth-
century records and, where available, earlier source material sometimes revealed a starting point for some customs much later than popularly held. Since the 1980s, the disclosure that a so-called traditional
practice is actually a comparatively modern phenomenon has been the
fate of a number of British annual customs.[4] Similarly, in the critical
discourse on dance that examines the uses of tradition in legitimizing
performance, it has usually been the researcher's role to interrogate
these tensions between the mythic past and the documented past, ex-
posing dances with assumed credentials of extreme longevity to be
more recent creations than hitherto believed.[5] Revelations about the
presumed antiquity of certain morris dances do not, however, provide
the principal focus for the historical and ethnographic exploration in
this chapter; for other pasts are at stake in this discourse, not least of
which is the past of myself as researcher. I wish, instead, to challenge
the neat division into mythic and documented histories through the
complicating factor of a personal history created through memory and
reflection upon my own documentation of morris dancing. In this respect, aspects of this chapter fall between the categories of ethnographic
writing characterized by sociologist Amanda Coffey as "tales of the
self" and as "partial/autobiographical."[6]

John Lofland and Lyn Lofland, in their guide to qualitative observation and analysis in ethnography, observe that "the norms of scholarship do not require that researchers bare their souls, only their procedures."[7] Revelation and re-evaluation of my past procedures as a researcher, quite obviously, make public the pitfalls of my former training in older models of ethnographic and historical inquiry.[8] The return to my past as researcher and to the intertwined pasts of those I researched has, more awkwardly for me, also highlighted my frequently unconscious construction of discrete selves and others as essential to pursuing the investigation. In carrying out the research, I had unwittingly drawn upon different versions of my own self, versions that drew upon personal experiences and senses of identity that I failed to realize profoundly influenced how I conceived of and treated the people who helped me in my study. Throughout the conduct of my research, however, I had believed that only one self was legitimately in operation in relation to my material, that of the scholarly self. Revisiting my ethnographic notes, correspondence, and, latterly, the field has demonstrated my comparative ignorance. Finding bias in the work of others, in the sense of past writings of scholars, is a critical directive in academia; finding it in the work of one's own is a less comfortable experience. In discussing such self-revelatory discourse, anthropologist Drid Williams points out that reflexivity serves no purpose for the reader and academic community unless made to inform beyond the personal and subjective.[9] Taking heed of this, my aims in this chapter are not to rehearse transformational experiences in my life as a dance researcher, purely for their own sake, nor merely to repeat criticism of the folk paradigm in which the concept of tradition has long been enshrined.[10] Both approaches in relation to the subject of this chapter would only posit a simplistic dichotomy between my present self and my past self. Instead, I wish to explore the mutually constitutive nature of the researcher and the researched, through my past and present attitudes toward the ethnographic communities, historical sources, and dancing.

Different Histories: Studying Morris Dancing in Northwest England

In the nineteenth century, the period for which most primary sources exist, morris dancers would appear at regionally specific holidays. As

performed throughout England today, however, the form is usually the
preserve of adult amateur enthusiasts. From the early twentieth century,
when the custom underwent the large-scale revival, morris dancing
transformed from a local cultural activity to that of a nationally distributed recreation, performed mostly at weekends throughout the summer
months. Morris dancing increasingly since the 1920s came to be perceived in England as a somewhat anachronistic affair, revived by aficio-
nados who came from a more privileged social and economic background than that of its former practitioners, who were principally drawn
from the laboring classes. Such a contrast was encapsulated by the early-
twentieth-century distinction made between the Tradition and the Revival. The former designated the genuine folk, the supposedly unedu-
cated, preferably rural, working classes. The Revival, on the other hand,
was dominated by the educated, socially and geographically mobile
members of society, whose reason for performing the folk repertoire
often stemmed from a false nostalgia for a vanishing cultural past.

In the mid-twentieth century, the folk performing arts underwent
a second national regeneration, in effect spawning a further morris revival in the late 1960s and 1970s.[11] These later-twentieth-century revivals
attracted a more socially diverse following, a phenomenon that remains
to be fully investigated. One result was a higher public profile for morris
dancing with, in some quarters, a strong emphasis on adhering to the
practices of the Tradition. These neo-traditionalists, here also referred
to as purists, in part sought to re-create the past through the re-
appropriation and reconstruction of regional variants. Unlike the earlier national Folk Revival that had tended to focus upon one geographically distinct form of morris dancing, the 1960s and 1970s movement
sought to revive regional variants. These different types of morris dancing are distinguished by the number of dancers, the type of implements
that the dancers carry in their hands, costume, choreography, and musical accompaniment. The northwest variety of morris dancing, which
formed the subject of my research, is typically performed by eight or
more dancers who carry decorated short sticks, semi-flexible rolled-up
handkerchiefs, or garlands. They wear brightly colored clothes and
wooden-soled shoes known as clogs. The music is often a brisk, almost
military-style rendering of popular eighteenth- and nineteenth-century
popular tunes, played by a mixture of brass instruments, concertinas,
melodeons, and drums, to accompany a processional street dance.

9.1. Manley Morris Dancers from Cheshire in Northwest England. Performing at a town shopping center for passersby, 1977. Photo by T. J. Buckland.

In the second half of the twentieth century, two broad approaches had come to typify the Folk Revival: the longer-established approach of revivalists who performed material regardless of its regional provenance, and the new approach of neo-traditionalists who sought to create regional identities in contradistinction to the older national Folk Revival. This latter aim was mainly pursued through close attention to the former contexts and practices of the Tradition. It was in this framework that I began my doctoral research on northwest morris in 1976.[12] Prior to this, I had never been engaged with the Folk Revival, nor indeed consciously exposed to dance practices categorized as the Tradition. Instead, I began my investigation with a background in ballet and modern dance and an undergraduate degree that included folk life studies.

Academic training continued to insist upon a critically neutral stance toward any subject intended for scholarly investigation—a normal practice for most researchers, and especially so in folk life studies, in the days when a positivist stance was the aim, well before reflexive

ethnography had gained widespread acceptance. Given the low academic status of dance and the absence of scholarly research into folk
dance in England at that time, my choice of topic was quite radical in the
context of an English university. Most of the limited publications available on English "folk culture" had been written within a nineteenth-
century evolutionist framework that had long been discredited in the social sciences.[13] Accepting without question the interpretations of the
English folk dance collector Cecil Sharp (1859–1924) and his followers,
most writers regurgitated the belief that morris dances were an ancient
tradition handed down from prehistory and thus beyond documented
history. Like many of my academic contemporaries in the study of folk
performance, I believed that the phenomenon of morris dancing could
be understood through access to a demonstrably lived past, identifiable
through rigorous scholarship and the evidence of tangible records. It
could also be explored as a lived present through ethnographic investigation of contemporary practice. I worked across the frameworks of European folk life studies, the British new social history, and North American folkloristics. My interests lay in the analysis of multiple and variant
forms of this dancing, in providing sociohistorical contexts for its performances, and in humanizing the activity in terms of individual agency
within social groups and institutions. Responding to the frequent integration of historical and contemporary concerns of the intellectual disciplines across which my research was principally located, I sought to
understand the phenomenon of morris dancing through both synchronic and diachronic perspectives.

The timing of my research, unexpectedly for me, coincided with the
flowering of interest in the revival of northwest English morris dances in
the 1970s and 1980s.[14] Revivalist performers were also searching through
local history libraries and traveling around to film and interview old
morris dancers. My purpose, unlike theirs, was not principally to collect
notations of dance and music for reconstruction, and I was sometimes
irritated by their unsystematic, highly selective inquiries that occasionally resulted in publicity pamphlets and short populist articles with no
academic referencing.

After over a year's research, it was clear that I could not investigate
every instance of morris dancing in the region, whether designated revival or traditional, within the time frame of a doctorate. Decisions on
how to limit the scope of my research were influenced by the attitude of
some revivalist dancers who jealously guarded historical sources for

their own revival of northwest morris dances, refusing to make them public. My period of research (1976–84) had also coincided with the contested emergence of women's morris teams within the national Folk Revival, a factor that similarly placed bars on my access to material. Being female meant that, in some cases, male revival teams, fearful that I would steal their dances, treated my inquiries with suspicion, despite my protestations of being a scholarly "honorary male" with no desire to perform or pass on morris dances. Even some female teams resisted my research, convinced that I would learn their dances in order to start up my own team. Rejecting most of the politically fraught contemporary scene, I eventually settled upon the period 1780 to 1914—the classic long nineteenth century—as one trajectory for my study. The other trajectory facilitated both historical and ethnographic dimensions. I would concentrate upon one unusual team in the region—the Britannia Coco-Nut Dancers—who demonstrated a comparatively continuous record of performance from the mid-nineteenth century to the present. Both the historical records of pre-1914 morris dancing and the Britannia Coco-Nut Dancers were unquestionably recognized as belonging to the Tradition. In the process of data collection and analysis, I hoped to shed further light on what constituted traditional practice.

By turns frustrating and fascinating, the revival morris teams thus became marginalized in my inquiry; though not before I had collected, in the manner of "ethnographic reconnaissance," some field notes, records of telephone calls, letters, and films of revival performances.[15] Through later family connections with northwest morris dancing and a growing involvement with the Folk Revival, I maintained an interest in the debates and performances, which continued into the 1990s. In 2001–2, I revisited some of the revival teams to find out what had happened to that passion for revivification of a distinctive northwest style of morris dancing in the 1970s and 1980s. In reflecting on my methodological procedures over this time span, it appears to me that several histories are at play, manifested through written and visual material, memory, and bodily reenactment. These constitute the history of northwest morris dancing in the long nineteenth century; the history of my own ethnographic and historical research during the late 1970s and early 1980s; the history of the revival of northwest morris dancing; the history of my return to the field in 2001–2; and the longer, less tidily defined history of my involvement with the Folk Revival from the late 1970s to the present day.

·

From the National to the Local: Aspiring to Be Traditional

The concept of tradition was a rallying call among several morris team leaders in the 1970s and 1980s, indicating their preference for a neo-traditionalism in revivalist practice that made their performances and policy distinctive within the larger national frame of the Folk Revival. Often rejecting the recent past of the early-twentieth-century first revival—as represented by the institutions of the English Folk Dance and Song Society (EFDSS), founded in 1911 as the English Folk Dance Society, and the Morris Ring, founded 1934—the neo-traditionalists often sought to return to an earlier lost but retrievable past, reinterpreting and discovering source material for nineteenth-century examples of morris dancing. It was thus believed that the notion of tradition might be given new life through the reexamination of the field manuscripts of Cecil Sharp and other early-twentieth-century collectors, or by finding new source material in newspapers, in photographs, or, indeed, from surviving morris dancers of the period and their relatives.[16] The other major source of inspiration constituted performances and practices of the so-called living tradition: that is, continuing teams that had been originally encountered by Sharp and his colleagues, or else teams that had apparently experienced little previous contact with the Folk Revival, such as the Britannia Coco-Nut Dancers.

In northwest England, one impact of the first major revival of the early 1900s had been to introduce the regional variant known as Cotswold morris to the area. Cotswold morris is the name given to the style of morris dancing found mainly further south in the counties of Oxfordshire, Gloucestershire, and Warwickshire, which formed the basis of the national morris revival. Even in the twenty-first century, the style dominates, and most of its practitioners are to be found in the south and midlands of England, as indeed are most morris teams, regardless of what style is performed. Cotswold morris is typically performed by six men in two files of three who, waving handkerchiefs and clashing sticks, perform in a light aerial style.[17] This style of morris dancing constituted the original repertoire of the Manchester Morris Men, the revival team based in one of the largest cities in northwest England. Largely made up of university academics, this team was established sometime prior to 1936.[18] During the 1950s, interest in retrieving local variants of morris dancing, through a mixture of oral history and reexamination of manuscripts of dances collected before the Second World War, resulted in the

9.2. Map of England showing main locations cited in the text. Map by Stephen Heath.

Manchester team adding northwest dances to its repertoire. In 1960, two team members published a survey of northwest morris dances in the *Journal of the English Folk Dance and Song Society.*[19] They listed their sources, plotted the dances' geographical distribution, considered the sociohistorical context of historical performance, and speculated on reasons for distinctive choreographic variants within the region. The collecting, publication, and teaching activities of the Manchester Morris Men were hugely influential. In 1960, only two adult male teams in the region performed local dances; by 1996, the figure had grown to thirty-four.[20] This growth occurred in the context of a growth in revivalist morris dancers across the country, some of whom espoused the neo-traditionalist cause.

There are two striking features in the citation of tradition in the northwest morris revival: the first relates to gender, the second to place. Searches in archives and for old morris dancers in northwest England had revealed a regional peculiarity. There had been female morris dancers in the past, a discovery that contradicted the nationally accepted view that morris dancing was an exclusively male activity. This revelation was at first considered problematic by the EFDSS and was clear anathema to the fiercely male bastion of the Morris Ring, most of whose teams performed Cotswold morris. History and the notion of tradition were cited to justify the exclusion of women from performing Cotswold morris, but as new research was disseminated through workshops and specialist folk revival magazines, it came to be more accepted that the northwest repertoire might legitimately be performed by women.[21] All-female morris teams performing northwest dances expanded in number, the most well known and influential being the Poynton Jemmers of Cheshire, founded in 1975.[22]

Interpretations of morris dancing and its relationship to place embraced another shift in thinking during this period of contestation. In the early 1900s revival, the concept of folk signified the older cultural practices of rural communities. Cotswold morris had mainly been performed in the nineteenth century by agricultural laborers;[23] thus, in this rather circular argument, its enactment by such personnel contributed to its authentication as a genuine folk activity. In contrast, the occupations of morris dancers in northwest England had frequently been those of coal mining, quarry working, hat making, or, more especially, cotton spinning.[24] The region, particularly in the city and hinterland of Manchester, is, in fact, considered to be the oldest in the world to undergo extensive industrialization and urbanization. This might be considered an illegitimate site for recovery of authentically traditional dances. A landscape of industrial towns and villages certainly contributed to the neglect of this part of England by Sharp and his colleagues as a potentially fruitful collecting ground for folk culture. According to the constructs of traditional and modern, the former term was properly applied to practices in rural contexts, whereas the industrial was recent and an aspect of modernity. By the middle of the twentieth century, however, as a partial consequence of the decline of the British Empire, the urban and industrial glory days of the nineteenth century were no longer perceived as standing in opposition to tradition but had emerged instead as a newly authentic industrial cultural heritage.[25] The industrial "workshop of the world" was now silent and the nineteenth century suitably distanced in time.

The criterion of "place" was to exercise yet greater force in the northwest morris revival. Place in the sense of the past origin of morris dances was an essential criterion for authenticity, but soon questions of place in relation to present performance were being raised. Cotswold morris dances had already been disseminated across the nation in the first revival, the dances taken away from their regional roots in a transmission that was regarded by purists as having weakened any attempt to honor genuine traditional practice. Was the same fate now to befall northwest morris?

Time, Place, and People: A View of and from the North

By the mid-1970s, following the Manchester Morris Men's example, most newly revived morris teams in northwest England performed a general repertoire drawn from specific communities across the region. The nineteenth-century practice of a specific choreography being performed exclusively by one team in one local community was no longer tenable to sustain twentieth-century audience and team member interest. Morris teams now needed several dances to entertain, and finding sufficient dances of local provenance proved a problem. The race to recover, and indeed to create, was on.

Another race had emerged that further troubled morris teams in the northwest. Across the country, a number of the revival teams were donning clogs and performing northwest morris dances. This situation caused an outcry from purists. New teams, formed in the locality of the dance's original provenance, sometimes sought to reclaim dances that were now in the national public domain. The rhetoric propagated by such neo-traditionalists placed a high premium on ownership of the dances through the criteria of locality and birthright. They thus positioned themselves as other to a national folk revival that they viewed as essentially southern. As noted above, the majority of morris teams, whatever repertoire they were performing, were located in the midlands and south of England. The strong sense of "northernness" was not peculiar to neo-traditionalist morris dancers in the region during this period.

On the contrary, it drew from and continued a long-held and deep feeling about northern England, often perceived by its residents in the twentieth century as marginalized and under siege from the more affluent south.[26] The decline of heavy industry and widespread closure of factories in what had been the engine room of the British Empire left a sense of economic and political neglect, made worse by the redundancies in the area during the years of Margaret Thatcher's premiership (1979–90). Such themes are evident in the correspondence in national folk periodicals complaining of the perceived appropriation of northwest English culture by southerners. For such neo-traditionalists, revival by northerners betokened authentic longevity, whereas southerners were merely swayed by passing fashion:

> A lot of us in the North West feel that after many years of being a social and educational backwater which no one South of Birmingham wanted to know about, it is now the "in thing" to dress in clogs and shawl and speak "Lanky" [i.e., Lancashire dialect].[27]
>
> Sometimes we think of it as the London attitude: squeeze the provinces dry so that we can have a good time.[28]

These territorial claims to cultural heritage were undoubtedly indicative of resistance to sociocultural and political changes in the region during the 1970s and 1980s, as economic resentment against the south's comparative prosperity grew. It is more than possible that for the ringleaders of the localized northwest morris revival, their historical sentiment had been reinforced by the very sources they consulted for reconstructive purposes. Around one hundred years earlier, a more articulate northern identity had begun to gain a profile. This found expression in newspaper articles; short stories, poetry, and books written in Lancashire dialect; published local reminiscences; and local histories.[29] It was often this very same material that late-twentieth-century morris dancers were drawing upon to resource their revivals. A detailed analysis of the expression of northwest identity within the Folk Revival must await future consideration, but suffice it here to say that in the more extreme instances, an exclusive regional essentialism was espoused:

> Personally, I don't like people in places like Devon or somewhere dancing Northwest morris, it just doesn't seem right. How can a Southerner for instance *be* something he isn't? You are a product of where you live, and your own area is ingrained in you, as part of your character. So someone from Devon, say dancing Lancashire morris dances is not

really going to put the dance across with anything near the same conviction as a lad who *is* a Lancashire morris dancer. One is a representation while the other is authentic.[30]

[It's] not a hobby or owt [anything] like that, it's much stronger
than a hobby, it's part of Northwest England, [a] British way of life. To
have your own local traditions is good and you've got to keep them
going, otherwise we'd all be the same, wouldn't we?[31]

Assertions of longevity in the area were manifest in the choice of team
names to correspond with those of the past, such as Preston Royal Morris and the Horwich Prize Medal Morris. The original teams bearing
these names had long ceased to function, and the revival personnel had
few links with the dancers, beyond residence in the locality and obvious
personal contact in seeking out the old dancers.

Distinctiveness is essential to the creation and maintenance of identity, but this emphasis also accords with Sharp's characterization of traditional morris as being continuously rooted in one place.[32] In 1910 he

9.3. Horwich Prize Medal Morris Dancers parading down the road at the annual
summer carnival in Adlington, Lancashire, 1978. Photo by T. J. Buckland.

had written: "Our experience proves that each village where morris dancing survives has its own tradition, its own dances and its own special methods of performance, all of which reflect no doubt the peculiar temperament and artistic sense of the community."[33] Although primarily concerned with the example of Cotswold morris, Sharp's declaration continued to exert a huge, shaping influence on the Folk Revival, including the neo-traditionalists of northwest morris dancing. The assertions of separate identity for northwest morris were nevertheless still rooted in the values of the first national revival. As Georgina Boyes has concluded, addressing here the term "the Revival" to the larger framework of the mid-twentieth revival of folk performances: "for all its apparent innovation and variety, the Revival was hidebound by historical theory. Determinedly producing a policy of authenticity, it became a more effective vehicle for Sharp's views than the English Folk Dance Society of the 1920s."[34]

Less directly, antagonistic commentary on women's morris further signaled older attitudes that drew upon an othering of gender that followed classic nineteenth-century divides. It was one that was often tied to an authenticity of traditional masculinist working-class culture.[35] Authentic morris dancing was acknowledged as the former preserve of the lower classes, and thus certain values associated with traditional working-class culture were espoused as desirable for reproduction within the Revival. In this respect, of course, pointing to the Tradition was a useful means of legitimating contemporary practice. Male dancers in the overwhelmingly middle-class morris revival of the twentieth century were often nervous about dancing in public for fear of charges of effeminacy and homosexuality.[36] This strong sense of a working-class male body as the only authentic vehicle for the performance of northwest morris in the revival was often manifested in a comparative emphasis on heaviness, discipline, and power in the dancing. Sometimes the historical record was willfully obscured with respect to the gender of previous performers, most notably in the instance of the Garstang Morris team, which was nationally known in the revival for its anti-female stance and for its emphasis upon "masculinity" in the dancing.

In 1996, the chief collector of their dances, the former wife of the team's leader, revealed that the repertoire had originally been founded upon her aunt's childhood morris dancing.[37] Such revelations were not made at the height of the team's fame. Where there was acceptance by other revival teams of female morris dancers on the grounds of historical precedence, there often tended to be a glossing over of the fact that from the late 1890s children and very young women had often been participants. If a men's team's traditional credentials were challenged on the grounds that the former dancers were female, a typical response might draw from a line of thinking popular among some members of the Morris Ring: that women had only acted as conduits of the tradition until such a time as when men could rightfully reclaim what was their legitimate heritage.[38] It was such thinking on the interrelations of past, gender, and place under the rubric of tradition that I was almost continuously to encounter when pursuing my doctoral research. And, in several respects, it was to permeate my own understanding.

Interpreting the Pasts of Others (and Selves)

In returning to past research in 2001, physically, intellectually, and emotionally, I discovered and rediscovered past selves, forcing me to reflect upon the conditions that had led me to construct others in order to carry out my research. During my doctoral research, I had remained convinced that my conceptions and values were distinct from those of the revivalists. It was axiomatic during that time that Tradition and Revival were dichotomous, although such a polarization was already beginning to be called into question in North American literature in anthropology and folkloristics.[39] Among purists within the English Folk Revival, however, such a division continued. If I entertained any such doubts about clear boundaries between the characteristics of traditional and revival teams, I could at least point to two clearly distinguishing criteria: the dancers' respective attitudes toward the past and their use of historical sources. There appeared to be a sharp contrast between the older, established Britannia Coco-Nut Dancers and the revived northwest morris teams.

From my ethnographic research of the late 1970s and early 1980s, it was evident that the Britannia Coco-Nut Dancers, and indeed most of their local community, were not engaged in uncovering source material to write history. Such archival pursuits were for outsiders, "university types," and students, who were often regarded as synonymous with members of the Folk Revival by some of the older Coco-Nut Dancers. Only one of the Coco-Nut Dancers I interviewed had experienced formal education beyond sixteen years in contrast to a sizable number of

9.4. Britannia Coco-Nut Dancers at Fylde Folk Festival, Fleetwood, Lancashire, 1980.
Photo by T. J. Buckland.

revivalist dancers. The Coco-Nut Dancers, though, had no compulsion
to demonstrate their traditionality—not only had the EFDSS provided
such authentication in the 1920s, but local oral memory could testify to
the nineteenth century and reputedly beyond.[40] The revivalist morris
dancers possessed no such public affirmation. My ethnographic research revealed that the Britannia Coco-Nut Dancers placed a high
premium upon the transmission of kinetic knowledge through local
human bodies.

> It's something that, you know, has been handed down and handed
> down by word of mouth and practical help in learning the steps. It's not
> something you can just go and pick a book up, read about, go and do it.
> Impossible. It's got to be—it's that sort of dance that it's got to be
> handed down from man to man.[41]

Such bodily continuity was much respected and coveted by many
revivalists.

In circumstances where immediate kinetic transmission was not possible, revivalists necessarily had recourse to other forms of documentation, highlighting anthropologist Paul Connerton's distinction between

incorporating and inscribing practices in the transmission of memory.[42] Written records and photographs of former local morris dancing were interpreted in local and national folk magazine articles, contributing to wider knowledge of traditional practices and announcing a team's revival/arrival with historical credentials.[43] Members of the Britannia Coco-Nut Dancers, on the other hand, were not at all interested in creating historiography nor, for the most part, in consuming it. Some individual members did possess an archive of the team's activities and articles written about them, but the sources for history and their own historiography were rarely discussed and almost never on display.[44] They knew who they were, and so did the local community; their national significance was annually affirmed by huge visiting audiences on their local day of dancing. Thus, it appeared that the writings of revivalist morris teams, setting out their own historical sources, positioned them further in opposition to the traditional team.

I distinguished myself from the revivalists in that my own historical inquiry into northwest morris teams and the past and present of the selected case study was more "sociological" in orientation. My agenda included details such as the age of the performers, their social status, occupation, and gender, the composition of the audience, as well as the constituent features of performance such as costume, music, instrumentation, repertoire, and contexts of performance. Inspired by the anthropological wave sweeping British social history and by the structural analysis of dance forms based on linguistic analogies, my approach to the records of the past was necessarily different from that of contemporary revivalists. I wanted to investigate what the Tradition was *really* like in order to understand the society that gave rise to these dances and what were the social, political, economic, and cultural factors that led to its transformation from a community-based adult male performance in the early 1800s to a predominantly competitive display by children, often of both sexes, that had developed with no relation to the Folk Revival by the 1920s.

It might be argued that the activities of nonspecialist historians of dance, as in the case of revivalist morris dancers, can be ignored by the academic: it is unlikely that amateur historians' representations will enter into professional discourse since, for most, publication in academic journals and in conference proceedings is not their intention. Similarly, the reverse may be true. In the instance of the English folk dance revival in the last third of the twentieth century, however, such a strict division does not reflect the fluidity of interchange that existed

between the personnel involved in academic study and in revival performance. My self-appointed role was comparable to that of those historians who "seem happiest at work puncturing legends, proving the
modernity of much of what passes for old, showing the artificiality of
myth and its manipulable, plastic character."[45] This indeed had been
an abiding interest from my undergraduate studies of other ceremonial
dance forms in England: an interest in the past as a resource for contemporary meaning, and a desire to de-mythologize the dominant theory of
the origins of morris dancing. To my mind, though, the use of the past
and belief in myths were what others did; as a trained academic, a professional, I considered myself to be outside this. From my position of
power I might perceive the reality: the disjuncture between the professed past of ethnographic revelation and the authentic past of historicity. Systematic academic investigation might demonstrate that claims to
ancient traditionality could not be substantiated after all. My identification and scrutiny of historical records on the past of the Britannia Coco-
Nut Dancers brought to light the strong possibility of a comparatively
modern origin for this so-called ancient tradition. Such a discovery pro-
voked a moral dilemma for me in terms of whether or not to publish my
findings.[46] In contrast, I felt less worried about revealing inconsistencies
in the historical record and in the claims of revivalist dancers. Many of
these revival dancers came from a similar social and educational background as mine, even if they had not been trained in folk life studies, history, or anthropology. Correcting, indeed dismissing, their use of history was, I considered, perfectly ethical; the revival dancers were not the
subject of my investigation, and their beliefs were not hallowed as the
Tradition. Their activities were tantamount to "invented traditions,"
symptoms of modernity and of a lesser order to the traditional.[47] In this
respect, these revival morris dancers, although equally employed in
investigating the past and using similar sources to myself, were other
to my academic self. The Britannia Coco-Nut Dancers were not only
other to my academic self but were also other to the revivalist dancers.
In my mind, they were the "real thing"—Tradition—demonstrable
through bodily continuity with the local past and authenticated through
written and oral records back into the nineteenth century.

By the 1970s in England, most purists and academic folklorists had
come to equate "folk" somewhat pejoratively with revivalist activity. In
an avalanche of criticism, serious researchers and purists had jettisoned
the concept in favor of the term "traditional." During the 1970s and early

1980s in England, within the newly positioned academic study of folk life studies, this label was considered by many academics to be a more faithful appellation, distinguishing between those activities that were inspired by the revivalist movement and those that continued outside of its remit. A new wave of university-trained folklorists within British universities also sought to distinguish their own work from that of past and present amateurs. In the debate, their fields of study were framed variously as popular, working-class, or vernacular customary practices, rather than as "folk" or "folklore." Such academics believed that legitimate and worthwhile academic interest lay in uncovering the reality of tradition, the past, and history.[48] Similarly, any ethnographic inquiry was to focus on the "authentic." As testimony to this move toward professionalizing the study of folk performance, a series of academic conferences and published proceedings was launched that expressly examined traditional drama and dance.[49] Designed to uncover the real history and practice of Tradition, these conferences, in fact, attracted numerous revival performers, who were also keen to learn more about the "real" Tradition.

By the mid-1980s, it seemed as though that thirst for historical knowledge of the Tradition had been assuaged among many revival morris dancers. Confidence in their own revival efforts had developed, boosted not least by the realization that some of these twentieth-century teams had been performing for longer on a regular basis than a number of the so-called traditional teams. This sense of self-worth among revivalist morris dancers found particular expression in an academic conference entitled "Contemporary Morris and Sword Dancing" in 1988.[50] If continuity of performance in one place was to be a major criterion of traditionality, then it was not surprising that the revival morris movement itself had now become an object of study, with many of the conference papers based upon personal experience and autobiography. The self-consciousness of the Revival, however, was evident in the emphasis upon self-documentation; unlike morris teams of the past, which had left scanty traces, revivalist morris dancers were keen to record their present activities with the intention of leaving fulsome records for posterity. The revival teams employed techniques of scholarly collection. In addition to minutes, photographs, journals, newspaper cuttings, and videotapes, data on the composition of teams were collected through distribution of questionnaires. Increasingly, comparatively new teams in the Northwest and elsewhere claimed traditionality. The Revival had become the Tradition, it was claimed, and deserved academic analysis.[51] Of interest to me, though, was the continuing use of this concept of Tradition as a legitimizing force in the argument. Through my increasing interest in anthropological theory, I could no longer justify, as in my previous research, valorizing one group of dancers over another as traditional. What became fascinating were the grounds of that valorization, and thus I shifted ground toward a meta-commentary on the discourse of morris dancing in northwest England.

In company with the anthropologically inclined ethnographer, today's historians and folklorists are interested in the uses to which understandings of the past are put, and in how representations, regardless of supposed verisimilitude, are constructed, by whom and in what contexts. As historians Raphael Samuel and Paul Thompson highlight, in parallel with more anthropological and cultural studies perspectives, significance lies not in "the reality content in our documents rather [it lies in] what they may tell us about the symbolism categories through which reality is perceived."[52]

Their statement obviously applies to all oral and archival testimonies, regardless of their date. Not only should the symbolic realities of testimonies of the researched be interrogated but also those—often less discernible—of the researcher. Over the years, I had come to view the revivalist northwest morris dancers not as impostors nor as poor historians but as fascinating in their own right. During my doctoral research, I had come to position them as other on three counts: first, as other to historical and ethnographic records of traditional dancing; second, as other to me (on the basis of the uses to which they put historical sources); and third, as other to me on the basis that I was not a morris dancer. By the late 1990s, however, this latter distinction had also dissolved.

Revisiting Ethnography and History: Personal Perspectives

In revisiting northwest morris teams in 2001–2, as a northerner by origin now living in the south, I came with the different academic persona of an established dance scholar, and with several years of participation as a Cotswold morris dancer. Any pretence at viewing the Folk Revival from a nonparticipant outsider position was over. As I now joined in practices of mixed and female morris teams, my body experienced what I had only rarely felt but often witnessed twenty years before. I remembered the boredom of watching many similar dances with little to interest me, so repetitive were the spatial patterns and arm and leg movements. Present participation tallied with my memory of joining in a very occasional practice in the 1970s before politics shut down my access and before I had stopped associating too closely with the revival morris teams. I admitted to myself in 2001 that the physical and mental boredom had served as a further distancing device, contrasting and elevating the more choreographically varied dances of the Britannia Coco-Nut Dancers. What I did not remember, however, were the sustained aerobic demands of the northwest morris dancing. I longed for the rise and fall of the contrasting dynamics of Cotswold morris, its opportunities to rest within the dance, the attention needed to remember steps, and how to control the handkerchiefs to make patterns in the air. There was no such individualism apparent in northwest morris, and my lungs, knees, and upper arms ached as I executed the seemingly relentless high skipping; my feet pounded into the floor, my arms fixed exactly in position, as I performed as a drilled member of a team. Participation in both styles had now given me greater understanding of contrasting dynamics.[53] It also provided a base for understanding discussions of how the dancers perceived regional identity, not just as a repertoire, but as a way of moving, both as an individual and within a group. My recent past experience as a morris dancer now proved a useful ethnographic entry point, making up numbers when too few dancers had turned up to rehearse, as well as providing me with a useful and enjoyable methodological tool.

On my return to the field in 2001–2, I discovered that a number of the teams had since faded away. The northwest morris revival appeared to have been a phenomenon linked to a particular generation, who, having now grown older, were either physically challenged by the dance style or had moved on to other activities. There was still a strong sense of regional identity professed among the continuing teams I interviewed, but time had softened the ferocity. Among those dancers who had joined in the 1990s, such passion for tradition, authenticity, and keeping the dances for only those in the Northwest was comparatively weak. Other reasons beyond a satisfaction of performing something old were now articulated as dominant, and it was mostly those dancers who had joined the team in the heyday of chauvinism who still professed historical and regional commitment. More recent recruits had little to say about the past, even when they were older members of the team in age. Dancing alongside a near seventy-year-old woman, I reflected on the

change with regard to age: previously it had been valued as an indicator
of Tradition; now it seemed to be a testimony to the new virtues of
maintaining youth and fitness. These dancers had joined because they
had seen, not the living continuity of local Tradition, but people of a
similar age to themselves, having a good time.[54] It was a group activity
for keeping fit. Indeed, for most of the recruits of the 1970s and 1980s,
physical enjoyment and camaraderie most likely always did outweigh
the rhetoric of the Tradition. It had always been the case that extreme
views tended to have been held by those with vested interests in the recovery of the Tradition.

I returned to the field as a published expert on the history of northwest morris dancing, uncertain of how much of my own profile as a previous organizer of conferences on Traditional Dance was known. Little,
it would seem, as many of the dancers I talked to had not attended such
events, either because they had become morris dancers much later or
else were not those personally driven to spearhead the setting up of the
team. The crossover between practitioners and academics interested in
traditional dance and music, so noticeable in the 1970s and 1980s, was
no longer discernible. The collecting and research into the past had
been completed; what mattered more to dancers was the present, looking forward to sociable events and meeting up with other morris dancers at folk festivals and weekends of dance.

In this final stage of my inquiry, though, a further manifestation of
otherness was to be revealed, a historical self that I had forgotten. By
the mid-1980s, I became known among the revival movement as a historian of northwest morris dancing. During this time, I received a letter
requesting help from a recently constituted team whose leaders had
moved from the south of England. Although the dancers had formerly
performed a variety of different regional forms of morris, they were now
located in Cheshire, a county in northwest England, and wanted to perform only morris dances from the locality. On rereading copies of our
correspondence, I am surprised that they ever replied to my boorish
letter in which I corrected their logo of a clog-shod morris dancer
in stereotypical Lancashire as opposed to Cheshire working-class dress,
and insisted that most Cheshire morris could only be accurately danced
in shoes, not clogs, and then only reenacted by children as the true original performers according to the historical record. There mirrored back
to me in these documents was not the objective scholar I had believed
myself to be, but the self-righteous academic historian and the partisan

ethnographer. Not only had I become totally bound by the directive of the Tradition, associating with those teams who operated such a policy, but a deeply felt anti-southern prejudice was also revealed. I had evidently taken it upon myself to protect the culture of "northern identity."

Conclusion

Undertaking reflexive ethnography in the present and reflecting critically upon the ethnographic records of one's past throw into relief the various selves and others that are created in order to carry out social investigation, whether or not evident to the researcher at the time of study. By shifting the focus of interest in my later fieldwork from the exclusive Tradition to an undifferentiated cast of northwest morris dancers, I realized that the exercise of otherness had almost blinded me to that which I shared with the dancers of the Revival. The demands of my scholarly task prompted the construction of my academic self against a field of amateur researchers and occasioned preferential evaluation and treatment of some people over others. My pursuit of authenticity, in the senses of setting the historical record straight and of paying more attention to the opinions and practices of so-called traditional dancers, positioned the latter as culturally more significant than their revivalist peers. Such privileging of individuals is a symptom of the notion of the "tradition bearer," an inheritance from classic folk studies methodology whereby some people's knowledge of older practices is valued more than others by the researcher.[55] The perceived authenticity of the practice is thus transferred to the authenticity of the person.

During the 1970s and 1980s, I had believed myself to be operating within a modernized folk life studies perspective but had failed to realize that the concept of Tradition had quietly transferred across from nineteenth-century studies to my own doctoral studies, escaping critical scrutiny. I had also believed myself to be relatively unbiased, pursuing the purity of academic rigor to uncover an authenticity of historicity. My northern upbringing, however, had resurfaced, erupting in a passionate defense of that which I clearly held to be an aspect of my own identity under threat.

The exact premise upon which any parameters for inquiry rest will rarely be fully discernible and will inevitably be enmeshed between the prejudices of the discipline(s) within which the research is conducted and those of the researcher's biography. This is particularly the case when working among past and present cultural traditions in dance practices of one's own country. Critical recognition of the fluctuating and situational dimensions of constructed selves and others in relation to the research aims and objectives is vital when conducting dance ethnography at home. Undoubtedly, as recent dance scholarship has demonstrated, the insights afforded as a result of collapsing the boundaries of self and other, of participating fully in the dance practices, and of resisting the classic anthropological demand to make the familiar strange are crucial correctives to a legacy of positivism and colonialism that has created hierarchies of knowledge and power.[56] The acceptance of a more public personal voice in ethnographic and historical writing since my doctoral days has widened debate and understanding of epistemological concerns in ethnographic and historical scholarship. The authority and authenticity of researcher and findings may be challenged, arguably resulting in a greater democratization of knowledge transfer, and the voice of the native researcher is gaining a welcome profile. Yet we must not automatically suppose that the voice of the native researcher necessarily guarantees an authenticity of knowledge in and of itself. Other historical and contemporary politics may well be operating, hidden in scholarly paradigms and in the history of the researcher herself, as this chapter has tried to demonstrate. And for the fuller revelation of that, we may have to look not only at the past and present but, assisted by the benefit of hindsight, await its unveiling in the future.

NOTES

Field and archival research undertaken in 2001–2 was made possible by a grant from the Arts and Humanities Research Council. Thanks are due to the morris dancers and musicians who selflessly helped me with this research, providing much of their own time, experience, and resources.

1. See John Forrest, *The History of Morris Dancing, 1458–1750* (Toronto, Canada: University of Toronto Press, and Cambridge, England: James Clarke, 1999) for discussion of the earliest records in England and for a critique of prehistoric origins.

2. For narrative accounts of the English folk dance revival movement, see Douglas Kennedy, *English Folk Dancing Today and Yesterday* (London: G. Bell, 1964), and Hugh Rippon, *Discovering English Folk Dance*, 3rd ed. (Princes Risborough, Buckinghamshire: Shire, 1993). For a more extensive critique of the folk

revival phenomenon from a cultural studies perspective, see Georgina Boyes, *The Imagined Village: Culture, Ideology and the English Folk Revival* (Manchester: Manchester University Press, 1993); a sociological view is offered by Niall MacKinnon, *The British Folk Scene: Musical Performance and Social Identity* (Bucks: Open University Press, 1993), and Michael Brocken's *The British Folk Revival, 1944–2002* (Aldershot, Hampshire: Ashgate, 2003) analyses the phenomenon from the perspective of popular music studies.

3. See Cynthia M. Sughrue, "Some Thoughts on the 'Tradition' versus 'Revival' Debate," in *Traditional Dance* (Alsager, Cheshire: Crewe and Alsager College of Higher Education, 1988), vols. 5/6: 184–90.

4. For examples see E. C. Cawte, "It's an Ancient Custom—But How Ancient?" in *Aspects of British Calendar Customs*, ed. Theresa Buckland and Juliette Wood (Sheffield: Sheffield Academic Press, 1993), 37–56, and in the same volume, Venetia Newall, "Up-Helly-Aa: A Shetland Fire Festival," 57–73.

5. For a case study of how these two notions of the past can work in relation to the construction of a dance as "folk" see Theresa Buckland, "'Th'Owd Pagan Dance': Ritual, Enchantment, and an Enduring Intellectual Paradigm," *Journal for the Anthropological Study of Human Movement* 11, no. 4, and 12, no. 1 (Fall 2001/Spring 2002; double issue): 415–52. As further examples of contested histories, see the chapters by Felicia Hughes-Freeland and Janet O'Shea in this volume.

6. Amanda Coffey, *The Ethnographic Self: Fieldwork and the Representation of Identity* (London: Sage, 1999), 122–26.

7. John Lofland and Lyn H. Lofland, *Analyzing Social Settings: A Guide to Qualitative Observation and Analysis*, 3rd ed. (Belmont, Calif.: Wadsworth, 1995), 13.

8. For a previous consideration see Theresa J. Buckland, "[Re]Constructing Meanings: The Dance Ethnographer as Keeper of the Truth," in *Dance in the Field: Theory, Methods and Issues in Dance Ethnography*, ed. Theresa J. Buckland (Houndmills, Basingstoke: Macmillan, and New York: St. Martin's Press, 1999), 196–207.

9. Drid Williams, "An Exercise in Applied Personal Anthropology," *Dance Research Journal* 9, no. 1 (1976): 16–30, and "Self-Reflexivity: A Critical Overview," *Journal for the Anthropological Study of Human Movement* 8, no. 1 (1994): 1–10. Helen Thomas in personal correspondence has reminded me that Williams's notion of the identity of self is neither multiple nor fluid.

10. For a summary discussion see Regina Bendix, *In Search of Authenticity: The Formation of Folklore Studies* (Madison: University of Wisconsin Press, 1997), 211–13.

11. There is no scholarly overview of this national phenomenon of further morris revival, but for insightful articles on the two regional types of morris in this chapter (Cotswold and northwest), see, respectively, Roy Dommett, "Extension of the Traditional Repertoire and Newly Conceived Traditions," *Lore and Language* 6, no. 2 (July, 1987): 33–64, and Derek Schofield, "Which Past?

The Influences of Tradition and Revival on the North-West Morris," in *Morris: The Legacy of the Past* (Morris Federation, Morris Ring, and Open Morris, 1996): 94–108 (available in the Vaughan Williams Memorial Library, Cecil Sharp House, English Folk Dance and Song Society, 2 Regents Park Road, London NW1 1AY).

12. Theresa Buckland, "Ceremonial Dances of the South-West Pennines and Rossendale" (Ph.D. thesis, Institute of Dialect and Folk Life Studies, School of English, University of Leeds, 1984).

13. Scholarly critiques of the concept of "folk" were published from the 1970s onward. For critiques of the concept of "folk dance" in English scholarship see Theresa Buckland, "English Folk Dance Scholarship: A Review," *Traditional Dance*, 1 (1982): 3–18, and "Definitions of Folk Dance: Some Explorations," *Folk Music Journal* 4, no. 3 (1983): 315–32.

14. See Schofield, "Which Past?"

15. The term "ethnographic reconnaissance" is drawn from Harry F. Wolcott, *Ethnography: A Way of Seeing* (Walnut Creek, Calif.: Altamira Press, and London: Sage, 1999).

16. For examples see conference proceedings from *The Evolving Morris* (Morris Ring and Morris Federation, 1990) (available in the Vaughan Williams Memorial Library, Cecil Sharp House, English Folk Dance and Song Society, 2 Regents Park Road, London NW1 1AY).

17. The classic descriptions of Cotswold morris dancing can be found in Cecil J. Sharp and Herbert C. MacIlwaine, *The Morris Book*, 2nd ed., part 2 (London: Novello, 1912–24), parts 4–5 (part 5 with G. S. K. Butterworth) (London: Novello, 1911, 1913).

18. For a history, see Manchester Morris Men, http://homepage.ntlworld .com/k.ashman52/mmm/index.html, last modified 23 January 2006.

19. Daniel Howison and Bernard Bentley, "The North-West Morris—A General Survey," *Journal of the English Folk Dance and Song Society* 9, no. 1 (1960): 42–55.

20. Schofield, "Which Past?" 95.

21. For a flavor of the debate see correspondence in *English Dance and Song* 36, nos. 3–4 (1974): 110, 150, and 37, no. 1 (1975): 29.

22. See Poynton Jemmers Northwest Morris, http://www.poyntonjem mers.net/.

23. See Keith Chandler, *"Ribbons, Bells and Squeaking Fiddles": The Social History of Morris Dancing in the English South Midlands, 1660–1900* (Enfield Lock, Middlesex: Hisarlik Press, 1993).

24. See Theresa Buckland, "Institutions and Ideology in the Dissemination of Morris Dances in the Northwest of England," *Yearbook for Traditional Music* 23 (1991): 53–67.

25. The left-wing sympathies of key performers and theorists in the folk revival movement from the 1950s positioned industrial culture, particularly song,

more centrally—see Boyes, *Imagined Village*, 210, 214–15, and Brocken, *British Folk Revival*.

26. For a historical consideration see Helen M. Jewell, *The North-South Divide: The Origins of Northern Consciousness in England* (Manchester: Manchester University Press, 1994). For a more contemporary appraisal see Rob Shields, *Places on the Margin: Alternative Geographies of Modernity* (London: Routledge, 1991), chapter 5, and on the 1980s in particular, pp. 231–44; also, Dave Russell, *Looking North: Northern England and the National Imagination* (Manchester: Manchester University Press, 2004).

27. Stan Gee, "Morris in the North West," letter, *Morris Matters* 3, no. 1 (1980): 30–32.

28. Julian Pilling, letter, *English Dance and Song* 39, no. 1 (Spring, 1977): 27.

29. This articulation of a northern identity has been considered in relation to sport. See Tony Mason, "Football, Sport of the North," in *Sport and Identity in the North of England*, ed. Jeff Hill and Jack Williams (Keele: Keele University Press, 1995), 41–52.

30. Roger Edwards, "Straight Lads from Lancashire," *Morris Matters* 7 (n.d.): 8–12.

31. Saddleworth Morris Men team member interviewed on ITV television program *Second Tuesday*, 1984. It should be recognized, however, that not all views expressed on this program were genuinely held; see Peter Ashworth, *Rushcarts in Saddleworth* (Saddleworth, Yorkshire, 1990), 44.

32. There is an extensive literature on theories of cultural practice and identity. See, in particular, Fredrik Barth, ed., *Ethnic Groups and Boundaries: The Social Organization of Culture Difference* (Prospect Heights, Ill.: Waveland Press, 1998); Anthony P. Cohen, ed., *Signifying Identities: Anthropological Perspectives on Boundaries and Contested Values* (London: Routledge, 2000); and Pierre Bourdieu, *Distinction: A Social Critique of the Judgement of Taste*, trans. Richard Nice (London: Routledge, 1984).

33. Sharp and MacIlwaine, *Morris Book*, pt. 3, 10.

34. Boyes, *Imagined Village*, 241.

35. On gender see Pauline Greenhill, "Morris: An English Male Dance Tradition," in *Ethnicity in the Mainstream: Three Studies of English Canadian Culture in Ontario*, ed. Pauline Greenhill (Montreal: McGill-Queen's University Press, 1994), 64–125. In this present discussion, the concept of class is considered as a social and cultural categorization; see Ivan Reid, *Social Class Differences in Britain: Life-Chances and Life-Styles* (London: Fontana, 1989).

36. Fear of the charge of effeminacy continued to be entertained by male morris dancers during my fieldwork: field notes, Manchester Morris Dancers, group discussion, The Mawson, Brunswick Street, Manchester, 29 November 2001.

37. Pruw Boswell, "The Lancashire Legacy," in *Morris: The Legacy of the Past*, 110–16.

38. For example, "David Welti Writes to WMF," *Morris Matters* 1, no. 2 (1978): 11. Such views were commonplace among many members of the Morris Ring during my fieldwork in the late 1970s and early 1980s.

39. The seminal article is Richard Handler and Jocelyn Linnekin, "Tradition, Genuine or Spurious?" *Journal of American Folklore* 97, no. 385 (1984): 273–91.

40. See Theresa Buckland, "'In a Word We Are Unique': Ownership and Control in an English Dance Custom," in *Step Change: New Views on Traditional Dance*, ed. Georgina Boyes (London: Francis Boutle, 2001), 49–59.

41. Derek Pilling, interview with author, 21 April 1981.

42. Paul Connerton, *How Societies Remember* (Cambridge: Cambridge University Press, 1989), 72.

43. See, for example, Julian Pilling, *The Royal Morris Dancers of Colne* (Colne, Lancashire: Colne Royal Morris Dancers, 1971); Sue Mycock, "Throstles Nest Morris and a Cumbrian Dance Tradition," *Morris Matters* 4, no. 4 (n.d.): 10–13; J. and T. Beasant, "The Marston Processional Morris Dance," *English Dance and Song* 43, no. 2 (1981): 4–5.

44. For a further discussion of the team's attitude toward history, see Buckland, "Th'Owd Pagan Dance."

45. Raphael Samuel and Paul Thompson, eds., *The Myths We Live By* (London: Routledge, 1990), 4.

46. The results were published in Theresa Jill Buckland, "Black Faces, Garlands, and Coconuts: Exotic Dances on Street and Stage," *Dance Research Journal* 22, no. 2 (1990): 1–12.

47. The concept of "invented traditions" derives from the seminal text *The Invention of Tradition*, which was edited by Eric Hobsbawm and Terence Ranger (Cambridge: Cambridge University Press, 1983); it should be noted, however, that Hobsbawm and Ranger's collection employs the concept within the specific framework of the nation-state and not in general.

48. See my introduction to Buckland and Wood, *Aspects of British Calendar Customs*, 9–21.

49. These include the "Traditional Drama" annual conferences at the University of Sheffield, 1978–85; the "Traditional Dance" conference series at Crewe and Alsager College of Higher Education, Cheshire, 1981–86; and the "Traditional Song" conference at the University of Leeds in 1982.

50. Published as "Proceedings of the Contemporary Morris and Sword Dancing Conference," hosted by the Centre for English Cultural Tradition and Language, University of Sheffield, 12 March 1988, special issue, *Lore and Language* 6, no. 2 (1987).

51. For example, John Seaman, "A Study of Contemporary Morris Dancers in Norfolk: Their Social Makeup and Their Motivation for Becoming and Remaining Morris Dancers" (MPhil thesis, Centre for English Cultural Tradition and Language, University of Sheffield, 1987). This shift is not restricted to

England; see, for example, Neil V. Rosenberg and Alan Jabbour, eds., *Transforming Tradition: Folk Music Revivals Examined* (Urbana: University of Illinois Press, 1993) and, on dance in particular, the papers on the theme of Revival: Reconstruction, Revitalization in *Proceedings of the 21st Symposium of the ICTM Study Group on Ethnochoreology, 2000, Korčula* (Zagreb, Croatia: International Council for Traditional Music Study Group on Ethnochoreology and Institute of Ethnology and Folklore Research, 2001).

52. Samuel and Thompson, *The Myths We Live By*, 1.

53. For a critical assessment of how bodily participation may inform understanding, see Sally Ann Allen Ness, "Being a Body in a Cultural Way: Understanding the Cultural in the Embodiment of Dance," in *Cultural Bodies: Ethnography and Theory*, ed. Helen Thomas and Jamilah Ahmed (Oxford: Blackwell, 2004), 123–44.

54. On the attraction of similar body types see Anthony G. Barrand, "Aesthetics and the Morris: Mutual Interactions of the Dance, the Dancers and the Environment," *Traditional Dance* 4 (1986): 105–32.

55. This celebration of the "tradition bearer" has developed into the system of "living human treasures" adopted by some countries. For further detail see http://www.unesco.org/culture/heritage/intangible/treasures/html _eng/method.shtml, last updated 31 August 2001. For an examination of the Korean example, see Judy Van Zile, *Perspectives on Korean Dance* (Middletown, Conn.: Wesleyan University Press, 2001), 51–62.

56. As examples, see Marta E. Savigliano, *Tango and the Political Economy of Passion* (Boulder, Colo.: Westview Press, 1995) and Barbara Browning, *Samba: Resistance in Motion* (Bloomington: Indiana University Press, 1995).

SELECTED FURTHER READING

CONTRIBUTORS

INDEX

SELECTED FURTHER READING

COMPILED BY THERESA JILL BUCKLAND

Dancing from Past to Present aims to stimulate further research into and debate on the use of ethnographic and historical theory and method in the study of dance as cultural practice. The following suggestions and reflections on literature relevant to such inquiry make no pretence to be inclusive or without bias. I include here key texts that have emerged through virtue of recurrent citation across this volume's chapters and elsewhere in dance scholarship. More localized references, even if essential to the interpretation of specific instances of dancing the past in the present, may be found within the notes of each individual essay.

ANTHROPOLOGY

Influential texts in anthropology that raise issues of history, representation, and power inequalities include the following:

Appadurai, Arju. *Modernity at Large: Cultural Dimensions of Globalization.* London: University of Minnesota Press, 1996.

Asad, Talal, ed. *Anthropology and the Colonial Encounter.* London: Ithaca Press, 1973.

Clifford, James, and George E. Marcus. *Writing Culture: The Poetics and Politics of Ethnography.* Berkeley: University of California Press, 1986.

Fabian, Johannes. *Time and the Other: How Anthropology Makes Its Object.* New York: Columbia University Press, 1983.

Geertz, Clifford. *The Interpretation of Cultures: Selected Essays.* New York: Basic Books, 1973.

———. *Local Knowledge: Further Essays in Interpretive Anthropology.* New York: Basic Books, 1983.

———. *Works and Lives: The Anthropologist as Author.* Stanford, Calif.: Stanford University Press, 1988.

Marcus, George E., and Michael M. J. Fischer. *Anthropology as Cultural Critique: An Experimental Moment in the Human Sciences.* Chicago: University of Chicago Press, 1986.

The following useful texts advance such lines of thinking in anthropology:

Fox, Richard G., ed. *Recapturing Anthropology: Working in the Present.* Santa Fe, N.M.: School of American Research Press, 1991.
Hastrup, Kirsten. *A Passage to Anthropology: Between Experience and Theory.* London: Routledge, 1995.
Herzfeld, Michael. *Anthropology through the Looking Glass: Critical Ethnography in the Margins of Europe.* Cambridge: Cambridge University Press, 1987.
———. *Anthropology: Theoretical Practice in Culture and Society.* Malden, Mass.: Blackwell, 2001.

ETHNOGRAPHY

There is a vast literature that addresses ethnography, but recurrent texts in this collection, or ones that are useful in characterizing and challenging practice at the turn of the twenty-first century, include the following works:

Amit, Vered, ed. *Constructing the Field: Ethnographic Fieldwork in the Contemporary World.* London: Routledge, 2000.
Coffey, Amanda. *The Ethnographic Self: Fieldwork and the Representation of Identity.* London: Sage, 1999.
Davies, Charlotte Aull. *Reflexive Ethnography: A Guide to Researching Selves and Others.* London: Routledge, 1999.
Emerson, Robert M., Rachel I. Fretz, and Linda L. Shaw. *Writing Ethnographic Fieldnotes.* Chicago: University of Chicago Press, 1995.
Williams, Drid, and Brenda Farnell. "Editorial Comments: Ersatz Ethnography." *Journal for the Anthropological Study of Human Movement* 11, no. 3 (2001): i–v.
Wolcott, Harry F. *Ethnography: A Way of Seeing.* Walnut Creek, Calif.: Altamira Press; London: Sage, 1999.

It must be remembered, of course, that ethnography is not a methodology restricted to anthropology. An essential volume that provides insight on its diverse practice is the *Handbook of Ethnography*, ed. Paul Atkinson et al. (London: Sage, 2001). Dance does not, however, figure in its pages, and the reader is advised to consult my edited collection, *Dance in the Field: Theory, Methods, and Issues in Dance Ethnography* (Basingstoke, Hampshire: Macmillan, 1999; New York: St. Martin's Press, 1999) for an overview of North American and European approaches to dance and ethnographic practice. Helen Thomas's chapter "Ethnography

Dances Back" in her book *The Body, Dance, and Cultural Theory* (New York: Palgrave Macmillan, 2003) provides a summary of emergent trends in the second half of the twentieth century of relevance to dance research.

HISTORY

With respect to the discipline of history, postmodernist and poststructuralist thought has resulted in ground-shifting texts, such as the following:

Certeau, Michel de. *The Writing of History*. New York: Columbia University Press, 1988. (Originally published as *L'écriture de l'histoire* [Paris: Gallimard, 1975].)
Foucault, Michel. *The Archaeology of Knowledge*. London: Tavistock, 1972. (Originally published as *L'archéologie du savoir* [Paris: Editions Gallimard, 1969].)
———. *The Order of Things: Archaeology of the Human Sciences*. New York: Random House, 1970. (Originally published as *Les mots et les choses: Une archéologie des sciences humaines* [Paris: Gallimard, 1966].)
White, Hayden. *The Content of the Form: Narrative Discourse and Historical Representation*. Baltimore: Johns Hopkins University Press, 1987.
———. *Metahistory: The Historical Imagination in Nineteenth-Century Europe*. Baltimore: Johns Hopkins University Press, 1973.
———. *Tropics of Discourse: Essays in Cultural Criticism*. Baltimore: Johns Hopkins University Press, 1978.

Debate has raged within the discipline of history over the problematization of knowing the past. Champions of postmodern approaches can be found in the following works:

Ankersmit, Frank, and Hans Kellner, eds. *A New Philosophy of History*. London: Reaktion Books, 1995.
Jenkins, Keith. *The Postmodern History Reader*. London: Routledge, 1997.
———, ed. *Re-thinking History*. London: Routledge, 1991.

Examples of balanced critiques, to my mind, of the extremes of postmodernist history can be found in these works:

Appleby, Joyce, Lynn Hunt, and Margaret Jacob. *Telling the Truth about History*. New York: W. W. Norton, 1995.
Breisach, Ernst. *On the Future of History: The Postmodernist Challenge and Its Aftermath*. Chicago: University of Chicago Press, 2003.
Evans, Richard J. *In Defence of History*, rev. ed. London: Granta Books, 2001.
Iggers, Georg G. *Historiography in the Twentieth Century: From Scientific Objectivity to*

the Postmodern Challenge. Middletown, Conn.: Wesleyan University Press, 2004.

David Cannadine's edited collection *What Is History Now?* (Basingstoke, Hampshire, and New York: Palgrave Macmillan, 2002) offers orientation in understanding early-twenty-first century perspectives in the practice of history.

ANTHROPOLOGY, HISTORY, AND FOLKLORE STUDIES: NATION, CULTURE, IDENTITIES

Recognition and analysis of the phenomenon of utilizing the past to reflect present concerns is best represented by Eric Hobsbawm and Terence Ranger's seminal edited collection, *The Invention of Tradition* (Cambridge: Cambridge University Press, 1983). Articulated within the framework of the rise of the nation-state, Hobsbawm's concept of the "invented tradition" has had far-reaching impact across a number of disciplines. In the same year appeared the influential *Imagined Communities: Reflections on the Origin and Spread of Nationalism* by Benedict Anderson (London: Verso, 1983) and Ernest Gellner's *Nations and Nationalism* (Ithaca, N.Y.: Cornell University Press, 1983), both of which underscored the emergence of the cultural within historical discourse. A further text central to stimulating debate on the construction of national identities through the significance of an invented past(s) is *The Ethnic Origins of Nations* by Anthony D. Smith (Oxford: Blackwell, 1986).

Within folklore scholarship, the valence given to the past in the present has come under regular critical scrutiny since the 1970s, as founding concepts such as "folk" and "tradition" became problematized. Key texts in this regard are Richard Handler and Jocelyn Linnekin, "Tradition, Genuine or Spurious?" *Journal of American Folklore* 97, no. 385 (1984): 273–91, and Regina Bendix, *In Search of Authenticity: The Formation of Folklore Studies* (Madison: University of Wisconsin Press, 1997).

Ideas relating to the articulation of various forms of cultural identity and the significance of the past have circulated in anthropological discourse, notably in the following works:

Barth, Fredrik, ed. *Ethnic Groups and Boundaries: The Social Organization of Culture Difference.* Oslo: Universitetsforlaget, 1969.
Cohen, Anthony P. *The Symbolic Construction of Community.* London: Tavistock, 1985.
Comaroff, Jean, and John Comaroff. *Ethnography and the Historical Imagination.* Boulder, Colo.: Westview Press, 1992.
Herzfeld, Michael. *Ours Once More: Folklore, Ideology, and the Making of Modern Greece.* Austin: University of Texas Press, 1982.

Tonkin, Elizabeth, Maryon MacDonald, and Malcolm Chapman, eds. *History and Ethnicity.* London: Routledge, 1989.

Paul Connerton's *How Societies Remember* (Cambridge: Cambridge University Press, 1989) is less concerned with the formation and expression of identity per se but addresses the notion of the embodied past in the present, a theme of key pertinence to this volume.

There is a considerable literature on the relation of history to anthropology that is impossible to list here, but texts of significance include these publications:

Cohn, Bernard S. *An Anthropologist among the Historians, and Other Essays.* Delhi: Oxford University Press, 1987.

Evans-Pritchard, E. E. *Anthropology and History.* Manchester: Manchester University Press, 1961.

Sahlins, Marshall D. *Historical Metaphors and Mythical Realities: Structure in the Early History of the Sandwich Islands.* Ann Arbor: University of Michigan Press, 1981.

——. *Islands of History.* Chicago: University of Chicago Press, 1985.

Michael Herzfeld presents a useful overview of the relation of history to anthropology in the chapter "Histories" in his volume *Anthropology: Theoretical Practice in Culture and Society* (Malden, Mass.: Blackwell, 2001).

The impact of the social sciences on the practice of history has also been much discussed, from Keith Thomas's "History and Anthropology," *Past and Present* 24 (1963): 3–24, and E. P. Thompson's "Folklore, Anthropology, and History," *Indian Historical Review* 3, no. 2 (1978): 247–66, through to early twenty-first century debate in the initial volumes of the journal *Culture and Social History: The Journal of the Social History Society* (vol. 1, nos. 1–3, 2004). Subdisciplines of social history and cultural history emerged from the 1960s onward with an extensive literature that has continued to grow and to have an impact on dance scholarship.

MOVEMENT AND CULTURAL EMBODIMENT

Most of the literature on cultural embodiment, as noted by social scientists who focus on dance, has tended to ignore the "moving body." For theoretical developments that go beyond Thomas J. Csordas's influential article "Embodiment as a Paradigm for Anthropology," *Ethos* 18 (1990): 5–47, and the work of other social scientists, see, for example,

Farnell, Brenda. "Ethno-graphics and the Moving Body." *Man: Journal of the Royal Anthropological Institute* (n.s.) 29 (1994): 929–74.

————. "Moving Being, Acting Selves." *Annual Review of Anthropology* 28 (1999): 341–73.

————. "Getting Out of the *Habitus:* An Alternative Model of Dynamically Embodied Social Action." *Journal of the Royal Anthropological Institute* (n.s.) 6, no. 3 (2000): 397–418.

Both Susan A. Reed in "The Politics and Poetics of Dance," *Annual Review of Anthropology* 27 (1998): 503–32, and Deidre Sklar in "Reprise: On Dance Ethnography," *Dance Research Journal* 32, no. 1 (2000): 70–77, provide surveys of the turn toward cultural embodiment in ethnographic approaches to dance in the late twentieth century. A critical consideration of such developments can be found in Sally Ann Allen Ness, "Being a Body in a Cultural Way: Understanding the Cultural in the Embodiment of Dance," *Cultural Bodies: Ethnography and Theory*, ed. Helen Thomas and Jamilah Ahmed (Oxford: Blackwell, 2004): 123–44.

DANCE, CULTURE, AND HISTORY

Drid Williams's *Ten Lectures on Theories of the Dance*, 2nd ed. (Urbana: University of Illinois Press, 2004) is a sustained scholarly analysis of anthropological approaches to the study of human movement. Reed and Sklar cited above provide surveys of late-twentieth-century developments that highlight issues of politics and embodiment in the dance literature. There is, however, a comparative absence of books that address more generally the field of dance as cultural practice since the impact of postmodern thought.

Critical reflection on historiography within mainstream dance studies has been better served given the centrality of history to these studies. The second edition of *Dance History: An Introduction*, edited by Janet Adshead-Lansdale and June Layson (London: Routledge, 1994) serves as a useful starting point. Susan Leigh Foster's edited volume *Choreographing History* (Bloomington: Indiana University Press, 1995) placed "the body" as central to historical inquiry in dance scholarship, with theoretical emphases upon the cultural and upon an interdisciplinary agenda. A helpful characterization of dance historiography at the turn of the twenty-first century can be found in Alexandra Carter's *Rethinking Dance History: A Reader* (London: Routledge, 2004). Lynn Matluck Brooks's essay "Dance History and Method: A Return to Meaning," *Dance Research* 20, no. 1 (2002): 33–53, largely eschews postmodern practices in the practice of dance history, yet poses a potential corrective against its more extreme versions. Essays devoted to discussion and advocation of the "cultural turn" in dance history include Amy Koritz, "Re/Moving Boundaries: From Dance History to Cultural Studies," in *Moving Words, Re-writing Dance*, ed. Gay Morris (London: Routledge, 1996), 88–103, and Norman Bryson, "Cultural Studies and Dance History," in *Meaning in Motion: New Cultural Studies of Dance*, ed. Jane

C. Desmond (Durham, N.C.: Duke University Press, 1997), 55–77. A collection dedicated to the cultural and the historical in dance studies is *Moving History/ Dancing Cultures: A Dance History Reader,* ed. Ann Dils and Ann Cooper Albright (Middletown, Conn.: Wesleyan University Press, 2001). It includes a number of seminal articles on dance, history, and culture. Of these, the most groundbreaking for its time is Joann Kealiinohomoku's "An Anthropologist Looks at Ballet as a Form of Ethnic Dance," not only for its anthropological reading of ballet, but also for its keen exposé of the hierarchical evaluation of the past with respect to Eurocentric notions of culture as "high art."

DANCING FROM PAST TO PRESENT

The following texts bring together, to a lesser or greater extent, historical and ethnographic approaches to the study of dance as cultural practice and offer a basis, together with the chapters in this volume, for further reflection on dancing the past in the present:

Albright, Ann Cooper. "Embodying History: Epic Narrative and Cultural Identity in African-American Dance." *Choreographing Difference: The Body and Identity in Contemporary Dance.* Middletown, Conn.: Wesleyan University Press, 1997. 150–78.

Buckland, Theresa J. "Dance, Authenticity, and Cultural Memory: The Politics of Embodiment." *Yearbook for Traditional Music* 33 (2001): 1–16.

———. "'Th'Owd Pagan Dance': Ritual, Enchantment, and an Enduring Intellectual Paradigm." *Journal for the Anthropological Study of Human Movement* 11, no. 4 and 12, no. 1 (Fall 2001/Spring 2002; double issue): 415–52.

Daniel, Yvonne. *Rumba: Dance and Social Change in Contemporary Cuba.* Bloomington: Indiana University Press, 1995.

Erdman, Joan L. "Dance Discourses: Rethinking the History of the 'Oriental Dance.'" *Moving Words: Re-Writing Dance,* ed. Gay Morris. London: Routledge, 1996. 288–305.

Foley, Catherine. "Irish Traditional Step-Dance in Historical Perspective: Tradition, Identity, and Popular Culture." *Dans Müzik Kültür, ICTM 20th Ethnochoreology Symposium Proceedings 1998,* ed. Frank Hall and Irene Loutzaki. Istanbul, Turkey: Boğaziçi University Folklore Club, 2000. 43–55.

Giurchescu, Anca. "The Power of Dance and Its Social and Political Uses." *Yearbook for Traditional Music* 23 (2001): 109–21.

Gore, Georgiana. "Present Texts, Past Voices: The Formation of Contemporary Representations of West African Dances." *Yearbook for Traditional Music* 23 (2001): 29–36.

Gottschild, Brenda Dixon. *Digging the Africanist Presence in American Performance Dance and Other Contexts.* Westport, Conn.: Praeger, 1996.

Meduri, Avanthi. "Bharatha Natyam: What Are You?" *Asian Theatre Journal* 5, no. 1 (1988): 1–22.

Noyes, Dorothy, and Roger D. Abrahams. "From Calendar Custom to National Memory: European Commonplaces." In *Cultural Memory and the Construction of Identity*, ed. Dan Ben-Amos and Liliane Weissberg. Detroit: Wayne State University Press, 1999. 77–98.

Ramsey, Kate. "Vodou, Nationalism, and Performance: The Staging of Folklore in Mid-Twentieth-Century Haiti." In *Meaning in Motion: New Cultural Studies of Dance*, ed. Jane C. Desmond. Durham, N.C.: Duke University Press, 1997. 345–78.

Shay, Anthony, and Barbara Sellers-Young. "Belly Dance: Orientalism—Exoticism—Self-Exoticism." *Dance Research Journal* 35, no. 1 (2003): 13–37.

Soneji, Davesh. "Living History, Performing Memory: *Devadāsī* Women in Telegu-Speaking South India." *Dance Research Journal* 36, no. 2 (2004): 30–49.

Thomas, Helen. "Mimesis and Alterity in the African Caribbean Quadrille: Ethnography Meets History." *Cultural and Social History: The Journal of the Social History Society* 1, no. 3 (2004): 280–301.

Usner, Eric Martin. "Dancing in the Past, Living in the Present: Nostalgia and Race in Southern California Neo-Swing Dance Culture." *Dance Research Journal* 33, no. 2 (2001): 87–101.

CONTRIBUTORS

THERESA JILL BUCKLAND is Research Professor of Performing Arts at De Montfort University, Leicester, England. Her publications include *Dance in the Field: Theory, Methods and Issues in Dance Ethnography* (editor, 1999), *Aspects of British Calendar Customs* (coedited with Juliette Wood, 1993), and chapters on dance and oral history in *Dance History: An Introduction* (edited by Adshead-Lansdale and Layson, 1983, 1994).

ELSIE IVANCICH DUNIN is Professor Emerita, University of California, Los Angeles, and dance research adviser with the Institute of Ethnology and Folklore Research in Zagreb, Croatia. She taught courses in dance ethnology in the former Department of Dance, UCLA, from 1966 to 1994 and has published extensively on social dance changes and their relation to sociocultural transformations.

FELICIA HUGHES-FREELAND is Senior Lecturer in Anthropology at the University of Wales Swansea. She has conducted research in Indonesia for over twenty years and has published widely on different aspects of performance in Java and on television and cultural transformation in Bali. She also makes ethnographic films, including *The Dancer and the Dance*. She is currently completing a monograph on Javanese court dance entitled *Embodied Communities: Dance Traditions and Change in Java*.

ADRIENNE L. KAEPPLER is Curator of Oceanic Ethnology at the Smithsonian Institution in Washington, D.C. She has carried out field research in Tonga, Hawai'i, and other parts of the Pacific. Her research focuses on the interrelationships between social structure and the arts, especially dance, music, and the visual arts.

LYNN D. MANERS, an aesthetic anthropologist, is editor of the *Journal of the Society for the Anthropology of Europe* of the American Anthropological Association.

239

He was guest editor of a special issue on Music and Dance for the *Anthropology of East Europe Review.*

JANET O'SHEA is Reader in Dance Studies at Middlesex University, England. Her doctorate, undertaken at the University of California, Riverside, examines politics of representation in twentieth-century bharata natyam. Her essays have appeared in *Asian Theatre Journal, Dance Research Journal,* and *The Drama Review,* and she has a monograph on bharata natyam forthcoming.

DEIDRE SKLAR, an interdisciplinary scholar, is the author of *Dancing with the Virgin: Body and Faith in the Fiesta of Tortugas, New Mexico* (2001). Her articles have appeared in *Dance Research Journal, TDR: A Journal of Performance Studies, Journal of American Folklore,* and other publications.

JUDY VAN ZILE is Professor of Dance at the University of Hawai'i at Mānoa, where she coordinates the dance ethnology program. She has published widely on movement analysis and Korean dance, and her extensive research led to her award-winning book *Perspectives on Korean Dance.*

INDEX

Page numbers in italics refer to illustrations.